THE BECKONING TIDE

HOLIDAYS IN MAYARO

A Memoir

Robin Mohamid

Copyright © 2018 Robin Mohamid

All rights reserved. No part of this work covered by the copyright herein may be reproduced or used in any form or by any means—graphic, electronic, or mechanical—without the prior written permission of the author.

ISBN 978-1-988344-06-5 (paper)
ISBN 978-1-988344-07-2 (e-book)

Production Credits

Cover design: Adrian So, Adrian So Design

Front cover photograph: Brandon Khan

Back cover photograph: Shivana Sharma

*This is dedicated to my parents, Hafiz and Gemma.
Thank you for all that you both did for me
and for giving me these wonderful memories.*

*For my sons, Joshua and Aaron, and my wife Vashti,
whom I love with all my heart.*

For all my family in Trinidad.

Contents

Mayaro 7
Chapter 1: Anticipation and Preparation 11
Chapter 2: Here We Come: The Start of the Holidays 22
Chapter 3: Peter, the River and the Junction 37
Chapter 4: Subash and Family, Peter for Dinner 52
Chapter 5: Rain and Jellyfish 63
Chapter 6: Pulling Seine, Roasting Fish and the Moore House 72
Chapter 7: The First Weekend and Visitors 89
Chapter 8: The Tropical Storm 111
Chapter 9: Galeota with My Cousins 132
Chapter 10: Day Trip to Tunapuna 151
Chapter 11: Fishing with Mr. Leeha 169
Chapter 12: Curried Duck Lime with Selwyn and Gatch 182
Chapter 13: Errol, Leon and the Trip to Rio Claro 193
Chapter 14: The Final Week: A Bittersweet Departure 204
Chapter 15: Going Back as an Adult 218
Chapter 16: Making New Memories 230
Chapter 17: From Trinidad to Canada 244
Chapter 18: The Last Days with My Mother 253
Chapter 19: A Final Journey to Mayaro with My Father's Ashes .. 263
Chapter 20: The Tide Still Beckons to Me…One Last Time 274

Mayaro

For those who know of it, just hearing the name Mayaro conjures up visions of vast stretches of brown sandy beaches fringed by the blue waters of the Atlantic Ocean, green coconut palm lined shores and an idyllic time at the seaside. For me, Mayaro is the magnet that draws out some of the best memories buried within the vast archives of a lifetime of experiences. As I raise my own family in Canada and as the years go by away from my birthplace and homeland, I found myself dreaming about, and remembering my childhood days vacationing in Mayaro. They sometimes flooded back with such intensity that it was difficult not to succumb to turning back the hands of time and pleasantly and vividly reliving those holidays. These were some of the best memories of my life, created with my family at the small seaside village of Plaisance in Mayaro. Each year for six years, we journeyed there to spend our annual holiday. This is my story of my holidays in Mayaro that started back in the year nineteen sixty-nine.

As a youngster growing up in Tunapuna in Trinidad, between the ages of six and eleven, each year my father booked his annual vacation to coincide with the school holidays from July to September. He reserved a beach house at Plaisance Village in Mayaro for about four to six weeks and took the family to the seaside to spend the holidays. These holidays provided me with some of the best memories of my childhood. For six years, we spent the holidays together in Mayaro and we all looked forward to these yearly family trips. It was a time when our family, with a few uncles, an aunt and a few cousins, spent quality time with each other, enjoying each other's company and enjoying a carefree time. Mayaro was the perfect canvas on which to paint these idyllic holidays.

My father had a good job as an airline manager and was the sole bread-winner in our family. My mother was the traditional home-maker. With only one income though, it was a challenge for my parents who had the difficult task to prioritize their spending between all our needs and wants, between the necessities and desirables. In the end, they managed to provide us with most of our basic needs. Taken in that context, some would say that we were quite privileged to be able to afford a vacation, considered back then to be a luxury. My father, however, worked very hard at his job and like everyone else, needed time off to recharge the proverbial batteries. His job with the airline provided us with flight rebates for foreign travel but he did not like flying. Overseas trips were also quite expensive and with the restrictions on the amount of foreign currency that could be purchased, it was never an option for my father. Those were not the only reasons though. He looked at his holidays as a time to be totally detached from work and to completely relax. He always loved going to the seaside and by the time we were old enough, his vacation decision was natural, and eventually expected and anticipated.

Mayaro is located along the East Coast of Trinidad. Back then it was a very rural area where the locals made a living from the ocean. If you took a trip through the Mayaro area, your first impression would be the coconut estates. The coconut estates and the Atlantic stood side by side separated by a wide beach that ran from Manzanilla to Galeota. Far and in between, you would stumble upon villages where locals relied on their wits to gouge a living from the sea. With names like Plaisance and Guayaguayare that reflected Trinidad's colonial past and rich heritage, these were the seaside villages where I spent holidays with my family and where I long to return to. My memories are so vivid that I can remember the heat of the sun, the feel of the sand, the aromas that abounded and I yearn to be there once more, to go back to a time and place where the biggest concern was how to prepare the fresh fish for our supper, or whether to play cricket or football on the beach.

As I reminisce about these past times, I am amazed at how vivid these memories are. It seems like it was just yesterday that these things happened. It is now that as an adult, in retrospect, that I understood the lure that Mayaro held for my father, in the same way it does for me now as an adult myself. Life was so simple then. It was a time when you could derive the most pleasure from the simplest things; when happiness was not measured by the size of your bank account or how much you had stashed away for retirement; when a simple gift like a shiny penknife could evoke immense joy; when eating a sno-cone with milk was a luxurious treat; when we took one day at a time and made the most of it. Sometimes we must slow down the frantic pace of our lives, step back, breathe and remember what is important. These are the days and the times that come back to haunt me and get me into such a nostalgic delirium that I cannot focus on anything else except these memories. It's then I realize that quality of life cannot only be measured in terms of material things, but more importantly by the time we share with our loved ones and what memories we create for our children.

If Vashti and I could create similar memories for our boys Joshua and Aaron, so that one day they too can look back as I am doing, and remember with fondness, then we would have been as successful parents as my mother and father. I long for the day when my boys are older and we visit Trinidad, when I can take them to Plaisance village and to Gill Street. Though the buildings may have changed, and some of the village folks no longer there, the memories of my holidays in Mayaro will remain. I long to tell my boys about those times and hope that they too will, in their future, remember what

Vashti and I did with them. I long to visit Mayaro once more with my brother Gerry and my sister Sherry. When we go there, this time as adults, I will read them this story and hope that they too will remember as I have, and I know that my mother and father will be watching and listening, and hopefully smiling.

Chapter 1

Anticipation and Preparation

As soon as the Christmas holiday was over, my father applied for his annual vacation. He applied for six weeks from the middle of July and all of August. In January, when he received confirmation of his vacation approval, he sat with my mother to discuss and finalize the dates. When they agreed on this, he confirmed the beach house reservation with the owners. My father had cultivated a good relationship with the owners and there was a standing yearly reservation. I guess because of his airline background and discipline, he wanted to notify them as early as possible to finalize the booking. When this was done and the deposit was paid to the owner's agent, he summoned us and informed us of the dates for our vacation. We received this news with great excitement and though the holidays were still some months away, we started dreaming about them. School usually closed at the end of June and re-opened the first week of September. This year we would leave on the Monday after school had closed and we would spend five glorious weeks in Mayaro.

    The next few months rolled slowly by punctuated by the Easter term examinations and by the short two-week Easter holiday. I was an acolyte at our St. Charles parish church and I spent most of the Easter holidays with the other boys helping to clean and prepare the church for Holy Week celebrations. We had practices for each of the masses during Holy Week and I oversaw training everyone on their duties. We did, however, manage to get some football and cricket games in between our duties at the church. After Easter, the final term of the school year was very tough and we all worked very hard to obtain good results. Good results always pleased our parents and set a good mood for the holidays. After what seemed like an eternity, the final school term came to an end, and as the last bell rung on the Friday afternoon, I grabbed my sister Sherry and gleefully joined our other cousins outside the school gates as we excitedly walked down Archibald Street towards my grandparents' house.

Archibald Street led to a T-intersection with Cemetery Street. My grandparents' house was on Cemetery Street. It was a large concrete building built in the traditional style on concrete stilts with the main house on the upper level and an open area underneath. There was a wide concrete staircase at the front that led up to the main house. There was a fairly large front yard. To the right of the front yard there were fruit trees including cherry, pommerac, orange and mango. Almost to the centre of the front yard, but slightly offset to the right, my grandfather Ralph, had an old wooden shed that he used to store and sort his newspapers. The entire yard was made of dirt and was swept each day with a cocoyea broom. When we got to my grandfather's shed, we put down our bags and gathered on the steps at the back of the house. It was always cool there in the shade of the giant chennette tree and plum tree. Sherry and the other girls, Rosemary and Michelle, sat at the top of the stairs talking about whatever girls talked about. The boys gathered on the landing and started spinning plans for the holidays.

As this was the last day of school, my mother allowed us some leeway before we had to be home. We enjoyed the extra freedom and hoped that the time would go by slowly. As we sat there talking, my grandmother Edna, made sada roti and with my other aunts, passed wedges of hot roti and butter to us which we thoroughly enjoyed. As the boys chatted, I silently looked at each of them. Two of them were very happy as they would be going with us on our Mayaro vacation. I knew the others were disappointed. As the time came for Sherry and I to leave for home, we picked up our bags and called out to our eldest cousin Angela to accompany us across the busy Eastern Main Road. As we walked silently up Hackett Lane, I know Sherry and I were thinking the same thoughts, only two more days to go.

My father did not have a car. It's not that he did not know how to drive, but I guess he never felt the need to get one. All of his working life was spent in the airline and transportation to and from work was provided for him. We lived all our lives in Tunapuna and everywhere was accessible and within walking distance. Sometimes I felt cheated because we were not able to pick up ourselves and go wherever and whenever we liked. In retrospect, however, my father used to drink fairly heavily and I could see why it was a wise decision for him not to have a car. When my youngest brother Gerard was born, my father stopped drinking and it was almost five years that he was on the proverbial wagon. So, whenever we planned our annual vacation, he made arrangements with two of his friends, Chestnut and Selwyn, to provide the transportation for us down to Mayaro. We needed two cars because apart from the five of us in my family, we always invited a few others to accompany us. This was usually my mother's older brother Roy, her younger brother Kelvin, his girlfriend Radica and two cousins. This year Ronald and Hayden were going with us.

Saturday morning dawned with my parents doing various chores around the house in preparation for our departure. While my mother did the laundry, we tidied up our rooms and packed away all our old books from the previous term. We had already presented our term test results to our parents. We both placed in the top five in our classes and our percentages were quite good, reflective of the high standard that our school, the Tunapuna Hindu School, prided itself in. As such, our parents were reasonably satisfied though they admonished us to do better next time. We had our booklists for the new school year and when the laundry was done, they took us to Charran's Bookstore to purchase the new books needed for the new school year that would begin in September. This was always exciting as well as daunting. The excitement of the feel and smell of the new books was mixed with a dread about going into a higher class. This anxiety did not last long though for as soon as we left the bookstore with bags in hand, we forgot about those uncertainties and concentrated on the upcoming journey to Mayaro. We wanted to take a leisurely walk back home along the Eastern Main Road, but my father urged us to quicken our pace as there were still quite a lot of chores to be done.

When we arrived home, after unpacking our books, we wrote our names and addresses inside each of them and covered them with brown paper. While Sherry and I did this, my parents sorted out the various linens and bedclothes that we would take with us. My brother Gerry sat glued to the television absorbed in the cartoons. They selected older sheets, pillowcases and blankets not wanting to take the finer stuff to be exposed to the salt air and sand. Next they rummaged through the closets to locate the beach blankets and beach towels. With all of the linens secured, they rolled them into tight little bundles so as to economize on packing space. By this time, we finished papering our new books and packed them into our book bags and stored them away in our closets for the new term.

My parents finished with the linens and moved to the kitchen. They needed to make a selection of pots, pans, crockery, plates, bowls, cups, glasses and various cooking utensils. This was a more painstaking exercise as these were bulky and heavy. Eventually they decided on two large iron pots, a rice colander, a large frying pan, two aluminum pots with covers and a variety of stackable bowls. There was a collection of enamel and plastic plates and cups which had served us well in the past and these were packed as well. My mother had a set of used cutlery which was appropriate for taking to Mayaro. All of the kitchen items were packed and stacked into two moderate sized boxes and taped close.

It was about two o'clock in the afternoon when we finished with the linens and the kitchen. The next chore was a pleasant one, going to Hi-Lo Supermarket to get the groceries. The supermarket was only two streets away from our house. We liked these trips as my parents were more likely to splurge a little and there would be treats for us. When we got there, we got a large shopping cart and I was allowed to push it. We made our way down each aisle while my parents selected the items that they wanted and checked it off their list. It was not practical to take everything we needed for the five-week holiday; there would be no space in the cars. Instead, they opted for items that were noticeably more expensive in Mayaro. Their selections included various canned foods and vegetables, tea, cocoa, coffee, sugar, flour, milk, rice, butter, oil, cheese, salami, toilet paper, mosquito coils, matches, toothpaste, soap, condiments and canned fruit juices. We would replenish items at the Mayaro Co-operative. In addition, there was an excellent market in Mayaro that would provide us with fresh fruit and vegetables as well as with fresh meat if we should so desire. However, with the abundance of fresh fish caught daily, meat would be eaten only on the odd occasion. We persuaded my parents to add some wafers and chocolates as a treat. When the purchases were paid for, because there were so many parcels, my father arranged for the groceries to be delivered to our house during the evening. We, however, kept our treats with us and made our way to the Tunapuna market to purchase seasonings.

We picked our way through the crowded market towards Sonny's stall. Sonny was the vendor from whom we usually bought our market items. On the list were chives, Spanish thyme, chandon beni, onions, garlic and hot peppers. These ingredients would be chopped and blended to make a local green seasoning that was versatile with both meat and seafood. They bought enough to make a large bottle that would provision us for the duration of our holiday. I always liked going to the market as it was always lively and colorful. The vendors who did not have stalls simply spread crocus bags on the road on which to display their produce and wares. Various smells permeated the air and nostrils were either tickled by a pleasant aroma or wrinkled when we passed the poultry depot.

When we finished with our purchases, we made our way to the back of the market near to where the huge immortelle tree stood. As we approached this area, a tantalizing aroma hit us. It came from the doubles vendor from whom my father always made his purchases. We approached his doubles box, perched in the carriage of a carrier bicycle, and my father ordered doubles for each of us. I ordered mine with slight pepper. The vendor deftly pulled his brown paper, slapped on two bara side by side, spooned the channa onto one of the bara and quickly added the hot pepper and bhandhania sauce. He did not fold the paper as we decided to eat the hot doubles right there. It was a bit messy, but absolutely delicious. Sherry and Gerry did not want doubles, so they ordered aloo pies instead. After eating our delicacies, we crossed over to the coconut vendor. My father ordered cold coconuts for each of us. I stood by mesmerized by the expert way the vendor handled the coconuts and his cutlass to hack them open. Sherry and Gerry each has a Solo Apple J instead. With our late lunch finished, we jostled our way out of the market and made our way home.

It was late afternoon, nearly dusk, when we got home and my mother sent us to shower and change our clothes. Just as I finished and made my way out to the living room, there came the sound of a vehicle honking its horn outside. I ran downstairs to help my father bring the parcels into the house. There was no need to unpack the boxes. The perishables, margarine, cheese and salami were packed separately in a bag and this went directly into the refrigerator. The other boxes were stowed away in the room adjacent to the kitchen. We then heard the front gate open and footsteps scampering up the stairs. It was the familiar way in which Kelvin ascended, two steps at a time. Kelvin lived with us and had done so since he was eighteen years old. He and Roy were our two favourite uncles and we had a special bond with them. Kelvin had just come from visiting his girlfriend Radica in Laventille. He announced that her mother would supply us with the usual offering of a bottle of her special homemade pepper sauce. Tired from the day's exertions, we settled down to relax after a very long day. Everything was in place. My father had made all the arrangements for the house, the date and time for departure were set, the transportation was arranged, the shopping was completed and the packing was done.

It was a tradition to invite two cousins to spend the holidays at Mayaro with us. Ronald was our automatic choice and he was included each year. The second was chosen from among the rest of cousins. This year, Hayden was also going with us. We all enjoyed Ronald's and Hayden's company. Five glorious weeks at a beach house in Mayaro beckoned, offering endless relaxation and fun. Ronald and I were the same age and Hayden was one year older. We all went to the same school and enjoyed each other's company immensely. My other cousins were a few years older so it was natural for the three of us to have a bond. They were both daring and sometimes a bit foolhardy, but always fun to be with. They too were as excited as we were and we could hardly wait for Monday morning.

Part of the excitement of going on holiday was the anticipation. As soon as dawn broke on Sunday morning, I sprang out of my bed. My parents were already up and about. My mother busied herself in the kitchen preparing breakfast. My father had taken his morning stroll to get the daily newspaper. Sherry and Gerry were also up and sitting in front of the television. Not for me though. I climbed onto the porch banister to get a better view of the street corner. The morning sun caused me to squint but I kept my eyes glued to the corner in eager anticipation of the boys' arrival. Ronald and Hayden would be at our house as soon as their mothers allowed. There was so much to do, so much to plan. Only a second stern command from my mother tore me away from the porch and got me back inside the house to sit down to breakfast.

Reluctantly I peeled myself away but the aroma of breakfast heightened my hunger. Breakfast during the holidays always had a languor to it. This morning there was bread and butter, a generous plateful of sausages and eggs, and the green jug of hot tea. Just as I started on my plate, there came the familiar sound of the creaky rusted hinges on the front gate. They were here. Ruff's excited barks and their all too excited squeals about the start of holidays heralded their arrival. Hayden was never one to refuse an offered meal and promptly took his place next to me while playfully poking his elbow into my ribs. Ronald tried to coax my mother to give him bread and butter with guava jam, while he sat grinning at the table. The meal was soon finished and we were eager to gather in my room to make up and go over our plans. After helping my mother to clear the breakfast dishes, we were excused and off we went to dream up our plans for each day of the holidays.

After much beseeching, we allowed Sherry and Gerry into the room to sit with us and allowed them to feel that they were involved in the planning effort. But soon they grew tired of our conversation and withdrew back to the television. Most of our discussions started with someone saying "remember when?" It was not so much planning but rather more reminiscing about past holidays and experiences. We tried our hardest to retrieve memories and felt elated when someone said a word or a phrase that brought them back in a flood. So the morning passed in glorious reverie. There was no special Sunday lunch today. My parents were busy doing other chores, besides which, no one really felt like being cooped up in the kitchen on the day before we were due to leave.

By the time noon rolled around and after a quick lunch of the previous evening's re-heated leftovers, we needed to get outdoors and find a release for some of the pent up excitement. We missed our daily game of cricket yesterday what with all our chores. Today, however, we arranged for a game and were expecting the other players to arrive soon. There was an almost daily ritual of windball cricket played with a tennis ball beneath our house. The yard was fully concrete and the space beneath the house was about twelve feet high. The length of the pitch was the width of the house, just over forty feet. The concrete provided an even bounce on the ball, but the short pitch was a bit daunting when facing the faster bowlers.

Just as we went downstairs into the yard, my other cousins and friends arrived for the game. I remembered seeing their faces and knew that each one of them longed to accompany us to Mayaro: my cousins Anthony, Derek, Ernest and Steve; my friends Brian Baptiste, Andrew Boodhoo, Vernon Ramlogan and Leighton Goodridge. As much as we would have loved to have them all accompany us, we could take only two, and Hayden and Ronald were the lucky choices. My parents were also very fond of these two and got along really well with them. The first tasks were to set up the wickets and draw the creases. There then followed the usual brouhaha with everyone trying to call the batting and bowling order. This exercise was quite rowdy and involved a lot of argument. Hearing all the commotion, my father and Kelvin came downstairs to see what was going on. Satisfied that it was only the call of the batting and bowling order, they good-naturedly decided to join the game. They even coaxed my mother to leave her chores and join us downstairs. Two other neighbors, Ray and Ras were out on their porches and hollered out to us that they were coming over to join the game. It seemed quite uncanny, but even Selwyn decided to pop in to see us and he also joined the game.

Pretty soon the game was in full swing. As if to execute some personal vendetta at being passed over for the Mayaro holiday, the other guys would put some extra zip when bowling to us and the ball more often than not struck us. This became a source of amusement for Kelvin and my father who referred to the blows as "body music." They in turn dealt their own blows to the others and it became a game of who could bowl the fastest and make the loudest noise when the ball struck the old kerosene pans that served as a wicket. However, it was all in good stead and there was no animosity. The game was as rambunctious and competitive as ever and the noise level attracted other neighbors as spectators. They cheered our shots and applauded the bowlers for their wickets. About mid-afternoon, Alfred the sno-cone vendor passed with his cart on his usual Sunday jaunt. It was quite hot and the adults stopped the game for a break. They hailed Alfred to stop and Kelvin went into the house to fetch some money. They bought sno-cones for everyone and we all thoroughly enjoyed the sweet cold syrup and shaved ice. My father brought out a tin of condensed milk that disappeared in a flash. After the sno-cones, my mother and sister passed around bottles of iced water to the thirsty players and we continued the game until dusk.

    As the sun began to set, we reluctantly abandoned the game and converged around the garden tap to wash sweat and dirt encrusted feet. There was the usual jostling to feel the cool water on our feet, hands and flushed faces. Before the game was finished, Selwyn left and went to Chung Lee's Bakery to pick up four quarts of hops bread and a case of Solo soft drinks. As we were washing up, my mother finished preparing sandwiches, one type with cheese and avocado, and the other with Vienna sausages fried with onions and ketchup. Tired from the game, we all gathered on the steps and on the landing to relax and enjoy the food my mother prepared for everyone. We were ravenous and we washed the tasty sandwiches down with mugs of cold soft drinks. My father and uncle were good at ribbing us at our foibles during the game and this was the prelude to an animated discussion.

    This evening was a bit different though, because as darkness wore on, there came the dreaded parting with my cousins and friends. I would not see them for five weeks. They would all come down to Mayaro with Aunt Jean one Sunday, but it would be only for the day. I was sad, but we could not invite them all to go with us. As they left, Ronald and Hayden reconfirmed the departure time for the next morning. We brought the cricket bats and balls and the football upstairs with us lest we forget them. I helped clear away the garbage and dishes from our meal on the stairs and then took my shower. After that, I finished packing my bag, mainly shorts, tee shirts and underwear. My mother looked after the packing for Sherry and Gerry. She ensured that there were enough long sleeved jerseys for the cool evenings. I ventured into the kitchen and observed my parents going over their checklist. They tried to think of everything, but whatever we forgot, we could buy at Mr. James' shop in Plaisance village. Kelvin would soon return with Radica and then all that would be left would be to sleep through one more night before we left for Mayaro.

Chapter 2

Here We Come: The Start of the Holidays

Monday morning, the day of departure, had finally come! My father woke us up at five o'clock in the morning. Sleepy eyed but excited, we made our way to the bathroom to do our toiletries. Radica and my mother prepared sandwiches to take with us to eat in the car. Showered and changed and after a cup of hot cocoa, we got all our personal bags together. Selwyn and Chestnut were already there and were having coffee. Roy was also there and he, Kelvin and my father took all the bags and boxes and stowed them in the trunks. It took some doing to fit all that we were carrying but they made everything fit. Meanwhile, my mother and Radica did a walk around the house to check that all taps were shut, that all appliances were unplugged and that all windows were shut.

With the house secured, we went downstairs. Our neighbor Ras came over to see us off. My father gave him some money as they had arranged for him to take care of the two dogs and make sure that they were fed. With our good-byes said and a last glance at our Tunapuna home, we climbed into the cars to begin our journey to our new home, at least for the next five weeks. There was one stop on Cemetery Street to pick up Ronald and Hayden. As the cars turned into Cemetery Street, we could see the two of them agitatedly waving to us to hurry up. They had been waiting on us since six o'clock. They quickly clambered in and by six fifteen we were on our way!

There were hardly any cars on the road at this time of day. My mother, Radica, my father and Roy sat in one car. All kids wanted to be in the same car so Kelvin sat with us in the other. Food always seemed to taste better when eaten outdoors. We did not have breakfast before we left and we greedily munched away on our cheese paste sandwiches as we set off, each of us silent with our own thoughts and anticipation. It would take just over two hours to get to Mayaro, so to pass the time we looked for familiar markers. The roundabout at Piarco that led to the airport was the first. As we passed the gas station, we could see an aircraft taxiing along the runway in the distance. The beacon of the Air Traffic Control Tower was clearly visible and we could see the beam of light change from white to green as it revolved. There was the grove of pine trees that marked the end of the runway and which was also a landmark to Mausica. As we neared Arima, we wrinkled our noses at the unpleasant odour of the poultry farms. As we were going at a fair clip the stench soon faded. The white rails and the tote board of the Santa Rosa racetrack soon came into view. I knew the racetrack well as my parents had taken me to the horse races there several times. We then passed the stone columns that marked the entrance to Wallerfield. We knew that we were leaving the towns behind as the concrete houses soon started giving way to vast stretches of open pastures and green fields.

The windows were rolled down and the cool morning air was refreshing on our faces. We could see the hills of the Northern Range and we tried to discern the highest points of El Tucuche and El Cerro del Aripo. The hills were very verdant and in some places where the foliage was densest, the green seemed almost bluish. We passed the farms of Wallerfield with cows and other cattle lazily grazing on the grass still moist with dew. As we came to a familiar T-junction, we got even more excited because this was another major marker on our journey. We referred to this spot as the point where we left civilization and ventured into rural Trinidad. We were approaching

Valencia. Valencia was not only a pit stop for travelers going on East Coast outings, but was also a launching point for trekkers into the hills of the Northern Range and to the north-eastern coast beaches of Toco, Matura, Balandra and Salybia. We knew that at Valencia there would be the mandatory stop at the famous Ponderosa Bar for cold lagers for Kelvin and Roy, and soft drinks for everyone else. The stop at the Ponderosa was a ritual that not only my family performed, but almost every family journeying to Trinidad's East Coast. We eagerly jumped out of the cars to stretch our legs and to see what treats we could salvage from the grownups on this brief stop. Reinforced with supplies of peanuts, channa and cold Coca-Cola, we continued on to the next leg of the trip down the notorious Valencia Stretch and on to Sangre Grande.

The Stretch, as it was known to locals, was an almost straight road that led from Valencia to Sangre Grande. It was notorious because of the amount of fatal accidents that had occurred on it. Because it was so straight, drivers were always tempted to speed. Our drivers, however, were not so inclined and we drove along leisurely with no traffic in front of, or at the back of us. We felt as if we were the only ones on the road at this time of day. We passed the clay quarry with its red earth. Kelvin told us to keep our eyes peeled to the right side of the road where the forest began. He told us that we might catch a glimpse of some of the forest animals. So we focused on the fringe of green trees and dense bushes. I guess he did that to get us to shut up for a bit, but alas we saw no exotic animals except for a mangy stray dog. Presently the road started losing its straightness and we found ourselves driving around curves. This was a sign that the Stretch was ending and that we were approaching Sangre Grande. It could not come too soon, as we normally felt a bit uneasy being on the Stretch.

We slowed down as we drove into Sangre Grande. We passed the familiar Ascot Cinema and exchanged an old joke about the name that my cousin Steve had made up. A little further on we turned left onto a one-way street that went past the bus terminal with its black asphalt made even blacker by oil and diesel stains. There were a few buses taking on passengers for the haul to Rio Claro, San Fernando and Port of Spain. We drove past the roundabout with the Police Station on the left. We wanted to stop at the Sea-Way bakery for cakes, but the adults declined. We did not stop at Sangre Grande and continued the journey towards the east coast. As we drove out of Sangre Grande, we noticed a change in the terrain. This sector of the trip took us through the cocoa estates of Trinidad. We saw the cocoa trees laden with brightly colored yellow pods or the duller purple pods. These trees produced some of the highest quality cocoa in the world. Companies like Cadbury and Hershey vied for Trinidad's cocoa to produce their chocolates. The trees looked different and the air smelt different. Because the cocoa trees demanded shade, there were huge immortelle trees everywhere. Their dense canopies created almost a barrier to the sun and this made the air feel cooler. There was not much else to see on this sector as the road literally cut through the cocoa estates.

      We soon left the cocoa estates and came upon another marked change in the flora. Instead of cocoa trees, there were now thousands of coconut palms. These were the coconut estates of the East Coast that provided an ample supply of water nuts for domestic consumption as well as rich copra to produce high quality coconut oil. Munching on peanuts, we started looking out for the distance markers along the coconut estates. As we descended a slight incline in the road, we spotted the signpost that said Caigual Trace. Chestnut lived in Caigual Trace. This was an important marker that indicated we were getting very close to the ocean. The bushes here were no longer lush and dense but were very short and scraggly. The earth was not rich and dark, but rather more of a sandy loam. It was, however, perfect for the coconut palms that grew tall and majestic. We were entering Manzanilla.

Manzanilla offered the first glimpse of the mighty Atlantic Ocean along the East Coast where there is vehicular access from inland. The beach embraced the Atlantic Ocean and stretched from Manzanilla all the way down to Mayaro and Galeota Point. As we drove into Manzanilla and passed a familiar uphill curve in the road, we craned our necks to see who would catch the first glimpse of First & Last Grocery and Bar. This was the penultimate marker on our trip and another institution for trekkers to the beaches. Since Valencia, we were in the car for just about thirty minutes and we needed not only to stretch our legs, but also to release and communicate our excitement. We bought fresh bread and vegetables at a stall conveniently located under the shop's awning and then boarded the cars again for the last hop to Mayaro.

There were five curves in the road to go and we knew them all. We counted them down as we drove on. We were all sitting forward with our eyes glued to the front of the cars. "I see it" was the scream from Gerry who was sitting with Kelvin in the front seat. Then we all saw the same vista as the car descended the slight incline. It started as a lush green canopy of palm leaves that quickly yielded a ribbon of blue and brown, the Atlantic Ocean and Manzanilla Bay. What a glorious sight! The first glimpse of the ocean evoked tremendous emotion and provided an overwhelming promise of a glorious holiday on its beach. The waves seemed to lumber to the shore with discolored foam. The water and the foam here had a brownish color caused by the outflow of the Nariva and Ortoire Rivers into the bay, but further out past the breakers, the sea was its usual deep blue color.

It was just before eight o'clock in the morning and the sun sent its rays streaming through the dense canopy of coconut branches. Without being asked, the drivers slowed their speed for all to drink in the spectacular scenery. The air was moist and smelt salty and we could taste the salt on our lips after a while. Everyone sat silently absorbing the moment. This was Nature at her finest. The coconut trees, uniformly planted and spaced on either side of the road, lurched up to the sky. Gravity, weight and the wind caused them to bend. Their palm branches almost met and formed a green vaulted arch that resembled a tunnel of brown trunks and green ceilings. It was almost like being in Nature's own Cathedral. The "coconut" as this stretch is known, is still one of the most beautiful, scenic drives on the island especially early in the morning when the sun is beginning its climb into the heavens.

It seemed like an eternity lost in silent wonderment and awe at the beauty of the scenery but it only spanned a few minutes. The road ran parallel to the beach and was almost straight. Because of the blast from the sea and the salty air, the surface was not smooth and there were lots of potholes. As the cars rumbled on we hoped that the drivers would speed up so that we could get to our destination faster. We absorbed all the beautiful scenery around us and marveled at the vast expanse of ocean beside us. The silence was soon broken with good-natured teasing as the dreaded Spring Bridge came into view. This was the one part of the journey that all the kids wanted to skip. I know we all felt the same way because we all fell instantly silent as the tires rolled over the first wooden planks on the bridge. There was always some trepidation at having to cross this bridge. The cars made their way slowly across the bridge and every revolution of the tires caused it to creak. The creaking was so eerie that we silently held our collective breaths while we conjured up frightful thoughts about falling into the dark Nariva River and being consumed by the thick muck and grotesque aquatic animals. Then, as suddenly as it had started, in less than ten seconds, it was over. Everyone breathed a collective sigh of relief, happy that this hurdle had been crossed. We were back on terra firma and rolling towards Point Radix.

Point Radix is the little peninsula that juts out like a nipple on Trinidad's East Coast. Point Radix was the last major marker on our journey and we knew that we were almost there. Only another fifteen minutes and we would be able to start our holiday. Point Radix was a hilly promontory and the road followed the natural contours and took us inland away from the ocean for a bit. We passed through a small village built on the banks of the Ortoire River. There was another bridge to cross here, but this was the Silver Bridge, built to take only one lane of traffic, and constructed from steel and asphalt.

As we traversed Point Radix, we left Manzanilla and entered Mayaro. There was no interest in looking at the scenery anymore as we anxiously counted the last few miles. There was just one more coconut estate to traverse and we would be there. A rattle, a bump, past the cattle grazing in the savannah, past the Lourenco horse farm, past the grocery store with its rusted ice bin, past the rickety old shack where the local whappie was played and then we saw the Junction! The Junction, as locals and visitors alike referred to it, was actually a fork in the road with a crown at the middle. Anti-clockwise to our right was the Naparima Mayaro Road and the Guayaguayare Road. To our left, the road descended to Plaisance Village. As the car turned left, less than a kilometer away, we saw the black asphalt of the road end as it met with the whitish-brown of the sandy beach. Past the football field, past the Co-operative, past the grog shop, past the array of two-storey houses, past the ice depot, hearts beating faster, past Mr. James' shop, adrenaline pumping away, right turn into Gill Street, past the bakery, past Assee's flats and there it was. Standing like a concrete dwarf among the giant almond trees, painted in its battleship gray, was our destination, Thackories Beach House. We were finally there and the holidays had begun!

The gates were open and we drove right in all the way down the driveway to our unit. My father always arranged to get the three-bedroom unit facing the sea. We thought it was the best of the seven units in the compound. The huge green windows in the living area were propped upright and the door was open. With a jerk, both cars came to a stop and we clambered out, bare feet touching the already hot, sandy asphalt of the driveway. Lloyd, the caretaker, was there with his wife. They had been cleaning and preparing for our arrival. My first action was to quickly glance around the surroundings. It was exactly as I had remembered from the year before. Nothing had changed. The coconut tree was exactly where it was supposed to be, right outside our bedroom window. The fence was still intact with its nails and tie wire rusting and flaking from the salty sea blast. The galvanized water tanks were still there though the owners had added two new plastic ones. My mother would be pleased that there would be a better water supply. The concrete benches were outside our back door and the laths looked like they were newly painted. Everything seemed to be as I remembered and rightfully it should be so. We did not want anything to change.

My cursory glance completed, the next duty at hand was to greet Lloyd and his wife. Lloyd was the caretaker and also a friend. He was also the dealer who set the prices for the fish with the fishermen and the buyers. He was also reputed to be the banker for the local whappie network hence his nickname "casa." He always looked out for us during the seines and made sure that we took some fish back home every time. It was good to see him again though his hair seemed to be a little grayer than I remembered. He had already taken my mother into the kitchen where he proudly displayed a spotless freezer containing two large carite and three large baichine. This was always his way of greeting us when we arrived. We knew that there would be fish for supper that night. He quizzed us as to our progress in school and was pleased when we told him of our results. He nevertheless felt obliged to give us a little speech about the value of education. We smiled with him and with his oratory done, we begged him to tell us if there were any new boats and what were the names. There were no new boats and all the captains were unchanged. He told us that the ocean this year was a little warmer than in previous years and because of this, there was a great abundance of fish. We thought that this was marvelous for there would be numerous seines. However, Lloyd explained that as there was so much fish, the prices had gone down. We could not follow this logic because if too much fish caused the price to fall, then why did they not cut back on the number of seines thrown.

With everyone disembarked and the greetings completed, the next job was to help unload the vehicles. We each took out our bags and placed them as instructed on the living room table. Next we helped with the linens and pillows. The heavier boxes we left for the men to bring in. The groceries were placed on the kitchen counter, the propane tanks were connected and stowed next to the stove, and my mother secured the perishables in the refrigerator. On the given signal, we scampered to our bedroom to commandeer the beds and dresser drawers. My mother and father had one room, Kelvin and Radica had another and the kids would share our usual room. Roy would bunk on the couch.

We opened the bedroom windows and dusted the mattresses. Even though Lloyd and his wife had cleaned the apartment, my mother and Radica insisted on doing it again themselves. We used a bottle of water to sprinkle the floor to keep the sand from flying and settling on everything. My mother swept the room thoroughly and we helped make the beds. There were two large beds in our room. Sherry and Gerry shared one closer to the wall and the three boys shared the other next to the window. It was not at all cramped, rather it was cozy at night when telling ghost stories. The space in the large chest of drawers at the foot of our bed was divided up with each of us bagging a drawer. We unpacked our things and stored them away. My father gave each child a small allowance for us to indulge ourselves at Mr. James' shop. We knew that we would supplement our cash reserves with some chores. With the bedroom taken care of, we turned our attention to the main living area.

The adults had not yet set up their rooms as they were busy cleaning and sweeping the main living area and re-sanitizing the toilets. The kitchen was self-contained and walled off from the living area. There was no door but rather an open archway that led from the dining area. The living and dining areas were an open plan. Six large green wooden windows ran the length of this area with a two-part door in the middle. The windows were the type that had to be pushed out and propped into an open position with a wooden plank. In the middle of the room there was the familiar orange painted table with four wooden benches. On the far right of the room, there was a large couch and two Morris sitting chairs all upholstered in dark maroon vinyl. Roy would make the couch his bed and we knew that he did not feel slighted at not getting his own bed. Roy was one of those people who needed very little to be happy and he had a joie-de-vivre about him that rubbed off on those he encountered. I guess that was the reason he and my father got along so well. Between the kitchen and Kelvin's bedroom, to the rear of the living room, was the face basin where we would clean our teeth and do our toiletries. The kitchen was small but practical. The sink area was constructed of solid concrete that would provide a flat, sturdy surface for preparation and ease of cleaning. The refrigerator was one of those old behemoths, rusted from years of sea blast, but whose working motor and compressor were a testament to the quality that craftsmen of yore took in their trade. With the tour of the apartment completed, we explored the compound as we had not yet been given permission to go down to the beach.

The Thackories compound was located on the beachfront side of Gill Street. There were seven units in three buildings. Facing Gill Street, there was a two storey main building that spanned the width of the compound. This building had four fine units but had no ocean view. In front of this main building, facing the ocean was another two storey building, half the size of the main. This one had two more units. We had the bottom unit, the fifth, while the top one, the sixth, was normally reserved for the owner. To the right of the ocean-facing building, was a small single house unit, by far the largest of the seven. At the back of the house unit, there was a large concrete deck that held a magnificent water cistern and three open air showers. We relished the thought of having our showers here. Between the main building and our unit, there were four large galvanized water tanks and two new plastic ones that were installed on high concrete supports. There was also another open air shower and stand pipe for rinsing purposes. In front of the two beach facing units and slightly to the sides, were four coconut trees. There was one tree wholly on our side, and the other three were in front of the house unit. In the middle of these two units there were five steps that led down to the beach. If you stood facing the sea, to the left of our compound, there was a six-foot brick wall that separated Assee's flats. To the right there was an empty plot of land used as a thoroughfare for access to the beach by other vacationers in the houses and units on the other side of Gill Street. At the back of our unit, facing the sea, there were two park-type benches that we used for our morning and evening gatherings. There was also a door that opened from our bedroom between the two benches. This made for easy access in and out of the unit and when held open, allowed a fresh breeze to flow through the entire unit.

With our exploration of the compound done, we returned to our apartment in eager anticipation of being allowed to go down onto the beach. I guess the grownups knew our thoughts and anticipated our collective plea. Radica sliced an orange sponge cake that her mother had sent and Kelvin poured soft drinks and ice into a mug. As my father gave the nod of approval to proceed to the beach, five eager children brushed him aside and our yells and screams added to everyone's excitement. I knew the adults were just as eager as they followed right behind us, their faces giving away their excitement. Kelvin and Radica set down the snacks and started a playful romp in the sand while Roy and my father engaged in a mock sprint. My mother sat on a log and surveyed all the activity taking place before her. The tide was out and left about fifty feet of beach before the ebb and flow limit of the water. There would be a lot of space for our cricket and football games later on; but those would wait because today we all wanted to wade and feel the sea water around our ankles. I scooped up a handful and splashed my face and arms.

My mother summoned us and doled out slices of cake and cups of cold drinks. Our excitement had taken our minds off food, but our exertions made us ravenous. We devoured our snack and, on instruction from my mother, returned to the apartment, which we would soon refer to as home, to change into our bathing suits lest we get our clothes wet and dirty. We knew that we would soon be allowed into the water and with youthful exuberance, dashed back to the beach. Kelvin and Radica had also changed and accompanied us into the water. With yelps and shouts of excitement, we ran into the water, splashing each other. We were allowed to go only up to mid-torso. Then I saw the first wave. Not large by any stretch of the imagination, crested with white foam, as it lumbered towards us. I dove through its middle completely immersing myself in its wake. The water was gorgeous and it felt like a warm swimming pool. The sun was brilliant overhead and the rays reflected off the surface of the water causing us to squint in the glare. By stooping in the water and kicking our legs out from under us, we floated on the surface. We swam in every possible manner and then started body surfing to the shore.

My mother, father and Roy also changed into their swimsuits and entered the water as well. They never ventured far out, but preferred to wade in up to mid-calf, lie prostrate on their tummies, support themselves with their elbows with their hands extended, palms flat on the sea bed and the water would float them with their backs to the waves. That way, by the time the waves broke and lumbered to the shoreline, it would gently cascade over them wetting their backs and their heads. This was how they enjoyed the water while chatting with each other. So we went on for hours on that first day at the beach and a perfect start to the holidays.

Time had no relevance to us what with five idyllic weeks stretching in front of us. We lost track of it and did not realize that my mother, father and Roy had left the water and returned home. It was not until Gerry complained of being hungry that Kelvin took notice of the time of day. The sun had long passed overhead and the coconut trees cast long shadows on the shore. He made us rinse the sand from our suits and return home. Reluctantly we did as we were told, took a last dive under a wave and slowly walked out to the shore. The late afternoon breeze was quite mild, but it caused goose bumps and Sherry's teeth even chattered. It was not cold, but we had been in the warm ocean for so long that our body temperature had to re-adjust. My mother heard us coming and had the towels ready. My father pointed us to the outdoor shower adjacent to our home and held out a bar of soap. We allowed Gerry and Sherry to go first and then we took our turn. We thoroughly lathered our bodies, rinsed off the suds and gladly accepted the towels proffered by my mother. We dried our hair and roughly toweled our skin luxuriating in the slight sting that it caused on our shoulders and faces that had already begun to show a dark tinge. We would soon be thoroughly burnt by the sun. With the towels wrapped around us, we stood in the driveway under the coconut tree, faces turned to the last crimson rays of sunlight rapidly descending in the west. We did not talk. Each of us I guessed was silently recollecting all the events of this first day in Mayaro.

Back in our bedroom, we quickly changed out of our wet things and donned dry shorts and tee shirts. My mother produced a bottle of lotion and instructed us to apply it generously. Freshly changed and bodies adequately moisturized with lotion, we drifted to the living area where a delicious smell permeated the air. We had skipped lunch and only had the one snack. We did not feel hungry during our romp in the sea, but now that we were warm and cozy in the house, our stomachs began to rumble reminding us that a meal was overdue. Radica anticipated our impatience and produced a jug of cocoa.

There were always two plastic jugs, a green one for tea and an orange one for cocoa. She poured us each a mug of steaming cocoa and handed us a few Bermudez vanilla cookies, also known as sweet biscuits, to tide us through until supper was ready. We coaxed my father and Roy to accompany us onto the benches outside and sipped our hot drink. Conversation was not hard to come by and we engaged in a discussion about the most recent Bruce Lee movie, *Enter The Dragon*.

When the ladies called that supper was ready, we did not need a second invitation to the table. We took our usual places and eagerly awaited supper to begin. There was a huge platter of country bread and butter, an absolutely enormous platter of fried fish, a simple salad of tomatoes and cucumber and the usual offering from Radica's mother, the bottle of reddish-yellow pepper sauce. We helped ourselves from the platters and salivated as we dug in. The fish had just been fried and was still hot. We made a mixture of ketchup, mustard and pepper sauce on our plates, flaked the fish onto the bread, spread some of our condiment mixture and made the most delicious sandwich ever. Getting us to eat fresh fish was never a problem. Again, there was more hot cocoa and we quickly devoured our supper. Slight burps were heard from my brother and sister causing an embarrassed smile on their faces. There was no scolding for them from the adults. We were not so lucky though when the three boys decided to see who could belch the loudest and longest. This first supper in Mayaro was perfect and everything we hoped it would be.

It was only seven o'clock in the evening, but the previous day's anticipation and our first day's exertions were catching up with us. After supper, we got the deck of cards and played a game of all-fours. The grownups got their own deck and started their game of gin-rummy. Even though they wanted to stay up all night, my sister and brother soon dozed off at the table and had to be carried to their bed. Determined to try and stay up as long as possible, Hayden, Ronald and I decided to take a stroll in the driveway hoping that the cool night air would erase the sleep that was fast approaching. The windows were open and the compound was adequately lit. We walked to the front gate and looked out at the street. The almond trees in the driveway opposite were silhouetted against the darkness and immediately our minds started imagining all sorts of weird things. Hayden wanted to cross over to the trees and do a bit of exploring around the old house at the end of the gap, but we decided that it was not worth the risk of getting into trouble on the first day. We would wait until the adults were a bit more relaxed and less restrictive on our movements. With that settled we walked back to the house and sat on the benches. The moon was bright and it cast a long silvery finger on the water. Far off on the distant horizon, the oil platforms were clearly visible in the dark night by the bright orange flames from the waste gas burn-off. We counted seven and realized that there was one more than the previous year. We listened to the waves as they broke and the hissing of the foam as it ran to the shore. A gentle breeze lulled us into silence and despite valiant efforts to keep awake we soon succumbed to our fatigue. After bidding everyone goodnight, we jumped into bed and snuggled under the covers. Within seconds, we were fast asleep and dreaming about the first day in Mayaro.

Chapter 3

Peter, the River and the Junction

Morning had not yet dawned, but I heard a noise coming from the kitchen. Rousing Hayden and Ronald, we got up and went to investigate. It was Roy. He was already up and making coffee. The house was shut and the light was on, so we sat on his still warm couch. He made fresh coffee in the old way by boiling the ground beans, adding the milk and sugar to the pot and then straining it into the cup. He poured a little into three cups and passed them to us with the warning not to tell my mother as we were not allowed to drink coffee. I guess that was what made Roy so special to us and why we loved him so much. He had had a hard life and he lived it very simply. We always thought he was an adventurer especially after hearing about some of his escapades when he was younger. Roy was my mother's older brother and Ronald's father. Kelvin was my mother's youngest brother. When he had poured his cup and lit his cigarette, he opened the door and we all went to sit on the bench and waited on the sunrise.

The scent of the tobacco in the early morning air was pleasant. The familiar cadence of the waves and foam was soothing and we silently sipped our hot drink. The wind was just a gentle breeze that carried the scent of the sea on it. The dew was moist in the salty air. There was just enough light to discern that the tide had come up to the wall of our fence during the night. Then it caught our attention. It started as a dull light on the horizon. Then it grew steadily in size and intensity until there was a silver and crimson aurora. We sat there with our eyes fixed to the horizon, watching as the sun rose in the east. The fiery arc was dull and we stared at it long enough to discern the corona. If you stared, it did not seem to move, but once you took your eyes away and then refocused on it, there was a visible increase in altitude. It was as though the sun did not want us to see it inch its way up. It cast a long golden beam across the horizon on the water which seemed to be calmer as if in response to the caress from the sun. As it rose higher, it was too bright to look at directly and we averted our eyes. The magnificence of this first sunrise seemed to hold a silent promise of good times and more good memories. As we sat there, the rest of the family awoke one by one, and they all knew that we were outside. They joined us and partook of the glorious canvas that was unfolding before our eyes. No words were necessary, no need to describe it, just an appreciation for God's creation and wonderment of life. In retrospect, as I sat there, I realized how insignificant we were in the grander scheme of things. The moment was shared by all and our spirit was refreshed and satisfied. Now we had to satisfy the body as the fresh morning air opened up our appetites and we all wanted our breakfast.

What was considered to be a chore in previous years had evolved into an anticipated ritual: the morning trip to Mr. James' shop to buy bread and newspapers. Changed out of our nightclothes and into our everyday wear, money securely stowed in our pockets and with a warning from my father not to dawdle, we began our first stroll out on Gill Street. Hayden was the eldest and was given charge over us on our stroll. We expertly ignored my mother's insistence on wearing slippers and proceeded barefoot down the driveway. The coconut trees were blooming and the wind had blown loose hundreds of little flowers that looked like confetti on the driveway. They felt slightly prickly under our bare feet and the asphalt was comfortably warm. We turned right onto Gill Street and walked past Assee's flats. The road was uneven and was dusted with fine sand blown by the wind. We walked past the almond trees on the right and past the little wooden shack that housed the bakery on the left. Just a few meters further we passed the High Wind Recreation Club and arrived at the corner of Gill Street and Plaisance Road. Directly in front of us was the old Chinese shop whose verandah still served the local fishermen a location to exhibit their catch. There was a small crowd peering over what looked like a very large grouper. We wanted to go have a look and Hayden agreed. We quickly crossed the road and approached the fish. It was an absolutely enormous grouper weighing about one hundred pounds. It has just been caught and its scales were still glistening with moisture. A change in the wind direction brought the fishy smell to our wrinkled noses. We were content to stand there gawking at the fish but Sherry threatened to tell of our deviation, so Hayden gathered us all and we proceeded back across the street. We went past the low wooden fence, turned left onto the next property and there was Mr. James' shop.

Mr. James' shop had its own unique character. It was an old wooden two-storey building painted in green. The shop was on the bottom and Mr. James lived above. There was a small sandy yard about ten feet in width from the road to the concrete verandah of the shop. It was littered with old crown corks strewn about in the sand. The shop was divided into two areas by a wooden latticed partition. On the left there was the grog shop that was always lively as I can remember. On the right there was the general shop that carried almost everything needed by locals and holidaymakers alike. We went into the shop and joined the line to await our turn to be served.

There were crocus bags of brown sugar that gave off a rich aroma of molasses. On the counter-top stood the glass case that proudly displayed the fresh hops, soft butter, yellow New Zealand cheese, logs of rich red aromatic salami, and fried eggs. This would be breakfast for many a fisherman as they came back from their morning jaunt on the sea. Next to the glass case was the kettle, Nescafe coffee, Milo and milk for those who did not want grog. Atop the counter were numerous glass jars that contained every imaginable treat: salt prunes, bubble gum, sweeties, chocolates, biscuits and a variety of other delicious temptations. The shelves were stacked from waist high to the ceiling and contained every imaginable type of canned food. On the highest shelves were dark bottles of Whiteway's Peardrax and Cydrax that were covered in dust. When it was our turn, Hayden ordered the loaves of country bread that we liked and two newspapers. In turn, we each ordered our treats and paid our money over. Holding on to our precious hoards, we merrily skipped out of the shop and retraced our steps back home.

As we walked back home, we stopped to pick up the almond pods that had fallen on the ground. Gill Street was not very long and just after it wound past Thackories, the road curved. There was an empty plot of land just at the curve and we spied a tall chennette tree. Taking careful aim, we began a game of trying to hit the tree with the almond pods as we walked. On hundred yards later we turned into our driveway and our game ended. We were greeted by a delicious smell emanating from our home. My mother was preparing scrambled eggs and we could hear the bacon sizzle in the pan as we entered the doorway. The windows were already opened, the living area had been swept and the breakfast items were laid out on the table. Radica took the bread to the kitchen to slice and my father took the newspapers from us. We each went to our drawers and stashed away our goodies to be enjoyed later in the day. While waiting for breakfast to be served, we took the football in the driveway and started a game of "raising" or keep-ups. The objective was to demonstrate ball-handling skills by keeping the ball in the air by chipping it gently with the feet, not letting it bounce or touch the ground and passing it off to another to do the same. We were so occupied until breakfast was ready and we were called to the table. We washed our hands and eagerly sat down in anticipation of a good breakfast. My mother dished out generous portions for everyone, Radica poured the tea and my father passed the platter of bread and butter. There was a bottle of homemade guava jelly that was a gift from Aunt Jean and we would do justice to it later in the meal once the bacon and eggs were dealt with.

    We were still at the table when we heard a familiar whistle. It had been a year since we last heard it, but we knew it quite well. It was our friend Peter the fisherman. He was coming up the driveway giving us his trademark whistle. There he was, familiar pair of tattered shorts, bare torso, hair bleached by the sea and the sun, uncombed as usual, his goatee in the same unkempt manner as his hair, but his eyes alive and twinkling. His raspy voice called out to my mother and father and we all jumped up in glee. Gerry was the first out of the doorway and he ran to Peter who literally picked him up and threw him into the air. He hugged Peter's neck very tightly and we saw that Peter was equally moved. We had met Peter a few years ago during one of our holidays. Roy had accompanied us quite a distance from the house to pull seine with the fishermen. Gerry was learning acrobatics at his school and was doing cartwheels and flips on the sand. The nets had just been hauled to the shore and the haggling was in progress.

    Peter had stepped aside from the melee to light a cigarette when he saw Gerry. Amused, he walked over to us. At first we kids were a little taken aback at Peter's appearance and his voice, but with Roy there, he reassured us that he just wanted to ask Gerry to do a few more cartwheels. Roy bade Gerry do a few more and Peter laughed out loud. He told us that he used to enjoy doing those tricks but a bad shoulder prevented him from doing so anymore. He introduced himself to us and told us that his brother, Kenny, was the captain of the boat *Spartacus* and this was their seine. We introduced ourselves to him and he and Roy lit another cigarette. He called Gerry over and shook his hand and told him that he must keep practicing. Then he took Gerry's hand and led him over to the overflowing baskets of fish. He pulled out a still wriggling eight-pound carite that was almost as tall as Gerry and gave it to him. He then shook hands with Roy and told us to call to him next time we saw him. And so our friendship with Peter had started.

Peter was always very comfortable around us kids, but he was a bit shy around my parents. He was a young man in his mid-twenties, but years of hard work on the sea made him seem older. There was, however, a gentle person beneath the rough exterior. He respected my mother and looked up to my father. We had to coax him to come inside and join us for breakfast. He told us that he heard from Lloyd that we had come back for vacation and he was impatient to see us again, especially his little friend Gerry. He accepted a cup of coffee but did not have anything else. He told us all that had happened since we were last here and brought us up to date on the local happenings and gossip. In return we told him about how we did in school and about what we accomplished in the past year. He was especially interested in what we did for Christmas. When we finished exchanging stories, he got up and excused himself and told us that Kenny was planning to go bank fishing later that morning all the way at Radix. With a solemn promise to return the next evening and have supper with us, he bade us good morning and left. My mother made a comment to my father that she suspected Peter would relish an invitation to spend Christmas with our family. The other grownups all agreed that my mother had a great idea. I knew that my mother and Radica would plan a very special supper for Peter the next evening.

After Peter's departure, we sat at the table listening to the adults talk about the hardship of life for the villagers. Kelvin opined that while it was physically demanding to earn a living from the sea, fraught with all the dangers and perils, he was not sure that our office jobs and our quality of life were any better. He argued that we were driven by an eight to four job mentality which inevitably got us into a rut. We were less active, more stressed and dying younger; whereas these villagers lived more in tune with nature, ate healthier than we did, and were in better physical condition than we were. They continued debating this for a while. At the time, we kids did not grasp the depth of what was being discussed, so we got the bat and ball and started a game of cricket in the driveway. We set up two old cardboard cartons as a wicket and proceeded in earnest with our cricket game. Gerry always wanted to bat first and we gave him three chances at getting out before we made him give up the bat. Sherry was treated in the same manner. By the time it came for our turn to bat, the adults joined the game and provided some more competitive bowling. The sun was high up by then and the driveway was bathed in brilliant sunshine. To get more weight on the ball, we got a bucket of water with which to soak the ball before bowling. Kelvin was most feared because he could bowl fast. If you missed the stroke, either you would be out if his aim was good, or you would be struck a nasty blow on your body. Kelvin and My father referred to this as "body music" and said it was good for building character.

My mother and Radica retired to the kitchen to prepare lunch while we passed the rest of the morning occupied with our game. We made it more interesting by playing to score runs and Roy declared that the one who scored the most runs would be duly rewarded. With that incentive, the game became more competitive and of course more boisterous. Hayden, with his knack of keeping one foot planted before his wicket to keep the ball from striking it, had scored the most runs and boasted of his cricket prowess. We challenged him next time to not bat with both the bat and his foot. My mother and Radica prepared a sumptuous lunch of beef pelau accompanied by sliced avocado and a cucumber salad. There was a huge jug of grapefruit juice with crushed ice and Angostura bitters. We lined up with our plates to be served directly from the pot in the kitchen.

Instead of eating at the table we decided to sit outside. There were not enough seats so we brought out the benches from inside and sat down to our outdoor picnic. My mother made the best tasting pelau and we thoroughly enjoyed it. Ronald, however, had a sweet-tooth and preferred bread and jam to a meal; but my mother saw to it that he ate what was given to him, though she would indulge him from time to time with a sweet snack. Most of us accepted a second helping and by the time the meal was eaten, we were thoroughly sluggish. The grownups wanted to take a nap and we wanted to go for a walk. Drawing us around him, my father made us each swear that we would obey Hayden's instructions and appointed him responsible for the jaunt. With that settled, we set off on our walk.

We had talked about and planned this long before and we knew exactly where we were going. We all wanted to visit the river that flowed out to the sea about a kilometer away from the house. To get there, we turned left on Gill Street and began our excursion. This part of Gill Street was lined with coconut palms on one side and a myriad of other tall trees on the other. As such, the tall branches and leaves provided a pleasant shade all along the road. There was no traffic on this road. The area was not deserted as there were other holiday houses located along it, but folks usually did not drive. There was no need to as everywhere was within walking distance and it offered the opportunity to rediscover the pleasure of leisurely walks. So we set off on our little adventure. As we approached the chennette tree that served as our target earlier that morning, we spied huge bunches of the fruit that looked ripe for eating. Without hesitation, Ronald, the most adroit of climbers among us, proceeded up the trunk and was soon perched on a branch from where he could reach out and pick the heavy bunches. He carefully and gently let them fall into our waiting hands. As the bunches fell, we caught them with upraised arms to allow us to cradle the catch and not bruise the fruit, in much the same way as a cricketer takes a high catch. When we had a good amount of fruit, we tied the bunches together with the stems and thus laden, we continued on our walk. The fruit was sweet and the flesh clung to our teeth just as we liked it. We cast aside the green skin into the bushes and when we sucked all the flesh off the seeds, we played a game of seeing who could throw it the farthest. We soon grew tired of carrying the chennette and we found a nice spot under a hibiscus bush to hide the bunches to take back home with us. So divested of our load, we approached the end of the paved asphalt road.

The end of the road marked the beginning of our adventure. We had to pass along a track with tall grasses and bushes on either side. Before we started, Hayden looked around and found a stout branch with which he armed himself; needless to say that Ronald and I did the same. There was nothing to fear, no wild animals, no man-eating savages, but we pretended that we were about to embark on an exploration of a lost world. We glanced around and made as if we had heard noises, but Sherry became startled and began to cry. We reassured her that there was no need to be afraid and that we were only pretending, otherwise we would have had to abandon the trip and take her back home. Having calmed her down, we gave her a stick to carry and this seemed to fortify her courage. We walked in Indian file along the winding track. The surface of the track was covered in fine dry sand blown over time from the beach. Underneath the sand was brown earth that seemed damp. The dampness of the earth indicated that we were approaching our destination. Without expecting it so suddenly, we turned a bend and came upon the old wooden bridge. This bridge spanned a small creek that had to be crossed before we got to the river where we planned on exploring. The creek was only about ten feet across but I must admit, the water was a dark rusty brown color and did seem a bit scary. We knew Sherry would be daunted by the prospect of crossing this bridge on foot, so Hayden and I held her hand and walked her gingerly across. Gerry had already run across and was making all sorts of scary noises in an attempt to ruffle her. She almost gave in to her fears, but we sensed this and scampered with her over the last few feet. Once on the other side of the bridge, we knew that we would not be get her to go back the same way, but we decided that we would cross that figurative bridge when we came to it. We walked past the familiar old almond tree, past the lime grove and came upon the wooden picket fence of the old beach house know as Sea Spray. We had arrived.

The river was ten feet from the fence and we rushed to the bank. The water level was not high as it was low tide. There were the three old coconut trees that grew from the bank and curved almost horizontally over the water. We picked a spot on the sandy bank and settled there for a while. Warm from our walk, we took our tee shirts off and soaked them in the water with which to refresh our faces and arms. We did not dare go into the water for fear that the younger ones would tell of our indiscretions. From where we sat, the beach was a short distance away and the terrain was flat enough that we could see the waves. The river was fairly wide at this point, almost fifty feet to the other bank. From here, it narrowed at the mouth and became a gentle stream that cut a narrow shallow channel in the soft sand and flowed out to meet the sea. We sat on the bank and peered into the water to see if anything was visible. To our surprise, there were dozens of old dried coconuts that had fallen and sunk beneath the water onto the gently sloping bank. There were hundreds of sireek crabs that had cut open the coconuts with their sharp claws and were feeding on the tough dry kernels. This was a sight that we had never seen before, so many in one place in their natural environment. We made up our minds to tell Roy and get him to come out with us back to this spot to catch crabs. We sat there watching the crabs until Hayden reckoned that it was time to return home.

Sherry of course did not want to return the way we had come, so we decided to walk along the beach back to the house. Gerry remembered that we had hidden the bunches of chennette under the bush and he wanted to take them back home for his mother. We promised that we would return and fetch them as we neared the house. With that issue settled, we walked at the edge of the surf, wading in the water as the waves swirled around our ankles. Sherry started gathering interesting shells and Gerry ran ahead of us chasing young jumping jack fish in a futile attempt to catch them. The rest of us engaged in short sprint races. When we tired of racing, we picked up sea balls and pitched them at an angle into the sea trying to make them skip over the water a few times.

We soon came upon an area of the beach where there had been a seine earlier that morning. We knew this from the dead sapatay fish that were tossed onto the sand on which the corbeaux were feasting. Sapatay is a fish with very leathery skin, hundreds of tiny bones and nobody bought them, so they were simply discarded on the beach. It was a waste but provided a feast for the corbeaux. There was also a dead stingray. Hayden had to pull Gerry back from getting too close to the ray. We saw that someone had broken off the tailbone lest some foolish person step on it. We saw a few jellyfish floating in the water and decided to continue our walk on the sand lest the tentacles come into contact with our skin. The distance to the house via the beach was shorter than the way we had come from the road, and we soon saw the gray walls of the house. Before heading home though, we left the beach, deviated across an open plot of land, came back onto Gill Street and found our hiding place where we had stored the chennette. This satisfied Gerry and he took his bunches and raced ahead of us to be the first to present them to his mother.

When we got back to the house, the grownups had already rousted themselves from their nap and were sitting on the benches outside enjoying the breeze. Roy and Kelvin were sipping on rum and coke and the others were having cold juice. We noisily broke the tranquil atmosphere and hurried to tell Roy of the crabs. He too felt excited for that was exactly the sort of thing that he enjoyed doing. He would have definitely gone back with us immediately, but as it was, we decided to go back the next day. Instead, we all changed into our swimsuits and went down onto the beach for a swim. We took the football with us into the water and started playing a game of catch and goalkeeper. We had not swum for the entire day and this felt good. We were tired and dusty from our walk and the water refreshed us. While we were in the water, the adults started teasing each other. The ladies complained about being stuck all the time in the kitchen and that they needed time to relax also. The chiding seemed to work for the men eventually gave in and declared that they would be preparing the evening meal. We joined in the fun and teased the men about their not being able to find their way around the kitchen. And so we went on, enjoying each other's company, basking in the warm water and feeling alive in Mayaro.

My father bade us come out of the water a little earlier than usual and had us take a fresh water shower before we went in to change into dry clothes. When we were changed he announced that we would all take a walk out to the village because he wanted to get some eggs. We wondered about the eggs, but we did not ask questions. When we were all ready, adults and children alike, we put on our slippers on my mother's insistence and proceeded to the village. The village was the area that surrounded Mr. James' shop. When we went past Mr. James' place we realized that we were going to walk, not to the cooperative, but to the Junction. This was exciting for we all enjoyed going up to the Junction. It was an exciting place to be. To get there we had to pass the savannah where the football matches were usually held. Once we passed the savannah, the road rose at a very slight incline to the crown at the top of the Junction. It took us about fifteen minutes at a leisurely pace to get there and we knew that there would be treats. We passed the Police Station on the left and the Health Center on the right. As we descended the crest of the Junction we saw the market ahead of us and the shops were to the right. We crossed the street and went into the largest of the shops. My father made his purchases and paid the clerk.

We stood outside of the shop gazing at all the activity around us. Taxis were arriving with returning workers from the oilfields; others were departing with workers going to the other towns. The corn vendors had their stalls set up on the pavement outside the market. We could hear the crackle of the coals as the kernels roasted and popped. The aroma of boiled corn also filled the air. A fat woman, with her hair tied up in a brightly coloured scarf, had her stall set up next to the corn vendor. She sold black pudding, a delicacy in Trinidad. A coconut vendor had his truck parked to one side and was expertly hacking open his ice-cold nuts with a couple of dexterous blows from his cutlass. Everywhere there seemed to be people coming and going. My father tapped us on our shoulders and we turned and were presented with Mr. Big ice cream cones. We gratefully accepted our treat and tore at the paper to get to the chocolate and vanilla ice cream and nuts. My father and Roy had roasted corn and the others had boiled corn. Roy also bought a quantity of black pudding and he made the lady liberally sprinkle pepper sauce all over. With our shopping done, munching on our treats, we started back home.

The shadows were beginning to lengthen as we turned into Gill Street. The bakery was open and a delicious aroma of fresh bread could be smelt. This was always a mandatory stop whenever we went out. The hot hops were baked in a wood-fired oven and had a unique taste. In addition, this bakery made the best coconut turnovers we ever tasted. The turnovers were a contrast of colors. The pastry dough was a brilliant yellow and the generous sweetened coconut filling was a brilliant crimson. Kelvin paid for the bread and turnovers and we quickened our pace to get home. Once home, the ladies prepared some tea, sliced a few turnovers, opened the back door from our bedroom and set themselves up on the benches outside. We did not want to disturb them so we concentrated on a game of go-to-pack. Meanwhile, the men took over the kitchen and busied themselves preparing dinner. We heard all sorts of noises coming from the kitchen but were deterred from investigating by the occupants. We left them alone and waited anxiously to see what they concocted for our supper. Whatever it was, though, it smelt good, and we continued with our animated game of cards.

With pride in their voices, they summoned all to wash up for supper and began to lay the table. We were surprised at the meal that followed. Kelvin prepared a simple dish of macaroni and cheese and my father had as his offering, baked fish with lots of onions and tomatoes. Roy produced a platter of hops and black pudding. There certainly was variety and there was a lot of food. All the dishes were tasty and were devoured with zest. We ate the hot dishes first and then tackled the platter of hops. Roy bought quite a bit of pudding and there was some left which he put on a plate with some pepper sauce. We ate that with our fingers. The younger ones and Ronald did not partake of the black pudding so we had more for ourselves. To make up for it and to their delight, my mother produced the bottle of guava jelly, grated some cheese and made one of their favorite sandwiches, almost a dessert. There were also the ubiquitous jugs of tea and cocoa. It was certainly an improvised meal, but one that was quite jovial what with all the teasing about culinary skills.

When the meal was finished, we took the benches and arranged them outside. Roy filled an old bottle with some kerosene, made a cloth bung, lit it and we had a flambeau. The breeze from the sea caused the flame to dance and the flickering produced a layer of soot at the top of the bottle. With the flame burning brightly, we could barely discern the fires of the oil platforms. Roy and Kelvin started telling ghost stories. My mother and my father joined in as well and they all recounted tales of experiences that they had whilst growing up. Some of these stories sounded incredible, but I knew there was truth to those that my mother told for I had some of those experiences with her while growing up on Freeling Street.

Gerry was perched on Roy's lap and Sherry sat on my father's knee. We three boys huddled next to each other as much for warmth as for reassurance. Even though we considered ourselves brave, there was still a feeling of trepidation listening to these stories. We shot glances around us at the shadows cast by the light of the flambeau, seeking to assure ourselves that there were no phantoms lurking in the dark. We all wondered if we had the courage to venture to the old stables across the road from us at night as we had planned. My mother saw that the younger ones were frightened by these stories so she stopped them, much to our consternation.

So, to prove we were unaffected by these stories, we decided to play a game of hide-and-seek. The adults, with the exception of my parents, decided to take part in the game as well. After elimination eenie-meenie-minie-mo, we all went to hide and Kelvin was the first to seek. As he discovered us one by one and we accompanied him to find the others, he tried to creep silently in the dark so as to frighten the hidden. Needless to say this was a very loud, animated game with lots of squeals and shouts and eerie calls. We continued for about an hour until the sandflies came out and we retired inside the house. We got out the cards whilst Radica made hot cocoa. We decided on the usual game of go-to-pack so that we could all play in the same game. While we played, Roy switched on the transistor radio and tuned in to a station that played mostly nostalgic songs. Everyone knew most of the tunes and there was a lively sing along that simultaneously accompanied our card game. As we sat there, I felt lucky to be so close to my family. I had seen other families torn apart by indifference and divorce and it felt good to have all those that that I loved around me. We retired to bed around midnight that second night.

Chapter 4

Subash and Family, Peter for Dinner

Despite going to bed at midnight the previous evening, we were up at the crack of dawn the next morning. We went through the morning ritual of joining Roy outside on the bench to look at the sunrise. This morning, however, all the adults were there. It was always a quiet time for all. The kids usually took this time to wipe the sleep from our eyes and to allow the breeze to fully waken us. I guess the adults may have used this time for reflection or whatever they did when they were silent. No one carried a watch or clock, and time was kept by looking at the sun. By the time the sun had sufficiently risen, we knew it was time for the other morning ritual of buying the bread and newspapers.

After we received the money from my father, we hastened out to Mr. James' shop. We did not linger on Gill Street but quickly made our way to the corner to see what lively action was taking place under the old shop. This morning the fishermen had caught two enormous hammerhead sharks. We eagerly sidled up to the crowd and peered at the fish that were displayed on the sand. We saw Peter among the fishermen and he came over to us. His hair was wet and his hands were covered with fish scales, but Gerry still jumped into his arms.

Peter's boat had been out banking all night and had just returned. They had caught a lot of red snapper and cavalli along with the two sharks. He took us to the basket and showed us the fish. We reminded him that he was supposed to have supper with us that night and he reassured us that he had not forgotten. After chatting with us for a short while, he excused himself as he wanted to get home and have a nap. Before he left, however, he handed us a large cavalli and told us to give it to my father who liked it for his fish broth. We took a last glance at the two sharks and then made our way over to Mr. James' shop.

We did not linger at the shop, as we had not touched our treats that we bought the previous day. We simply got the bread and the newspapers and made our way back home. We were eager to do so as we had planned to play cricket on the beach immediately after breakfast and we wanted to get as much playing time before the tide turned. As we turned onto Gill Street, we saw two cars parked in front of Nadens Apartments, the coral colored building obliquely opposite Thackories. We considered the beach to be our private domain and regarded other vacationers as intruders into our space. As such, we were curious to catch a glimpse of the newcomers. We slowed our pace down and walked slowly past Nadens. We could not see the people as they were probably inside unpacking their belongings. Disappointed at not seeing them and at the thought of having to share "our" beach with them, we made our way back home.

Radica caught sight of our dejected looks and enquired about them. When we told her, she just laughed and told us to cheer up that there was more than enough beach for all. She gave me a hug and we all felt better. While waiting on breakfast, we sat under the coconut tree and engaged in a conversation about all the species of fish that we knew. It was not long before my mother called us in to an eagerly awaited breakfast. This morning there were salami sandwiches made from thick slices of fresh bread and for a change, a jug of hot Milo. This was a very filling breakfast and we were eager to finish it so that we could start our game. As soon as the signal was given that we could leave, we scampered to grab the balls, bats and wicket. The adults promised to join the game and we tried to coax them to finish their cups of coffee and proceed to the beach.

The tide had receded and there was a wide flat area of beach. The sun had already started drying the sand and it was compact enough to get a good bounce on the ball. We set up the wicket and drew the batting crease. Of course we could never agree on the length of the pitch so Roy intervened, took about twenty steps and drew the bowling crease. The other adults soon arrived and the rules were established. We decided to play for runs: over the fence and into the Thackories compound was four; into the Assee compound was six and out; plumb past the gnarled coconut tree behind the bowler was six; along the ground past the same tree was four. There was the usual bucket of water with which to soak the ball. Kelvin took charge of setting the field and the game was underway. Some encouraged the batsman, others the bowler and we were soon engrossed with our exertions. My mother brought out two plastic bottles of frozen juice for refreshment. It was a fun way to pass the morning though it did make us filthy. With the sand to cushion us, we felt more inclined to dive to stop a shot or to take a catch. I played in my usual position as wicket-keeper. I made some valiant diving saves when the bowlers strayed down leg-side and took some good catches when the batsman got an edge especially off Kelvin's pace bowling. Needless to say the din was terrific as we all became excited about either one thing or another during the game.

It was my turn to bat and I had been at the wicket for about five balls when we heard my name being shouted. Everyone turned in the direction of the voices. Then we saw them. It was Subash and Vinod, two brothers whom I grew up with in El Dorado when we lived with my paternal grandparents. They had come down to the beach and had seen us. They ran over to greet me. They knew my parents but did not know my siblings or the rest of my family. I proudly introduced them around and especially to my cousins. Subash was the same age as Ronald and I; Vinod was the same age as Hayden, one year older than we were. Their parents followed behind them and as they also knew my parents, there was a sort of reunion on the beach. The game was temporarily forgotten as the reunion unfolded and the introductions were made. Our parents had not seen each other for over five years. They explained that they had just arrived that morning and were staying at the Nadens apartments only for a few days until Sunday evening. That explained the cars that we had seen earlier and I felt relieved to know that it was Subash and his family and not total strangers.

With the introductions out of the way, we invited them to join the game. They declined saying that they still had some cleaning to do, but that Subash and Vinod could stay. They accepted my mother's invitation to supper that evening and the game was taken up once more. Subash and Vinod were avid cricketers as well and they provided more competition to the game. During one of the water breaks, I noticed Vinod and Hayden chatting I felt glad that they were getting along. As for Subash and Ronald, they were very much alike and I knew that with my friends and my cousins getting along well, the rest of the holidays would be brilliant. There were two more boys with which to plan our jaunts and wanderings. And so we spent the rest of the morning playing cricket. When we each batted twice, the scores were tallied and like on the first day, Hayden again scored the most runs. When we finished the game, we were hot as the sun was blazing down on us. We had our bathing suits on and everyone dashed into the water. The water felt cool on our flushed skins and we luxuriated in the feeling.

After about an hour or so, hunger reared its head and it was time to seek out lunch. We had to improvise seeing that nothing was prepared. As we got to the house and started rinsing the salt water off, Subash's parents saw us and came over. His mother had a basket with her and she approached my mother. She brought aloo pies, curried channa and mango anchar with her. She offered us this for our lunch. My mother felt awkward as there were so many of us, but she insisted and the two families eagerly partook of her basket. Kelvin and Roy poured mugs of Solo soft drinks and added lots of ice. We sat under the shade of the coconut tree to our impromptu picnic and we thoroughly enjoyed the meal.

The adults chatted away catching up on the last five years with my uncles and aunt getting to know the newcomers. We, however, had closed that chronological gap earlier on the beach and instead focused on planning the rest of our vacation together. It was unsaid, but understood, that Subash and Vinod would be part of any plans that we made. Kelvin and Roy mixed rum and coke for themselves and Subash's father. My father and the other ladies only had coke. There was half of a watermelon in the fridge and they cut wedges for us. The watermelon was cold and it soothed our tongues as the anchar was a bit peppery and spicy. The ladies soon left us outside and made their way inside to plan for the evening meal to which Peter was invited. We stayed outside with the men and listened to their conversation about fishing. Suddenly Roy got up, went inside and came back out with a large brown bag. He asked if Subash and Vinod could accompany us on a little adventure. We had totally forgotten about the crabs and just like Roy to remind us about it.

With permission given for my friends to accompany us, seven excited kids set off down Gill Street with Roy. Our destination was the river and crab catching. There was no dawdling this time, as we wanted to get to the crabs as quickly as possible. We set a tidy pace and within ten minutes we were on the riverbank peering into the water. Roy undid his brown bag and revealed the contents. There was a quantity of thick string or twine, the type used to tie boxes, as well as some chicken skin. We looked at him inquisitively and he showed us his plan. He took a portion of chicken skin and tied it to the end of a long piece of twine. He then made his way to the edge of the riverbank and dropped to his knees. Slowly he let the string into the water and allowed the chicken skin end to sink to the sandy bottom.

The river here was only about two feet deep and the water, though it seemed to be a brackish brown color, was clear and we could easily see the chicken skin on the string. Within a few minutes, about a dozen crabs warily approached the bait. Still holding onto his bit of string cleverly wrapped around his index finger, Roy instructed Vinod and Hayden to cut seven bits of string and tie some chicken skin onto them as he had done. Quickly the boys did so and passed a string to each of us. Roy then had us space ourselves along the riverbank and lower our strings into the water. As we were doing this, he got the first crab. A fairly big one had locked its claws around the bait and started tugging at it. Roy felt the tug and responded by slowly drawing his string out of the water. He explained that if we jerked the string or pulled it too fast, the risk was greater that the crab would let go. He successfully drew the crab up onto the bank and approached it from behind to grab hold of its claws. With the claws raised high and open in a defensive posture, it let go of the string and it was easy to grab the claws when approached from the back. Once he had a firm hold, he carefully dropped it into the brown bag he had brought.

After observing Roy's technique, we were eager to try it for ourselves. The crabs seemed to be hungry as very soon there were dozens of them approaching our strings. Roy bade us continue with our slow technique as any sudden movement or action would scare them away. We continued for the rest of the afternoon with our crabbing and when Roy decided it was time to return home, we counted about two dozen. We would have been content to catch them all, but Roy told us that we had caught more than enough and that we should leave the others to get bigger. He promised to definitely come crabbing again. As with our previous trip to the river, we returned home via the beach and once again hastened our steps, anxious to show off our catch. With excited screams, we called out to the others as we entered the Thackories compound. Roy got all the buckets that we had brought and began to empty the crabs into them. The adults stood by admiring the amount that that been caught and we felt proud of our accomplishment. My mother and Radica were a bit squeamish about cleaning the crabs so this task fell to the men. We had fun catching the crabs but were not eager to see them killed or cleaned. Subash and Vinod returned home and we five were sent to shower and change. We were having guests for dinner.

    We showered outdoors and wrapped ourselves in our towels and stood under the coconut tree just staring out at the ocean. I was content to stay there for a while but my mother's stern commands made us go into the house to shed our wet things and get into some decent clothes. Decent meant proper shorts and a fairly good jersey. We applied lotion to our legs, arms and faces, brushed our hair and we were done. Our faces had already begun to burn and had taken on a much darker tint than before. We decided to stay out of the way of the adults who were busy preparing for our dinner guests. We got out some sheets of paper and some pencils and played a word game called boy-girl-animal-place-thing. One person was told to start and would say the alphabet silently. When told to stop, the letter that the person stopped at was told to everyone. We then had to scramble to jot down a boy's name, a girl's name, an animal, a place and a thing that started with that letter. The first person to finish would yell stop. We would compare answers and award points. Ten points were awarded for unique words, five points for common words. We would continue until the page had no more room. The scores would then be tallied and a winner declared. This game occupied us right up until dinnertime.

    Instructions were called to put the game away and to help set the dinner table. Just as we put the finishing touches, Subash and his family arrived. As there were so many more people, we borrowed some benches from their home to supplement ours so that there would be seats for all. The ladies gathered in the kitchen, the men busied themselves in the house and we crept outside to sit on the benches. This was undoubtedly our favorite spot as we inevitably congregated there. There was a small coalpot which the men set up on a table just outside the living room. It took some effort but eventually their combined efforts won out and the coals were lit. The steady breeze from the sea ensured that the coals were constantly fanned and glowing and every now and then we heard a crackle as some embers burst.

    We looked forward to dinner very much, not only for the delicious dishes that we anticipated, but it was fun to have a lot of people sharing at the table. As we gathered around the coalpot and were enjoying the warmth that emanated from it, we heard the Peter whistle and glanced up to see him coming up the driveway. He obviously took care to dress himself. His natty hair was combed, something we had never seen before. He had shaved the stubble from his face and he smelt like lilacs. He wore a pair of blue jeans and a short sleeved white cotton shirt that was ironed. We were so accustomed to seeing Peter coming out of the sea, wet hair, bare torso and wet shorts that seeing him like this made us stare. I guess he must have felt a bit uncomfortable because he made a comment about not wanting to shock us by his appearance. My mother came out to greet him and quickly put him at ease by introducing him to our friends. The men had set up a makeshift bar outside and they were helping themselves. They allowed us to pour our own soft drinks. Peter usually preferred to have his drink neat, but he requested a glass and had a long one poured. The odours that wafted about the air tickled our noses and we were eager to get things moving.

    The ladies brought out a huge basin of chicken that was seasoned and pre-cooked. This would go onto the grill to finish cooking and would be lavishly basted with home-made barbecue sauce. Kelvin took charge of this task and we begged him to allow us to help with the basting and turning of the meat. Under watchful supervision, we each had our turn and chided each other as to whom we thought had charred their pieces. The radio was turned on inside the house and the combination of the music, the breeze, the warm grill and the odors all lent to a truly cozy ambiance. When the music changed to a reggae song, Hayden did an impromptu dance and soon had us kids doing likewise, much to the amusement of the adults. Meanwhile, the ladies finished laying the buffet and put the finishing touches on the other dishes for our dinner. As we did not have enough dinnerware, we used disposable plates, forks and knives. These could easily be dumped afterwards with no worry about washing up. It took just over an hour to barbecue all the chicken and when it was done, my father passed the basin to my mother who then announced that the meal was ready.

My mother, Radica and Subash's mother prepared a lavish spread. There was potato salad with beets, fried rice, coleslaw and buttered rolls to go with the barbecue chicken. There was also curried crab and dumplings. There was enough food to feed an army, and as we were a small army, we dug in to this repast with much gusto. Peter was definitely shy and seemed reluctant to dish out his dinner. Radica took him by the arm and led him to the buffet and helped him dish out. She piled his plate high with food and he seemed a bit overawed by the amount. After we had eaten our chicken and all the trimmings, we all wanted to try the crab that we had caught. My mother dished out for us and we attacked our platefuls. I guess it tasted that much better seeing that we caught the crabs ourselves. We sat at the table for quite a long time. There was no need to rush. It was a leisurely meal and Peter overcame his initial shyness. He actually finished his barbecue and had some crab and dumplings. We spent the better part of three hours at the table and at the end of the meal the men complimented the ladies on a superb dinner. We also added our endorsements as they beamed with delight.

After dinner, Radica prepared coffee for the adults and my father fetched a bottle of brandy. We continued sitting around the table engaged in conversation. Peter was the center of attention as there were numerous questions posed to him about his life. He told us stories of his childhood growing up in Mayaro. His tales of his experiences out on the ocean on a boat held our attention steadfastly. There was one time they had gone out overnight and set the boat adrift while banking for snapper. When they tried to start the engine to guide the boat to another spot, the engine sputtered and refused to jump to life. They were very far from land and the current was strong. With the engine dead and the boat drifting, the current could easily have taken them in the direction of the area where the Atlantic Ocean met the confluence from outflows of the mighty Orinoco and Demerara rivers of Venezuela and Guyana.

It was apparently quite a serious situation to be caught in without an engine, as the current flowed down the South American Coast towards Brazil and then swung out into the Atlantic between Africa and the Americas. Fortune smiled on them that night because a ferry taking drilling supplies out to the oil platforms of AMOCO spotted them and came to their assistance. There was an engineer onboard the ferry who looked at the engine and was able to repair it. After thanking the crew of the ferry, and God, they pointed the boat in the direction of land and sped home. They had been drifting on the high seas. Who knows what may have happened to them otherwise.

We were all amazed at the story Peter told us. He went on to explain that this incident made him realize how short and fragile life was and that we must all enjoy and live each day to the fullest. He also said that he may not have much material possession, but he did thank the Lord every day for providing him with good health and an easy spirit. From the looks on the faces of the adults, you could tell that they listened to this simple fisherman and they knew what he had just said was profound. It was then we realized that Peter had spent all his life in Mayaro. He had never been to the large cities of San Fernando or Port of Spain. Whatever he needed he could get in Mayaro so there was never a need for him to leave. In a sense it was sad, but how many people would have gladly exchanged their stressful worlds for his peace of mind. It is now that as an adult, in retrospect, that I understood the lure that Mayaro held for my father, in the same way it does for me now as an adult myself.

They sat until after midnight talking and enjoying each other's company. It was not until we realized that Gerry and Sherry had left the table and were fast asleep on the sofa that we took notice of the time. Subash's parents and Peter thanked my family for the invitation and bade everyone a good night. We wanted to stay up a bit longer but my father sent us to bed with a warning that if we didn't, we would feel the effects in the morning. Reluctantly we retired to the bedroom, but instead of going to sleep, we stayed up a while longer whispering about make believe adventures on the high seas. Eventually sleep overtook us and we succumbed to blissful oblivion.

Chapter 5

Rain and Jellyfish

The next morning, Ronald shook us to wake us up. Sleepily we rubbed our eyes and asked him what the matter was. He pointed out a strange noise to us and we cocked our ears to hear it. It sounded like hundreds of pebbles falling onto glass. We realized that everyone else was still asleep, so we quietly crept out of our beds to investigate. As we crept into the living room, we heard gentle snores coming from Roy and we tiptoed so as not to awaken him. The room was dark as the windows and doors were still closed, but the darkness seemed to be more pronounced for that time of morning. Usually there would have been some light filtering through the cracks in the wood. We quietly approached the door and undid the bolt that fastened the top half. We seized the frame firmly and gently pushed it open a bit to peer outside. As soon as we started pushing it open, we were struck by stinging pellets of rain. That explained the strange noise and the darkness. There was a strong gusty wind blowing and it was driving the rain hard against the building.

    I guess that we may have relaxed our grip on the doorframe for the next thing that happened was a strong gust blew against the open frame. We lost our hold on it and the wind caused it to blow open and bang hard against the wall. Of course the noise woke Roy who immediately came to the door to see what was happening. It also woke Kelvin and my father who joined us at the door. There were stern looks in our direction but eventually everyone focused on the raging wind and rain outside. The rain was falling so heavily that it took on the appearance of a curtain. The sky was black and the clouds were low and heavy. It would pour like this for a while yet. After a few minutes, we closed the door and retreated back to our bedrooms. The darkness made it feel more cozy and we snuggled back under our covers. We left the bedroom door open so as to see when the adults were up and stirring about. Until then we stayed in bed quietly hugging our pillows.

It was still raining heavily outside when my mother and Radica peered into our bedroom to see if we were awake. We immediately sprang out of bed and put on our slippers without being asked to. Roy had found a stout cord, opened the top half of the door just a little and tied it to the main frame so that it would not blow wide open. The room felt a little cool so we retrieved our blankets and wrapped ourselves in them as we sat on the sofa. Needless to say that we could not venture out this morning to Mr. James' shop for bread and newspapers. While we sat there, Sherry and Gerry awoke and joined us on the sofa. As we each took turns to do our morning toiletries, Kelvin and Roy started a game of all fours. We decided to pair up with partners and the losers would have to leave the game and make way for a new pair. We were so absorbed in the game that we completely forgot about breakfast.

Our usual ravenous morning appetite was dulled by the sumptuous meal from the previous night. It was, however, approaching ten o'clock in the morning though the time was unknown to us. It was not until about eleven o'clock that we started feeling hunger pangs and our enquiry was met with a quick answer. We were told to wait just a bit longer. Some anxious minutes passed before my mother and Radica appeared with a tray full of fried bake. They were doing this while we were absorbed in our game. To accompany the bake, they prepared a platter of tinned sardines with onions, tomatoes and hot pepper. There were also slices of cheese and the usual jugs of hot cocoa and tea. This late morning brunch was really appreciated, as fried bake always seemed to be the proper food on a cool rainy day when stuck indoors. When we had our full, the leftovers were cleared away and we were instructed to tidy up our room and make our beds. We did so quickly and returned to the living room with a burning question.

Boys being boys, we all desperately wanted to go out into the rain to play; of course mothers being mothers we were given an emphatic no. Disappointed and a bit vexed, though we did not dare show it, we sulked at the table. Even my father did not challenge this maternal edict. Opportunity, however, always had a strange way of manifesting itself and when it did, it was most welcome. As we sat there gloomily looking out at the rain, we heard Subash and Vinod calling out to us. So excited were we that we overturned the bench in our haste to rush to the door. We looked at them enviously for they were thoroughly soaked and smiling from ear to ear. My father opened the top half of the door fully and looked out over the wall to the Nadens apartments. There he saw Subash's parents who gave him the thumbs up that they knew where their boys were. They had a football with them and were passing it back and forth to each other. They bade us come out and join them and we turned to my father this time.

In a flash, Kelvin tore off his shirt, pushed us out of the way and vaulted over the lower part of the door. He ran into the rain and played a mock tackle at Vinod for possession of the football. Almost simultaneously we again chorused our plea to my father who, probably remembering his boyhood days, gave in and told us that we could go. This was met by a loud protest from my mother, but my father coaxed her into calming down. We squealed with joy and were about to take our jerseys off when my father told us we could go but had to keep our tops on. It was an attempt to placate my mother and it was a small price to pay for freedom. We thrust open the door and leapt out into the driveway.

The rain felt gloriously cool against our warm skin. It was still raining heavily and the wind had not died down. The raindrops stung our skin as they hurtled down from the sky. At first we had to blink them out of our eyes, but we gradually got used to them and soon they were oblivious to us. We got some old dried coconuts to use as two goals and divided ourselves into two teams of four. Pretty soon a lively animated game of small goal football was underway in the driveway. The rain created large puddles everywhere and it was a source of amusement to stamp into a puddle and splash the opponent in an attempt to win the ball. Within a few minutes, Roy and my father joined the game and the action became more intense. You had to be alert to dribble with the ball and not lose possession because there was not adequate space in the driveway to allow for creative football. It was a fast game of touch, pass and try and score. We did not become winded as quickly as the rain kept us cool. When we were thirsty we opened our mouths and caught the raindrops on our tongues. When we grew tired we took a short rest on the bench at the back of the house. We sat in the still falling rain and it was fun to sit on a wet bench completely drenched to the bone.

As we sat catching our breath, we looked out at the ocean. It was quite choppy and the waves were high. The wind augmented the choppiness and whipped the white foam at the crests. The ocean seemed to be a deep azure as there was no sunlight to penetrate the water. The sky and clouds were so thick, low and black that it made the horizon impossible to distinguish. One or two brave corbeaux were aloft and seemed to be motionless in the air. The beach was deserted and all the boats were pulled up high onto the beach. No one was venturing out on a day like this. Peter had taught us that fishermen gained a healthy respect for Mother Nature and the power of the open ocean.

The coconut trees on the shore bent and swayed in cadence to the gusts that blew in from the ocean. It was not a storm by any means; there was no lightning and no thunder. Rather, it was one of those systems caused by the Inter Tropical Convergence Zone, or the ITCZ, that frequently made their way up from South America and into the Caribbean. It had probably started earlier that morning and would probably move off by mid afternoon.

While we were resting on the bench, my mother opened the bedroom window just a crack and told us to come to the main door for a drink. We obliged and she produced a jug of cold orange juice to quench our thirst. As we had a late brunch, we were not hungry and with the jug emptied, we restarted our game of football. Just as we started, Subash's parents wandered over and were welcomed in by my mother. My mother and Radica soon had pot of tea for the ladies to savor while Subash's father joined in on the game. Sherry and Gerry opted out of the game, returned indoors and busied themselves with a compendium of board games that we brought along for days like this. Everyone seemed content with their particular activities and three separate groups focused on what they were doing. It was not until about two in the afternoon that the rain seemed to lessen and presently it stopped altogether.

The clouds were slow to break up, and when the sky started clearing, we saw a beautiful rare sight. Out over the ocean, through a break in the clouds, rays of silvery light filtered and fanned out. It was a very ethereal sight and the rays looked like delicate silver fingers. Apparently there was still moisture in the air for, as though by magic, slowly before our eyes, a brilliant rainbow appeared. We called out to those inside to come and witness this marvelous spectacle. My mother made the younger ones put on their slippers and soon we were one group standing there marveling at the glory of Nature.

As we were already thoroughly soaked from the rain, we decided to have a swim to round off the day. My parents secured the house and the entire troupe made its way down to the beach. Even though the breeze was cool, the water was surprisingly warm. It was still a little choppy and we were only allowed to venture in up to our waists. The adults stood around watching us like hawks lest we try and gain a few yards further out. The turbulence of the waves during the past few hours caused the water to churn up a lot of seaweed. It felt really creepy with all this seaweed around us; every time a piece brushed against our legs, we jumped for fear it was some sea creature waiting to pounce on us.

My aunt Radica was lounging in the shallows near the water's edge when she cried out loudly. Her cry attracted us all and we ran over to see what the matter was. Kelvin was the first at her side and discovered that a jellyfish had stung her. He pulled her from the water onto the sand and saw the area on her leg where she had been stung. Her leg was red and we could see the marks from the tentacles. Of course we were all immediately ordered out of the water. Kelvin took a handful of wet sand and rubbed the leg so as to try and remove the stingers. Meanwhile, Roy located the cause of her discomfort and pulled it out of the water with a stick. Her leg, however, started getting numb and Subash's father suggested that she be taken to the Mayaro Health Center and ran home to get his car. Kelvin quickly carried her back to the house. The poison from the jellyfish was potent enough to warrant medical treatment but only in rare species would such a sting be lethal. We wanted to stay around and observe the jellyfish but my mother would have none of that. Instead we made our way back to the house to see Radica off. My mother, Subash's mother and Kelvin went with them to the Clinic. They tried to comfort her as she was crying from the pain and numbness. We all felt sorry for her and hoped that the doctors would soon be able to ease her suffering.

When the car left the driveway, we were all sent to shower and change. My father told Subash and Vinod to do likewise and to rejoin us when they were changed. Within half an hour we had done so and the boys had made their way back to our place. We sat quietly around the sofas because I think we all probably felt that we shouldn't be enjoying ourselves when Radica was injured. My father observed our gloomy silence and guessed at our thoughts. In his typical manner, he tried to cheer us up by challenging us to a spelling game. This brightened us up and we enthusiastically began with him as the moderator. Roy produced a bottle of split channa and we munched on these while engrossed in the game. Vinod and I were the best spellers and it came down to the two of us to do battle for the right to be called spelling champion of Mayaro. The others had taken sides and cheered us on vocally. When Vinod made a mistake I saw his error and correctly spelled "rhombus" to earn the victory. We were soon in better spirits and my father and Roy left us to our own devices. We continued noisily teasing each other and did not observe them slink away to the kitchen to prepare supper.

The sun had receded by this time but the clouds gathered again with a renewed threat of rain. It had rained so heavily earlier on the moisture seemed to have awakened the mosquitoes and sandflies. They were out in abundance and were soon a discomfort and a nuisance. Seeing them and feeling their bites as well, my father produced a bottle of citronella oil and we generously applied the strong smelling oil to our exposed limbs. Roy lit a few mosquito coils as well and placed them around the room. The air was cooler and we put the lights on as it suddenly seemed darker. Somehow the scent of the citronella oil combined with the wisps of smoke from the coils repelled the little pests and we were able to sit a little more comfortably. Sherry and Gerry went to the bedroom and returned with their blankets, spread them on the sofa and curled up. They were not tired, but the sudden darkness and moist air made the room feel cool and the blankets allowed them to cozy up on the sofa.

We all felt like doing the same. Hayden turned to me and asked if I thought that Radica was okay because they were gone a long time. His question was poignant and we lapsed into an uncharacteristic silence. I guess we all hoped that the sting was not too serious and silently wished that they would soon return from the Clinic. As we sat there pondering on Radica's well-being, it seemed our prayers were immediately answered for we heard a car turn into the driveway. We sprang up off the sofas and shouted to my father and Roy who needed no second call. The car pulled up to the doorway and my father opened the door. Kelvin came out from the other side and with my father, they helped Radica gingerly out of the car onto her feet. They supported her on both sides and slowly she made her way into the house and sat down on the sofa. My mother went into the kitchen and made her a cup of tea.

      We all wanted to ask the same question but had to wait until she had made herself comfortable on the sofa. When she seemed all right, my father enquired as to what happened at the Clinic. When they arrived at the Clinic she was immediately attended to by the doctor on duty. He examined the leg and commended Kelvin for successfully removing the stinger. It was not serious and was a common complaint seen by the Clinic staff. However, he acknowledged the discomfort and the numbness in her leg. He administered cortisone and antibiotics to help with the poison and with the pain. However, instead of releasing her, he wanted her to remain for a while for observation. As such they had no choice but to wait with her. When the doctor had satisfied himself that the medication was working by testing for feeling in the leg, he released her. He told her to take regular Panadol if she had any pain. He told her that she should be back to normal within a day or two. After that they left the Clinic and returned home. With Radica all tucked in on the sofa, Kelvin hovered around looking helpless. The grownups teased him a bit about his demeanor and even Radica joined in. It was so strange seeing him this way, I guess he felt helpless to do anything to alleviate her pain.

      Once she settled down and was resting comfortably, it was only then that we took notice of the time, prompted by the rumble in our stomachs. We only had brunch earlier that morning and it was fast closing in on seven o'clock in the evening. This would be improvised and my mother insisted that

Subash's parents stay and partake of the makeshift meal. His mother left for home and soon returned with a few cans of tuna. My mother dished out some food for Radica along with another cup of hot tea. Kelvin took it to her and helped feed her dinner. As soon as the meal was on the table, we all heartily partook of it.

There was some barbecue chicken left over from the previous night, left over fried bake, fresh bread and butter, a copious tuna salad, slices of cheese and tomatoes and of course the usual jugs of hot cocoa and tea. It was by no means an elegant meal, but it was hearty and it satisfied us. By the time the meal was over, I guess everyone was tired because Subash's parents excused themselves and retired to their home. Reluctantly Subash and Vinod went with them and I must admit that I was a bit relieved, as I also desired my bed. We cleared away the dinner table and my father started locking up the house. It was only about nine o'clock in the evening, but bed beckoned to us all and soon we were fast asleep from the day's exertions.

Chapter 6

Pulling Seine, Roasting Fish and the Moore House

The next morning, we three boys awoke as usual before the others and made our way to the living room. Roy was already up and he gave us the okay to open the door and windows. What a difference from the previous morning. The clouds from the night before had cleared and the sun was already starting its heavenly climb. The asphalt in the driveway was still damp but the moisture would soon evaporate and dry things out. We made our way to the fence and looked out at the beach to see where the tide was. It was low tide and we saw a familiar sight down the beach about a half-mile away to our right. It was a seine and it had just started as we could spy the boat letting the nets into the ocean about a half mile from shore. We squinted and counted about ten persons on the shore holding onto the lead ropes. We grew excited for since we arrived four days ago, we had not yet gone out to help pull the seine.

We ran back to the house and excitedly told Roy about it. My father was just making his way from the bedroom at this time and we directed our question to him. He strolled outside with us and we pointed it out to him. He approved of us going to the seine but admonished us to be careful when the nets came to shore. Before allowing us to leave, he made us change into some older jerseys and put on our bathing trunks and suggested that we might want to hail out to Subash and Vinod, as they had never been to a seine. We quickly ran over to their compound and whistled for them. They were already up and about when we ran up the stairs. We told their parents that we were going to the seine and they gave the boys permission to join us. They also changed into their bathing trunks and we quickly set off down the beach.

As we walked towards the seine, we waded in the water at the water's edge. It was surprisingly warm and it felt good as it swirled around our feet. The weight on our heels caused our feet to sing slightly into the soft sand and we marveled at the clear ripples of the water reflecting on the sand. It was still relatively early in the morning and the cooler air mingled with the warm rays of sunlight to produce a fine mist at the edge of the coconut trees lining the beach. As we walked, we picked up sea balls and threw them into the water trying to make them skip and skim the surface. The air had a familiar salty smell to it and we felt excited to be on our own for a short while. The shallow water was crystal clear and we could see small fishes darting around chasing after each other. We stamped our feet as much to scare the fish as to splash each other with water. Soon we closed the distance on the fishermen.

As we approached the seine, we saw that there was still a long way to go before the nets were ashore. By this time, the boat had already discharged the nets and was making its way to the shore. It slowed just beyond the breakers and two boys jumped into the water. Their role was to hang onto the nets and to make sure that the corks were not entangled with the lead sinkers. We quickened our pace and soon we were there. We waded in and chose spots where we would be up to our waists in the water, and grabbed hold of the rope. This allowed us to be pleasantly splashed by the oncoming waves. There were about thirty people all pulling on the ropes. About half of them worked for the captain of this seine. Most of them were adults who lived in the village, but there were quite a few whom we knew to be vacationers like ourselves. We recognized some of their faces from the previous years and one or two of them in return recognized us and asked if we were back for the holidays. The captain was quite visible and vocal, shouting instructions. He would stand still for a while and look at the waves as this gave him an indication of the strength and direction of the current. He would then holler new instructions to his people who would in turn guide the seine.

Pulling the seine to shore was very strenuous. The seine consisted of a net about fifteen feet wide and about nine hundred feet long. There was a rope running lengthwise on either side of the net. On one side of the net there were lead sinkers, on the other side there were corks. The rope was long and toughened from being constantly immersed in the salty waters. The technique was very simple. The boat would scout the waters to locate the fish. The captain read the signs and acted upon his instinct from his experience.

Once the spot was chosen, the boat would tack back towards the shore. One person would take hold of one end of the rope, dive into the water and swim towards shore. There would be usually a few helpers on the sand waiting to lend a hand to hold onto the rope. In the meantime, the boat would swing around and slow its speed. Other helpers on the boat would begin letting the nets into the water. The nets would be lowered with the lead sinkers first. The lead would cause the nets to sink and the weight would pull the width of the nets into the water. The corks on the other side of the net would halt the descent of the net and the result would be a net suspended in the water that extended down about fifteen feet below the surface of the water. The boat would continue its movement parallel to the shore so that the nets would form an arc. When the final bit of net was lowered into the water, the boat would then make for the shore and as it approached the breakers, another person would dive off holding onto the other end of rope. When this other end of rope reached the shore, the rest was manual labor. Sheer muscle power was required to pull the two ropes and guide the nets to shore.

Usually someone at the back of the helpers would shout encouragement to the others to create an atmosphere of teamwork. This was done in cadence with the waves and the ebb and flow of the water. Usually the current placed additional weight on the nets and the strain was visible on the arms and shoulders of all. These were men of the sea and had grown up doing this every day of their lives. Their sinewy limbs were burnt brown by the sun and their muscles rippled from hard work.

Just as the task of pulling the seine began to seem interminable, there was a shout that the corks were sighted. This had the effect of lifting all spirits and the dauntless efforts would soon reap its reward. We strained to catch sight of the corks and were equally heartened when we saw them bob just at the breakers. Hand over hand, with a more determined effort, the rope seemed to come to an end and very shortly we were holding onto the nets. Two helpers were charged with the task of wading further out into the water to hold the lead down. This was done to prevent any fish that had not yet been trapped in the net from swimming under and escaping. At this point we had to be careful and cautious with our feet in the water. The danger was treading on porcupine fish, catfish or stingrays. The captain gave the order for the two lines to close in so as to narrow the expanse of net. With the lead being held down and the helpers pulling the top portion of the net, it was very difficult for any fish to escape. There was seaweed clinging to some parts of the net but as yet there was no sign of fish. With about twenty feet to go, we saw a carite trapped by its gills on the left side of the net. The action became a lot more agitated and the more senior fishermen shouted instructions to us all. By this time, we gave up our place to the seine workers, as they needed to roll the nets to the sand and start the unloading.

The water bubbled with the mad frenzy of writhing fish trying to escape their doom. We all grew excited for this was what the whole effort was about. Fresh fish being hauled out of the nets to be put on ice into baskets to be taken to the markets for sale. Obviously the seine workers took control of the proceedings and shouted at any bystander who attempted to take the larger more prized fish that was worth a lot more money. We were, however, allowed to pick up the smaller fish. We had each secured bits of vine to which we knotted a small stick at the end. Thus armed, we tread cautiously in the water and pulled the nets apart and started collecting the small fry. Once we got hold of one, we thread the vine through its gills and mouth and allowed it to slide down. The piece of stick tied to the end of the vine prevented it from falling off our makeshift string. We occupied ourselves in this manner until there was nothing left in the nets. Our strings were full of butterfish and young carite and we each secured about ten or so. This was quite enough and the adults back at home would not relish the task of cleaning so many small fish.

We started our journey back home and were wading in the water dragging our strings of fish behind us when we saw the rest of my family coming towards us. We hastily ran to them and proudly displayed our prizes. Gerry wanted to touch the butterfish and had to be cautioned lest the slippery scales cut his hand. Vinod gave him his string to hold and he was as proud as punch to carry it. We had a decent haul and Roy told us that we could help him clean the fish. It was a leisurely walk back to the house and I know that we each wanted the rest of the holidays to be like this. It was still low tide in some places along the beach, there were pools that had formed in depressions on the sand. One of these pools was about six feet across and about half a foot deep. The water in it was quite warm and we waded through it and rinsed the fish off in it. As we approached the house, my father suggested that we rinse the sand off our bodies before coming in. We did not need a second invitation so we handed over our strings to the adults, tore off our jerseys and raced into the water, much to the consternation of my brother and sister who did not have their bathing suits on. Kelvin decided to take a short romp in the water with us and after about half an hour, we reluctantly left the water and went to the house.

    My mother handed us some towels and we walked over to Roy who was taking the fish off the strings and putting them into two buckets of seawater. He did so to keep them moist because we would have breakfast before tackling the cleaning. We tried to inveigle my mother to allow us to do so at once, but she would have none of that. Subash and Vinod returned home to ask their parents if they could help us clean their own strings of fish. After a hastily eaten breakfast, we were eager to start the task of cleaning the fish. My mother told us that once it was done properly, she would prepare them for our lunch and dinner. Just as we finished breakfast, Subash and Vinod came scampering up our driveway to help clean the fish. It was a beautiful day and a cooling breeze blew from the ocean tempering the sting of the sun.

    My father and Kelvin brought out the wooden benches and some plastic chairs and the adults set themselves up under the coconut tree. Roy brought out some knives and two large enamel basins. We crowded around him and he admonished us to be quiet or he would not allow us to help. Scared that he might carry out his threat, we calmed down and awaited his instructions. As there were not enough knives, he quickly crossed over to Nadens to get two more from Subash's parents. When he returned, he went to the large water tanks that supplied the compound with water and locked off the valve. There was an outdoor pipe and tap next to the outdoor shower. He turned the tap on and water from the main slowly trickled out. He explained that he did this so as not to waste the water in the tanks. There was a short raised concrete culvert about four feet in length surrounding the pipe and we took our places sitting on it. The water ran very slowly and it felt great under our feet.

    Roy took one of the butterfish in his hands and showed us how to hold it so as not to let it slip from our grasp and cut us with its scales. He showed us how to run the knife safely against the scales to get them off. He stopped occasionally to rinse the loosened scales under the water. There was a basin placed under the tap to catch most of the scales as they fell and were rinsed off. When the scales were removed and rinsed, he held the fish in his palm, belly down, and showed us how to take the dorsal fins off. He then placed the top of the fish against the flat of his palm and secured his grip on the sides of the fish with his fingers. In this way, the underside of the fish was exposed. He then placed his hand under the running water and with the knife, cut open the belly. The blood ran out and was soon washed away by the water.

Once the belly was cut open, he put down the knife, inserted his fingers into the cavity, and pulled out the innards. Once the innards came out, he threw them into a plastic bag that he had brought out for this purpose. All in all, it was not as unpleasant a task as we had thought. The smell of the innards was not as powerful as we had imagined since the fish was freshly caught. He then rinsed the fish again under the water, pulled back the flap from the belly and ran his fingers again along the cavity to make sure all the innards were out. Once this was done, he threw the cleaned fish into one of the basins, which he had filled with water. When we assured him that we had followed his every step, he gave us five boys each a knife and we eagerly took a fish each in our hand to begin. Sherry and Gerry were too young to be given knives so they settled for doing the final rinse of the fish.

Maybe it was our youthful innocence and exuberance, but we relished cleaning the fish. We pretended that we were performing an important task and that everyone was dependent on us to feed them. Needless to say this would be a task that in future years, we would not approach with quite as much enthusiasm. It took us the better part of the morning to complete all the fish and even Roy had to agree that we had done a superb job. There were young carite, young cavalli, a few small red snappers and mostly butterfish. Subash's parents by this time wandered over to join my parents, and this became a part of their daily routine. We called our parents over to show them what a good job we had done. Subash and Vinod started picking out the fish that they had cleaned when their father stopped them. He asked us if we had ever roasted fish on a spit. We told him that we had had fish fried, stewed, baked and curried. He then asked us again if we had ever roasted fish ourselves to which we answered no. Some of the best memories are those that occur impromptu and this was to be one of them. He turned to my father and told him of his plans to build a fire to roast the fish. Both my father and Roy agreed at once for they had enjoyed roast fish before and vowed that it was the best way to have fish.

With that settled we were told to go collect dry kindling for the fire. The men went over to the empty plot of land to the right of Thackories to locate wood for the fire and to build the spit. We all soon returned to our compound and had everything we needed to build our fire. The men selected a sandy spot near to the coconut tree, against the brick wall. The wall would provide shelter from the wind but would allow enough air to circulate to keep the fire going. They dug a long shallow hole into which they placed the kindling. They then arranged the larger pieces of wood to fuel the fire. When this was done, they sunk two stout poles into the sand on either end of the hole. They cut grooves at the top of these poles. Next they placed a thinner longer pole across the top with the ends resting in the grooves of the upright poles. In this way, the fire, heat and smoke would be spread evenly along the improvised spit rather than be concentrated in one circular place as is the case with campfires.

The kindling was very dry and it caught alight with the very first match that was struck. When the kindling was ablaze, the men rearranged the wood so that it would start to burn and then smolder. The objective was not to get a roaring fire going. Rather it was to try and control the flames, produce some smoke and generate enough heat to cook thereby imparting a smoky flavor to the food. While they did this, we stood silently observing and taking mental notes of all that was done. Meanwhile, the ladies took the fish inside and lightly seasoned them with salt and pepper and some of the ground seasoning that we brought with us. When they were done, they placed all the fish into one large basin, covered it and brought it outside to us.

Subash's father showed us how to take a spit rod, take a fish in our hands, open the mouth and thread the fish onto the rod. This was quite easy for we were used to threading fish onto our vines. He made us hang them close to each other on the rod and when the rod was fully loaded, he showed us how to place the rod horizontally across the spit with the fish hanging down and their heads pointing up. He told us that this method of cooking was used in olden days to smoke meats to preserve them from rot. It was a slow method of cooking and one had to be patient. As we stood there grinning at our accomplishments, juices from the fish trickled down and spluttered in the fire. The aroma was very pleasing and we were anxious to sample the finished product. It took about fifteen minutes for the first batch to be done and Roy got another rod ready and allowed my sister and brother to prepare the next batch onto the rod. Subash's mother got a platter ready and took the first batch as it came off the roast and covered it with aluminum foil to keep it warm. It took five batches to finish cooking all the fish and there really was an enormous amount when it was all cooked. My mother sliced a couple loaves of bread and buttered them to go with our roast fish. Kelvin made two huge jugs of lime juice and he put in crushed ice and Angostura bitters. We decided to have our meal outdoors. The small coffee table was brought out to rest the platters. We used paper plates and had a garbage bag nearby for the bones. The fish was exquisite and it tasted all the more delicious because we had foraged for it, cleaned it and helped cook it. The wood produced an agreeable smoky flavor to the flesh. I ate the fish by itself and then had the bread. There was plenty for everyone and at the end of the meal, when everyone had their full, there was still fish left over.

During this time the tide had turned and it was high by the time the meal was over. My mother had Sherry and Gerry take a cool shower and told them that they should take a nap. They enjoyed the shower but protested at having to take a nap. To coax them, my mother opened the bedroom windows so that they could hear us under the coconut tree. Pretty soon, the breeze took its toll and they both fell asleep contentedly. The adults also were lulled into silence by the breeze especially after such a satisfying meal. Anticipating a favourable response, the five boys sought permission to go wandering for a while. It was about two in the afternoon and we were told that we had two hours before we had to be back. We gathered ourselves up and proceeded quickly down the driveway. We left so quickly that my mother did not notice that we went barefoot. We had no plans except a desire to go wandering by ourselves hoping to stumble onto some sort of thrill.

Walking abreast of each other, we turned left on Gill Street and were just about to start our stroll. Hayden asked what we wanted to do. At first no one had any idea and just as we seemed stumped for ideas, Ronald came up with a capital suggestion and we immediately agreed with it. His was a simple plan. Obliquely opposite the Thackories compound, there was a long sandy driveway which led to an old house owned by the Moore family. The old house was painted blue and yellow and the paint had faded over the years from the salty sea and sand blast. At the back of this house there were old stables that were once full of horses. The Moore family used to train thoroughbred racehorses and used these stables to accommodate the animals when they brought them down to Mayaro to exercise them on the beach. It was good exercise for the horses to run in the soft sand and swim in the surf as this built strength. It used to be a grand sight watching the grooms lead the horses into the water to swim. Anyway, Ronald said that he heard the stables were haunted and he wanted to go and explore a bit. At once we agreed that this was a great idea and we halted our footsteps. Turning around slowly, we cast a glance at the property and wondered silently what we would find.

From the road it seemed that the property was overrun with bushes and there was a desolate look about the place. We looked at each other seeking reassurance that none of us was afraid and with a steeled bravado, we slowly walked to the other side of the road and peered down the driveway. We knew the house was empty for we had observed it during the past five days. No one was about and it seemed no one was due to arrive soon. The pitch was warm but not hot and as we tread our first steps on the sandy driveway, it felt noticeably cooler. The driveway was about one hundred feet long and was lined on either side by tall coconut trees. From the right of the driveway, it was about ten feet to the concrete wall that marked the boundary with the adjacent property. The bushes grew densely right up against the wall. The driveway ran at an angle down to the house. From the left of the driveway, it was another sixty feet to a chain link fence that marked that boundary. The bushes were dense though only about knee high. We could not see to the back of the house but we could make out the tops of tall breadfruit trees above the roof of the house.

We held our collective breath and listened hard for any sound. There was none from the property or from the deserted road. Hayden gave us the signal to start walking and we did so very slowly and cautiously. No one knew what to expect, but it was a thrill simply knowing that we were trespassing on private property. It lent to our heightened sense of adventure. With the adrenaline pumping, our confidence grew as we ventured further down the driveway. As we neared the house we saw the surroundings better. The house was built on concrete and wooden stilts about six feet off the ground. There was a wide wooden stair with no rails to the front that led up to the door. Subash wanted to go and explore under the house but Vinod promptly said no.

He explained that the place was cool and dark and we did not know if there were snakes nesting under the house. At the mention of snakes, we all looked around for we were surrounded by bushes and we had not thought of this before. This made us a bit more nervous and uncomfortable. We had come this far and were not about to quit our exploration, though we were uneasy after Vinod mentioned snakes.

As we neared the house, the sandy driveway forked into two pathways that ran past either side of the house. There were fewer bushes on the right side so we took that pathway. We bent into a crouch as we stealthily crept past the house. It was not a very big house and the pathway soon curved to the back giving way to the row of stables. We were immediately awe struck for there on the closed up stables were large white painted crosses. This sight caused the hair on our hands and the backs of our necks to stand on end. We had heard that country folk painted crosses on buildings, but this was the first time we actually saw it. The crosses were supposed to ward off the dreaded soucouyant. A soucouyant was supposed to be an evil creature, usually an old woman, who had the ability to turn herself into a ball of fire and travel about the countryside in search of blood. Usually she preyed on humans but also on large animals. The location of these stables and the relative isolation seemed to us to be a prime hunting ground for the soucouyant. Hayden knew a lot more about the legends of the forests and he recounted to us some of his knowledge.

It was very eerie standing there looking at the crosses on the stables. At the back of our minds we knew that there was nothing to fear for it was broad daylight and we knew that the soucouyant only preyed at night. It was then that Ronald had the bright idea to see if there was a way into the stables. I did not know why he wanted to do so, but I was not going to show the others that I was afraid or scared. I guess I was not the only one who felt this way for we all asked each other if we really wanted to go in. Of course everyone said yes to show their bravery. With that settled, Ronald led the way around to the back of the stables. Again, for no reason, we crouched and went in single file. At the back of the stables there were two coconut trees and four breadfruit trees. At the bottom of these trees the ground was covered with dry leaves that had fallen long ago. All around the stables there was a ring of fine dry sand that widened to the rear. The bushes at the rear were not as thick as at the front and it made us wonder why. Hayden suggested that this was so probably because not as much sunlight penetrated to the rear. This explanation was adequate for us until Vinod reminded us that the soucouyant did not like light and that this was a prime area for them. That made us a bit more uneasy, but we held steadfast to our plan of exploration.

We approached the stables from the right side and made our way to the rear. There were no windows nor did there seem to be any way in. As we made our way around the rear to the left side, we gazed upon a loose plank of wood about three feet from the ground. The plank had partially fallen to one side leaving a small space. This sight caused the adrenaline to pump even faster through our veins. This was the way into the stables. We exchanged glances with each other for reassurance and to bolster our daring. We crept quietly up to the open space and peered in but did not see anything as it was pitch black inside. Did we dare go in? Immediately we conjured up images of being attacked by strange malfeasants but we were determined to explore inside and shook these images from our minds. Vinod decided that he was the eldest and he would be the first to enter. With that settled, we moved the plank a bit more to widen the hole for him to squeeze through. Hayden followed him, then Ronald, then Subash and finally me.

It was pitch black inside and we could not see each other. We huddled together listening keenly for any sounds from within. As our eyes gradually adjusted to the darkness, we began to see each other and slowly discerned our surroundings. The floor was covered in fine sand and littered with old straw.

There was a musty smell mingled with one of old manure that tickled our noses. The walls were bare and did not hold the array of old implements that we hoped would be there. I guess we applied our memories of old western movies and hoped that this stable would be like those. As our eyes grew more accustomed to the darkness, we fanned out to explore our surroundings. Hayden gave a loud gasp that immediately alerted our attention. We rushed to his side and looked in the direction that he was pointing. On the stable door, painted on the inside, was another huge white cross. There was nothing too remarkable with that, but as our eyes followed his finger, we all jumped at what we saw. The sight made our hair stand on end and caused us to break out in goose pimples all over.

On the ground, there was a large flat stone that seemed to be tainted with some sort of liquid that had dried out. Around this stone there were about a dozen burnt out candles and some feathers. I had read about this before in a book on the legends and practices of Trinidad and knew that this was a place where some sort of black magic had been performed. The stone was the altar, the candles were consistent and the feathers meant that a cock had been sacrificed. Maybe a voodoo or a shango ritual had taken place here. As I explained this to the others, Vinod and Hayden were eager to leave. Unconsciously we made the sign of the cross to protect ourselves from evil and quickly made our way to the gap through which we had entered. The hair on our necks stood straight and we could not leave this place fast enough. One by one we exited and as the last one came out of the stable, we cast a last glance back at the hole in the wall, regrouped and quickly moved away from the rear of the stables.

The afternoon's adventure made us suddenly feel very tired. Maybe it was because of the rush of adrenaline. As we regrouped in the roadway, we discussed the events that had just unfolded and each of us felt that we had just had a close encounter with the supernatural. We were all eager to get away from this place as we turned to return home. Slowly we traced our steps along Gill Street and turned into our driveway. As we did so, Hayden stopped us and told us that he thought we had better not mention our adventure to the grownups for fear that there may be some consternation to be put up with. We saw the logic in his argument and all agreed not to divulge anything to the others. Our pact thus made, we quickened our paces until we got to the apartment. There were still about two hours left before dusk and we decided to noisily encourage the others to go for a swim.

They had all taken a nap and were just about rousting themselves when our noisy embellishments stirred them to their feet. Everyone agreed that a swim was a good idea as they had all been rather lazy that day. Hayden retrieved the football and we made our way down to the beach. While waiting for the adults to arrive, we set up two goals using piles of sea balls and began a game of small-goal football. Hayden and I formed one team and the other three boys formed the other. The tide had receded but it left the sand quite soft and our weight caused our feet to sink when we ran. It was rather tough because it burned up more energy and we soon grew tired with our exertions. As we collapsed panting on the sand to rest, the adults made their way down the steps. Kelvin ran up and kicked the ball into the water and waded in after it. Kelvin and Radica started a game of catch with the ball in the water. This looked less strenuous and we joined in. Sherry and Gerry contented themselves building a sandcastle on the shore.

My mother, my father and Roy took up their usual prostrate position in the shallow and Subash's parents soon joined them. The water was warm and felt incredible. We positioned ourselves with our backs to the waves so that they crashed onto our shoulders giving us an aqua massage. The time passed rather quickly and before we realized it, dusk was upon us. We reluctantly rinsed the sand from our bath suits and made our way out of the water and up to the apartment. Subash and his family bid us good evening and made their way to their home. My mother passed towels to Sherry and Gerry who had finished their showers. The three boys all huddled under one shower to enjoy the feel of the fresh water as it washed off the salt from our bodies. The wind was a bit nippy so we gladly made our way to the bedroom to change. We did not linger over this but rather hastily donned our dry things and proceeded to the living room to see what the others were up to.

My mother and Radica brewed a pot of tea and relaxed on a bench they had taken outside and set up under the coconut tree. The other grownups were seated on the bench outside our bedroom and were chatting away. Sherry and Gerry retrieved the goodies that they had purchased earlier and were happily munching away on salted prunes, Toronto chocolates and bubble gum. Hayden and I brought another bench outside and the boys installed themselves there and we began a lively discussion about what we thought the other cousins were doing back in Tunapuna. It's not that we were nostalgic or homesick, but we thought about them. We soon grew tired of just sitting and needed to get moving. Hayden started singing some of his favourite reggae songs and soon had everyone chiming in. Hayden was a good dancer and we looked to him to show us the latest dance steps. Of course he came in for a lot of chiding from Kelvin and Roy when he tried to show us his version of a two-step and three-step dance. His antics brought guffaws from the adults who had grown up with their versions of the two-step and three-step from the fifties and sixties. In retaliation, he retorted that his dance was modern reggae as opposed to their ancient moves. But it was all good-natured ribbing.

While we were sitting there enjoying each other's company, we realized that the first week was almost over. It was already Friday. The first few days always seemed to go by slowly, but the realization that one week was almost gone brought on some anxiety in our stomachs. My father rationalized with us that we should look at it, not as one week already gone by, but more positively that there were still four more weeks to go. I guess he did make sense as we tried to see it that way and it did make us feel a little better. As we sat there, the salty breeze, the sound of the waves and the hissing of the foam lulled us into silence. It was uncanny for we all felt silent almost at the same time. I guess each one had their private thoughts at that moment. It was totally relaxing just to sit there and look out at the ocean in the fading twilight.

The ladies retreated inside to prepare dinner and they called out to us when it was ready. We all picked up our benches and returned to the house. That night our dinner was a very simple one of steamed rice with corned beef with cabbage. The simplicity of the meal by no means underscored how delicious it was. When the meal was over and the table was cleared away, we sat down to our nightly ritual of cards. Subash and his family were at their apartment and would not join us that night. I guess they felt that they should not be over all the time, which in a way was fine with me because sometime you needed your own space. We played game after game of all-fours and just as it was beginning to get a bit monotonous, my mother made an announcement that lifted the sleep from our eyes and got us all excited.

We had forgotten that she had extended an invitation to Aunt Jean to come down and spend a weekend with us. My mother reminded us that tomorrow, Saturday, Jean and Sundar would be coming to spend the weekend, and that she was almost sure that some of our cousins would be coming as well. That announcement brought an abrupt end to our card game and we got up from the table and made our way outside to the bench to discuss plans for the cousins' arrival. We speculated on who would be coming and whether Jean would bring any of her tasty coconut drops. We would have stayed up all night talking were it not for my mother's insistence that we retreat to bed. So with smiles on our faces in eager anticipation, we reluctantly snuggled under the covers and continued in hushed whispers until one by one we dropped off to sleep.

Chapter 7

The First Weekend and Visitors

My father had to rouse us the next morning because we were still asleep having drifted off at about 2.00 am. He asked us to do the morning ritual of going to Mr. James' shop. We did not linger over this as we eagerly wanted to get back to await Jean and Sundar's arrival. We all knew that Sundar liked to get an early start and anticipated their arrival anytime. We made our purchases quickly and did not dawdle on our way back. While waiting on breakfast, we all congregated on the bench at the back of the house and resumed our excited chatter from the night before. Sherry wondered whether any of the girl cousins would be coming. In a way we felt sorry for Sherry, as she was the only girl to us four boys. In addition, the only prospects for company for her would have been Michelle or Rosemary. We told her that she would have to wait and see who came with Jean.

    As we sat there talking about taking the visitors to pull seine and to catch crabs, we were summoned to breakfast. We took our usual places around the table and helped ourselves to hot cocoa from the steaming jug. It was only about 7.30 in the morning and the day stretched in front of us with an exciting promise. When the meal was placed on the table, we took turns helping ourselves and were just about to delve in with great gusto when we all heard the same sound. There was the sound of car tires crunching over the small pebbles and gravel at the foot of the driveway and then the distinctive sound of Sundar's bullhorn. They had arrived, and quite early at that!

My mother's admonitions to remain at the table were politely ignored as we rushed from our places at the table into the driveway eager to catch a glimpse of the arriving car. As it approached, we could not see who was in the back seat to satisfy our curiosity. We saw only Sundar at the wheel, Jean in the passenger seat and Steve in the back. Surely it was not only the three of them. The car came to a stop just in front of the doorway and then, quite suddenly, the back door was flung open and we could see the crouching figures hiding from us. Steve alighted from the back and was followed by Ernest, Anthony, Derek and Rosemary. We screamed with excitement at seeing our cousins, but we could not have been happier than Sherry. She was absolutely delighted that Rosemary had come! This was the first time that Rosemary had made the annual visit with Jean.

Sherry and Rosemary interlocked arms and ran giggling into the house and planted themselves on the sofa to talk about whatever girls talk about. As for us boys, we slapped each other on the back and exchanged playful arm punches. Ernest and Rosemary were Ronald's brother and sister. We could not stop grinning and the exchange of news about what was happening in Tunapuna caused a terrific din. Sundar came out of the car and opened the trunk. We all lent a helping hand to carry the stuff out into the house. On their way to Mayaro, they had stopped at the Sea-Way bakery in Sangre Grande and Jean had bought fresh loaves of bread. While my mother and my father were welcoming Jean and Sundar, Radica and Kelvin retreated to the kitchen to get more hot cocoa going and to cut more bread for our extended group.

With the greetings taken care of, Roy and my father re-arranged the benches at the table to accommodate our seven visitors. We re-took our places at the table and continued our interrupted meal. The boys all sat on one side of the table with me in the middle and Ronald and Hayden on either side of me. The excitement opened up our appetites and the platter of bread and butter practically disappeared, so much so that we had to ask for replenishment from the kitchen. A bottle of freshly made guava jam presented by Jean was devoured with great relish and we could not seem to get enough cocoa. With our appetites sated, we listened in to what the adults were talking about, but as their conversation did not interest us, we asked to be excused from the table and promptly proceeded outside to the bench. The first order of business was to find out about the others in Tunapuna. We learned that everyone was fine and that the others also wanted to come to Mayaro. We understood their disappointment and we missed having the others as well. But the most exciting bit of news was that the football team was formalized and that Hamil was our coach. The team was to be called Brooks United, named for Mr. Brooks of the Coast Guard who frequently did weight training by Hamil and who agreed to sponsor our uniforms. This was fantastic news and already we were anticipating the return home to get involved with the football team. With all the news on Tunapuna exchanged, it was our turn to tell the others what we had done during that first week we were in Mayaro.

   We were recounting our adventure down to the river and our crab-catching exploits when Derek interrupted us. He pointed down the beach to where a lot of people were gathered. He wanted to know what was happening there. Derek had been to Mayaro several times in the past, mostly on day-trip jaunts. However, he had never seen a seine being pulled. When we explained the mechanics of the seine to him, he got all excited and wanted to promptly go and join in the proceedings. We did not need to be coaxed and hurriedly went to seek permission from the adults still having coffee at the table. With admonitions to be careful and not to go into the water, we were granted leave to proceed to the seine. But first we had to change out of our day clothes into our beach suits. We quickly donned our beachwear and excitedly raced down the steps to the beach and practically ran in the direction of the seine.

Ernest and Anthony were the eldest and they were in charge of the group of eight children. With a steady pace and trot being kept by all, they ensured that we did not stray into the water. As we passed the massive, old tree that we believed was deposited on the beach by the current all the way from the Orinoco in Venezuela, Ronald called out to us to stop. He had spotted a green coconut branch that looked like it had just fallen. He wanted to stop and strip off some of the leaves to get the strong, supple fibrous rib. He explained to Derek that this was to be used to string any fish that we would forage from the seine. He re-assured Derek that he would show him how to do it and with that, we set of once more. It took us about another five minutes before we were at our destination. I looked at Derek and could see the wonderment in his eyes.

We had arrived at the seine just in time to allow Derek to participate. There was still a fair amount of rope to be pulled in, so we bade Sherry, Rosemary and Gerry to remain high up on the shore, and the rest of us boys waded into the water to grab hold of the rope and help with the pulling. We had to separate into two groups, as there was not enough room on one side to accommodate all six of us. Derek quickly got the hang of the hand over hand technique and we all strained every muscle trying to outdo each other. Pretty soon there was a shout and I explained to Derek that the corks were sighted and that this meant that the nets were quite near. I pulled him aside and pointed to a spot just beyond the breakers where the line of red and white corks could be seen. I pointed out to him the boy who had been tasked by the captain to swim out to the corks and hold the lead down. I could see Derek drinking in all that I was telling him and could picture what was going through his mind. I know because that's how I felt the first time I saw a seine and my father explained it to me.

As the nets were pulled in, the arc narrowed and pretty soon all the volunteers, like ourselves, were made to leave go of the ropes and nets to allow the seine workers to manoeuvre the nets to the shore. We were all standing up to our knees in the water just about ten feet from the nets and we saw the silvery writhing and splashing of the fish. As we were allowed to pick up any small fish that we could pry loose from the nets, Ronald positioned himself next to Derek and showed him how to do it without damaging the gills. He then showed him how to keep a firm grasp on the fish with one hand while threading the end of string through the side of the gills and through the mouth. With the first one done for him, Ronald handed the string to Derek who set about foraging for himself. While the others were absorbed with their efforts, I pried myself away from the melee and stepped back to look for Sherry, Rosemary and Gerry on the shore. Sure enough they were there, safe and sound, chatting away with Lloyd. My mind at ease, I returned to help the others.

Very soon, the nets were picked bare and the helpers had started unfurling them and shaking out the seaweed that was caught in the mesh. I looked at our five intrepid foragers and realized that they had gotten a pretty good haul. Of course, Ronald being the most dexterous had the biggest string. They dragged their strings through the water to wash the sand from the fish and we re-grouped on the sand and joined Lloyd. He was quite impressed with our haul. He explained that they had caught a pretty large shoal of kingfish, which everyone was happy about. Kingfish was prized by the hotels and restaurants and usually fetched top dollar. He was about to hand us one when I stopped him. I explained that we had more than enough this morning and that there was still some in our freezer at home. I told him, however, that if there was another seine tomorrow, we would accept his offering then. He seemed contented with that compromise and we bade him good morning and set off for home.

The walk back home was leisurely and as the sun was a fair way up and the heat rising, Ernest and Anthony consented to Sherry, Rosemary and Gerry wading in up to their ankles as we made our way home. They gleefully splashed each other and darted after the young moonshine that simply eluded them in the shallows. With a watchful eye on them from time to time, we six boys picked up sea balls and tried to strike an agreed target on the Orinoco tree. It was a picture perfect day with absolutely blue skies and hardly any clouds. The water seemed to be almost crystal clear as it lapped our ankles. Further out, the tint seemed to me more aqua than azure. There was just a gentle breeze that was enough to cool. With the breeze came the distinct heady aroma of the Orinoco tree that had lain on the sand there for as long as I can remember.

Elsewhere in the distance, you could see the outline of another seine being pulled, but it was too far away to want to venture on another long walk. We were all anxious to get back home and go swimming. It was that type of day that beckoned you to just simply relax with not too many exertions. As we walked, we spied several sand dollars, a type of brittle starfish. Steve and Ronald began treading on them and crushing them with their toes much to the consternation of the younger ones who wanted to collect them. Ernest intervened and chastised the two delinquents as much to stop their destructive actions as to placate the upset youngsters.

As we neared the house, we saw that the grown-ups had already installed themselves on the beach in front of the house and were just relaxing in the beautiful morning sunshine. We quickened our pace to get home that much faster. The adults were very impressed with our haul of fish casting an observant eye on our prized strings. Sundar volunteered to take the lot off our hands and clean them. With absolutely no hesitation, we promptly handed the fish over and then asked whether we could go into the water. There was no need to don our bathing suits as we already had them on for the seine. With delighted shouts of glee when permission was given, we scooted into the water splashing each other as we jumped into the gently rolling waves.

Kelvin and Radica accompanied us as usual and gave us the signal to halt any further distance. With the water just midway up our torsos, we felt that we could have encroached a few feet further by stealing a few inches every so often. However, Kelvin would have none of that and reprimanded us sternly with a threat of sending us to sit on the shore. So we resigned ourselves to the imposed border and busied ourselves playing water fights. This was a simple game played by using the flat of the palm held slightly at an angle and briskly striking the top of the water in a forward motion so as to create a fast moving jet of water directed at an opponent. The target was usually the eyes as the salt would cause the victim to have to blink, shut their eyes or stop and wipe their eyes. This would render the victim vulnerable to more aquatic assaults and eventually concede. We tried to see who could splash the most accurately directed jets. With Kelvin enjoying this type of horseplay as much as us kids, it was inevitable that he would emerge the victor, though Anthony did give almost as good as he doled out.

With the water fight abandoned, we simply bent our knees and spread our arms so as to have the water up to our chins. As the waves loomed, we instinctively turned our backs to them so that they would break on our backs and necks rather than our faces. The sun by this time was intense and the water felt really cool and wonderful. We formed a semi-circle in the water and started talking about all that had happened back in Tunapuna during the week that we had left. Anthony and Ernest jockeyed verbally to see who would be first in recanting events, but Ernest conceded and Anthony was given the honor of so doing. We had left Tunapuna last Monday morning and it had been a week that we were gone. Anthony told us that the old gang from Cemetery Street did practically the same routine stuff that they normally did during the holidays. Except that during the last week, there were two bits of extraordinary adventures for them.

The morning we left for Mayaro on our vacation, the usual gang had gathered at my grandfather's old shed in the morning. They had been up quite early to see Ronald and Hayden off and had already had their breakfast. Anthony, Derek, Ernest and Steve were joined by Leighton, Andrew, Brian and David. With not much else to do, they started an early game of cricket in the road. There was practically no traffic on the street so there were hardly any interruptions. By 9.00 am, they were joined by the Shoon brothers, Glen, David and Roger, as well as by Harper and Hamil. With thirteen odd players, they called out to and coaxed Glen to join to even up the numbers. Teams were chosen and a cricket match started. However, by starting at such an early hour in the morning, it was inevitable that by noon, when the sun was at its pinnacle, there were extremely exhausted players who were ready to abandon the game to seek out some cool refuge.

With Roy on vacation in Mayaro with us, Hamil inveigled Krishna, one of the close neighbors, to wake up from his nap. Krishna had an open-tray flat-bed truck. Hamil proposed to Krishna to take the entire bunch of players to the Caura River. As it was indeed a very hot and sunny day, Krishna did not need much convincing. He readily agreed and the whole gang merrily set off for Caura River. They went up to Guava Hole and spent the rest of the day bathing, diving and catching cascarob and guabin.

The next bit of excitement for them was the next day when, after a game of football in the road, hot and tired, they retired to the shade of the back steps of my grandmother's house. They then planned a "raid" on the coconut and fruit trees in the nearby lot. With lookouts posted for the watchman and the dogs, Anthony, Leighton and Andrew scaled the fence and proceeded to divest the fruit trees of some of their loads. With the illicit gains safely thrown to the lookouts and a hasty retreat beaten, they made a bucket of chow using oranges, mangoes and cucumbers. The coconuts provided the means to quench their thirst and cool the peppery heat from the chow. These two bits of news from Tunapuna did cause Hayden, Ronald and I to be a bit envious that we had missed out. And sensing this envy from us, I guess the others felt a bit better that they had one up on us. With that out of the way and the ice broken, we resumed our swim until we were called in to lunch.

With seven visitors, space at the table was premium and we were allowed to take our plates and sit at the sofa and use the coffee table. Lunch was simple meal of hotdogs topped with coleslaw and was made more enjoyable with the addition of the visitors. It was very hot and the heat seemed to permeate into the living room. The only respite came to us in the form of huge jugs of water with chunks of ice thrown in to chill the drink. We jostled to wipe the condensate from the outside of the jugs with which to wipe our brows. After the meal, Jean opened all the bedroom windows and the bedroom door at the back of the house. Sundar had brought a huge yellow tarpaulin with him and in the shade at the back of the house, he spread the tarpaulin on the ground. We brought out the cushions from the sofas and he arranged them on the tarp. In that way, we could all lie down and rest in a group using the bedroom and the makeshift tarpaulin bed. Normally we would have relegated Gerry and Sherry to the bedroom, but allowed them the first choice. Sherry and Rosemary opted for the bedroom and Gerry eagerly joined us outside. We just lay there enjoying the shade and the odd cooling breeze coming in from the ocean. We did not sleep but rather just rested a while.

The respite from the heat and from our morning exertions was welcome but was short-lived. Subash and Vinod had gone on a trip with their parents to visit a relative in Guayaguayare and had just returned. They came to look us up as this was to be their last night in Mayaro before they went home. As they sought us out at the back of the house, they were surprised to see my other cousins as they would not have known they were coming to visit.

We were almost all the same ages and from the same hometown, so camaraderie was easy. I introduced them to the others and they greeted each other. With that out of the way, and with us just content to relax in the shade, Derek suggested that we start a game of cricket or football. This sounded good to the rest of us but with so many more people, the driveway would be too crowded. So Anthony was delegated to approach the adults for permission to play in the road on Gill Street. The adults decided to join and pretty soon there were two captains appointed and two cricket teams selected. Everyone joined in including the ladies and the girls. As there was never really any traffic on Gill Street, we were assured of a practically un-interrupted game.

The game took off and was played with much enthusiasm by all. The tall trees on the western side of Gill Street assured us of adequate shade and diminished the direct heat. However, our enthusiastic play rendered us hot and sweaty very soon. As if by coincidence, we heard the tinkling of a bell and turned in the direction of the sound. Coming down Gill Street from Plaisance Road was a sno-cone cart. He pulled up to us with a huge smile on his face and explained his appearance. He had been out in the village near the Chinese shop plying his trade when he saw us on Gill Street and thought he'd come down to see if we wanted sno-cones. A rhetorical question if we have ever heard one. We abandoned the game and encircled his cart. With a beaming smile, the sno-cone vendor pulled up in front out driveway while my father went home to fetch the money. There was pineapple syrup and guava syrup which we eagerly wished to try half and half. Normally in Tunapuna we only got the red kola syrup. This would be a welcome change. There was also coconut ice cream served in cones which the ladies and the girls opted for. With everyone served, the vendor collected his money and gave us a hearty goodbye, smiling obviously at such a big sale in one shot. We all just left the cricket gear there and just sort of sat on the low wall outside Nadens while we enjoyed our icy treats.

While we were so occupied, Roy checked the scores and announced that once again, Hayden was the top scorer. This was the third time that we played cricket and the third time Hayden had top-scored. Roy was never one to renege on a promise and reminded us that he had promised a surprise for the highest run scorer. That piqued our interest and Hayden, beaming, urged Roy to produce the surprise. Roy nipped back to the house and returned in a flash. He had his hand in his pocket and fished out a gleaming new penknife with a key holder ring at one end. He ceremoniously awarded the penknife to Hayden, who, being as clownish as Roy, made a grand gesture of acceptance. That made us all laugh. We finished our sno-cones and ice cream and were all contented to just relax the rest of the afternoon there when Subash's mother reminded us that we were all invited over to their place tonight for supper. At that signal, my parents bade us all go back to the house and get cleaned up.

My parents knew about the invitation but had deliberately not told us to keep it a surprise. It certainly was and we looked forward to going out for supper. My mother, Radica and Jean retired to the kitchen to prepare their contribution to the meal. The rest of us were charged with taking our showers. Sherry and Rosemary used the indoor shower. The boys opted to use the outdoor showers on the concrete deck at the back of the compound. These showers were not connected to the water tanks so there was no fear of depleting the tank levels. With this luxury, the eight boys noisily crowded into the open air shower stalls to shower as much as to poke and tickle each other. There was such a din that Kelvin came out to admonish us to keep it down. Rather boldly, Anthony, who had a mouthful of water, sprayed Kelvin. Well who told him to do that? Kelvin was not upset, but took it as a challenge and chased Anthony up and down the compound trying to catch him. This caused much ruckus and squeals egging Anthony on to run faster, and urging Kelvin to "catch 'im and tap 'im up." Kelvin eventually was able to grab hold of him and pin him to the ground. In mock play, he administered a series of knuckle cuffs to Anthony's triceps causing then to "frog." After making Anthony plead for mercy and say he was sorry, Kelvin laughingly released him. All the while, the rest of us were screaming with laughter at the horseplay. A sharp reminder from my father to hurry up with our shower put paid to any dawdling. We quickly toweled dry and returned to the bedroom to dress and apply lotion. We were supposed to go over to Nadens for supper at 7.00 pm and as such had about an hour to kill.

While the ladies took their showers and dressed, the men were charged with keeping an eye on the kitchen. Jean opened the bag of goodies that she had brought and produced some of her special coconut drops and some of the biscuit-cake that she had bought at Sea-Way bakery in Sangre Grande. We gladly accepted the proffered treats and happily munched away. Her coconut drops were always tasty with just the right amount of sugar, coconut and flour, not too soft and not too hard. When we finished out treat, we helped the men carry our benches over to Nadens so that there'd be enough seats. With that done, we had to go back home and wait on the ladies. They were not long and soon enough we were all on our way over to Nadens for what was expected to be a grand supper.

Subash's mother had made paratha roti with curried goat, stewed chicken, aloo and channa and pumpkin. This was a feast! We had not had roti and curry in a long time and the odors simply made us salivate. My mother, Radica and Jean brought sweet rice and a Dundee sponge for dessert. It was a sumptuous repast and we all delved in heartily. There was a table in the main room at which all the adults sat. Then there was another table on the porch where we kids sat. The usual mosquito coils were lit and placed about the rooms so there was no disturbance from the annoying sandflies. It felt like we were at an Indian wedding, feasting on such delights especially when the huge glass jug of cold Solo soft drink appeared. And just like at Indian weddings, the flavors were mixed: cream soda, banana and red, all making for a delicious beverage. As we ate, I paused and looked around at the rooms. Here I was, surrounded by my family and friends, not a care in the world, and I realized how lucky I was.

With a superb meal relished with gusto, we all gravitated to the porch, or gallery as we used to call it. The porch was long and ran the entire length of the house upstairs. The men moved their table onto the porch and we helped them with the benches. With two tables set up, the children had one and the adults had the other. The men pulled out a deck of cards and they started a game of knock rummy. It seemed that they wanted to make the game more interesting as they were playing for five dollars a pot. Sherry and Rosemary contented themselves sitting on the stairs and playing their girls' games. The boys on the other hand, started our own game of all-fours. We played in teams of two and winners stayed on the table. We divided ourselves into pairs: Subash and I, Ronald and Steve, Hayden and Vinod, Ernest and Anthony. Derek was left without a partner and so we allowed him to choose anyone as his partner at his turn. It was still pretty early in the evening as we were all absorbed in our card games. The ladies settled themselves on the sofas indoors and contented themselves with a pot of tea and conversation.

As we finished the first round robin of our game, with the prospect of sitting and waiting for our next turn, Subash, as was his wont, grew restless and soon he beckoned me to follow him. Curiosity triumphed and I eagerly followed him down the stairs into the courtyard below. He looked gingerly around and glanced up a few times before putting his hand behind the large potted palm at the bottom of the steps. Of course I wanted to know what he had in his hand but he shushed me and pulled me into the shadows. Then he showed me what it was that he fished out. It was an opened packet of Broadway cigarettes and a box of Three Plumes matches. He told me that his father had left them on the top of the trunk of the car earlier when they were in Guayaguayare and he did not seem to miss them. Of course Subash was beaming at his purloined articles and tried to inveigle me to go with him across the road to have a smoke. That meant that we had to get permission to leave the compound. So we decided to bring the rest of the boys in to our plan and seek permission from the adults. We hastened up the stairs to tell them we wanted to ask permission to go across the road to sit on the wall facing the sea opposite the old bakery. We did not tell them about the cigarettes though. They agreed as they were also getting bored with the card game. With permission sought and reprimands to keep within sight of the house, Vinod fetched his big torch and we clambered down the stairs leaving a pleading Gerry with the girls and the adults.

    The other guys relished this opportunity to go on this nocturnal jaunt and we picked our way through the almond trees aided by the light from Vinod's torch. We quickly arrived at the broad, low wall that faced the sea. The guys all jockeyed for seats. Subash then revealed his secret. With the exception of Derek, they all were game to have an illicit smoke. Subash handed out the cigarettes and Vinod used the box of matches to light everyone up. We had all smoked cigarettes before in Tunapuna, usually stolen from Roy's packet, on the old train line overlooking the cemetery. But those were usually shared smokes. This time we all had our own cigarette. It made us feel grown up and important. As we crouched down behind the wall having our smoke, we heard the music from the jukebox at the High Wind bar drifting across the air. We enjoyed the scent of the tobacco and the slight buzz that we felt from the nicotine. As we took the last drags and snubbed them out in the sand, Subash pulled out a packet of Mint Spangles and passed it around. This was to try and get rid of the smell of cigarettes from our breaths. Just as the mints were being passed around, we heard a shout from Kelvin that he could not see us. Vinod gave a lusty reply and waved the torch in the direction of the house. This seemed to satisfy the adults and we were glad that we could stay here a bit longer.

We sat on the warm sand on the beach and absorbed the moonlight. The moon was not totally full but it certainly was bright. The guys engaged in a lively discussion about cricket at the Queen's Park Oval and the Test Matches that had been played there. We recounted the day when my father took all my cousins to the Oval to see West Indies play against New Zealand. We fondly remembered sauntering up Cemetery Street to Narinesingh's Supermarket to buy Smarties and Holiday Foods Corn Curls for our trip to Port-of-Spain. We vividly remembered queuing up for the PTSC bus in front of the Hosein's house and the eight-mile trip to Port-of-Spain. It was fun remembering getting to Ariapita Avenue, crossing the road to the Oval, the high walls, the even taller immortelle trees that cast a cool shade on the western side of the Oval on Havelock Street, and the scent of the manure from the police horses while we walked to the entrance. From going through the turnstile one by one, to getting our chairs right up at the fence on the grounds in front of the Dos Santos Stand, to my father negotiating with the drinks vendor for cold coca-cola for us, to buying pallet from the ice-cream vendor.

We heartily recalled when Terry Jarvis was posted on the boundary right in front of us and how we heckled him. We teased Derek to remember when he asked Terry Jarvis to allow him to use his mouth to go number one so that he would not have to get up and go to the bathroom. This recollection caused huge guffaws. We all agreed that we should ask my father and Kelvin to take us to the Oval for the next Test Match against India. And so we passed the next hour or so in lively conversation and recollection until a loud whistle from Roy bade us return to the house. As we neared the house, Vinod advised us to use the stand pipe in the yard to wash the sand from our feet as well as to attempt to wash away any lingering scent of tobacco. After bidding our hosts thank you and goodnight, we included our goodbyes to Subash and his family for they were leaving very early the next morning and we would miss their departure. With a solemn promise to keep in touch more often when we returned home, we bade them goodbye and we crossed leisurely to the Thackories compound and sought out our beds while the adults locked up the house for the night.

The next morning, Anthony tried to wake everyone up very early but only succeeded in rousing Hayden and I. Everyone else just ignored us and pulled the covers over their heads glad at the extra space on the beds. The three of us tiptoed through the living room and quietly opened the door. Roy awoke but was satisfied that we were only venturing outside to the benches. We walked around the compound and peered through the wooden fence to see if there was any activity on the beach. There was a seine far off in the distance but we decided it was too far away to even try and get permission to go. So we just sat on the steps leading down to the beach and chatted about the plans for the football team when we all returned to Tunapuna. Gerry and Ronald soon came outside and joined us. As we got up to make our way back to the house, Kelvin was already up and was opening the windows.

While we all waited our turn at the sink to brush our teeth and wash our faces, breakfast was being prepared and there was a delicious smell of hot country chocolate. As we had all had a late night, no one was in the mood to spend a long time in the kitchen, so breakfast was quite simple but hearty. We all tucked into a huge platter of bread and butter and hot country chocolate. There was the usual bottle of guava jam as well as some cheese and salami. Hayden made a cheese and jam sandwich that prompted us to follow suit. The combination was good and we tucked in. The coffee for the adults smelt good and we wished unsuccessfully for some. It was amazing to see the platter of bread disappear and caused my mother to jokingly wonder aloud if we would eat them out of house and home as she sliced another loaf to replenish the platter. There was no rush that Sunday morning. Breakfast was leisurely and slow and not until the last drop of chocolate was drunk did we wrest ourselves away from the table.

We would have been contented to just laze around the house that morning, but Steve and the other boys who were visiting, were anxious to not waste time around the house. They wanted to play football on the beach. However, my mother insisted that before we were allowed to play, we should help with some of the household chores. Anthony, Ernest and Hayden were assigned the task of cutting up carrots and sweet peppers; Steve and Derek were given cucumbers and tomatoes to peel and slice. Ronald and I were assigned to cleaning the table, sweeping the house and making the beds. Gerry, Sherry and Rosemary were exempted from these chores and were allowed to engage in an animated game of tag outside in the driveway. We did not mind doing these chores as there was still about an hour to wait before the tide was out far enough for our game, plus we did feel like we were contributing to the meal preparations. As we finished the chores and were donning our bath suits, Lloyd the caretaker drove up to the house. He greeted my folks and presented us with a grop of coconuts. These were young green nuts with sweet water and he told us there was medium jelly. My father thanked him for the gift and said that he'd reserve the coconuts for us for our water break from our football game. With that, we all, except for the ladies, trooped out of the house down to the beach for our football game.

        Captains were selected and the two teams chosen. The tide was low and it left a wide swath of beach, more than fifty feet wide. So we decided to play with big goals instead of small goals. That was good news as I played goalie and relished the opportunity to block some shots and show off my skills. Besides, the sand was soft and would cushion the dives. What followed was an animated display of football, with as much noise, chiding and horseplay as displayed skills. The sun was high overhead and seemed to direct its heat on us. Presently we were all drenched in sweat and sometimes, when the guys played the ball into the water, there'd be a scramble to splash about and cool down.

When Hayden, our central defender, tripped Kelvin, play stopped and everyone agreed that deserved a penalty shot. I steadied myself and focused on the ball. Kelvin took the shot himself and I anticipated correctly, low to my left and I was able to parry the shot. That brought excited shouts and taunts from our team. With the game tied at 2 – 2, my father said that the next team to score would be the winners. That made the game really tense and competitive. An angled snap shot from Anthony caught me off guard and slammed into my chest. I could not hold the shot as it rebounded into play, but sharp defending from Hayden and a timed tackle averted the danger. As the ball went into touch for a throw, Roy collected the pass and laid it back to me. Instead of picking it up to throw it downfield, I trapped the ball and looked up and saw Ronald free on the right side near to the water's edge. I deftly chipped the ball to him and he in turn collected it cleanly, beat an onrushing Steve and was clear on goal. Delightedly he tapped the ball in and we had won the game. Exhausted and hot, we slumped into the water's edge to cool off and to catch our breath. Roy then bade us come back up to the house for coconuts. He was quite deft with the cutlass and quickly had the coconuts opened and we all enjoyed the cool refreshing water. As we were done with the water, he hacked open the shells for us and cut us a spoon with which to eat the sweet jelly. Thus refreshed, we made our way back to the water for a swim.

The water was gorgeous and surprisingly clear. After our coconuts, we were sated and not very hungry. Presently the ladies made their way down to the beach and joined us in the water. They had decided that they'd get in a decent swim and then we'd all have a late lunch. That suited everyone fine and there was a royal romp in the water. Carefree and leisurely is how best to describe that day spent in the water enjoying each other's company. Talk was easy and spontaneous and there was not a worry in the world. And so we spent the better part of two hours in the water until Jean said it was time to get cleaned up and prepare for their departure. We all rinsed the sand from our suits and made our way back to the house.

As Jean and the visitors were leaving, they had to shower with fresh water and change into their dry clothes. The rest of us just roughly toweled off and dried ourselves in the sun. We then made our way to the table in anticipation of a good Sunday lunch. We were soon rewarded with a sumptuous repast. It was a typical Sunday Lunch of red beans, stewed chicken, macaroni pie, but instead of white rice, there was a cookup-rice. A huge jug of freshly squeezed grapefruit juice and a cucumber and tomato salad rounded off the meal. It was a noisy table made all the noisier by recollections of the football game. But no one was scolded as I guess the adults allowed us some leeway with the soon departing visitors. With lunch devoured, Sundar produced a huge watermelon and neatly carved up wedges for everyone. For this, we all moved outside under the shade of the coconut tree and to the comfort of our benches. The other benches from inside the house were brought outside and we installed ourselves in a wide semi-circle. After we had washed the sticky juice from our hands, Sundar was always a stickler for that, we enjoyed the breeze and the shade and the smell of the salt in the air.

It was about three in the afternoon while we were relaxing outside when we saw a boat passing in front of the house. We heard Gerry's name being shouted and looked in the direction of the voice. It came from the boat and we made out Peter waving to us. He was beckoning to us and pointing to the shore. We knew instantly that they had been out banking and were coming back to shore. They would need help to "jock up the boat" or in other words, pull the boat out of the water and safely up onto the shore. We at once noisily asked if we could be allowed to go. Permission was given but Steve, Anthony, Ernest and Derek had already changed into their dry clothes in preparation for departure. Jean saw the disappointment on their faces and made a compromise with Sundar to delay their departure. They were given permission to change back into their trunks and happily did so in quick time. We then all set off down the beach including the girls and the ladies.

It was only a short distance to where the boat had landed and was bobbing up and down in the water. Peter and Kenny were already out of the boat and were unfastening the engine. When they were done with that task, Peter saw us and beckoned us to him. We gladly took up our positions on either side of the boat. The boat was of the pirogue type about thirty feet long and quite heavy. The technique was simple. We'd wait until the next wave came and in the surge, we'd use the force and direction of the water to guide the boat to the sand. This called for timing and Peter called out the cadence. This was a very pleasant task as it meant getting wet and being splashed by the waves. Very soon the keel of the boat wedged into the sand on the shore and from there it was sheer muscle power and rhythm to pull it safely to the top of the shore. This was done in practically the same way with Peter calling the cadence. There were about thirty willing hands, including ours, helping with this.

The cadence was a simple call of 1-2-3-up, rest, and start over. Each pull gained us about a foot. It took a good fifteen minutes to get the boat fully parked safely in its position on the shore and then allowed to slump to one side propped up by a stout plank. When the "jocking up" was completed, the next task was to off load the boat. For that, Peter and Kenny had some of the younger village boys offload the nets and rods and gasoline tanks. Next they had the baskets brought out and they offloaded their catch. They had been out banking and had been lucky to come upon a shoal of grouper and red fish. There was an enormous grouper weighing about sixty pounds.

We were happy for Peter and Kenny as their catch would fetch them a tidy sum of money from the fish vendors waiting to buy the catch. In his usual way, Peter sauntered over to our group with two large red fish which he handed over to my father. My father hesitated and told Peter no, but Peter was adamant that he accept this as a gift and my father thanked him but admonished him that if he continued giving away fish like this to us, we would no longer come to see him at the boat or at the seine. Peter in an unusual twist told my father that if he did not come, the fish will still find a way to get to him and that as a fisherman, if he could offer us fish as a gift, he would be offended if we did not take it. With that matter settled, my father invited both Peter and Kenny back to the house for a drink.

    We made our way back to the house quickly with Jean urging the four boys to go and shower again and change back into their dry clothes. Roy produced a bottle of Scotch and poured generous glasses for the men. As they made their toasts outside, my mother decided to give one of the red fish to Jean to take back with her. This involved finding some plastic bags and packing some ice to keep the fish cool for the drive back to Tunapuna. It was already four in the afternoon and Sundar was anxious to get going. As Peter and Kenny left, we gathered around the car. Roy and Kelvin helped Sundar load the trunk with their belongings. Sundar offered to leave the yellow tarpaulin with us and my father gratefully accepted his offer. Jean and my mother embraced and the men shook hands. We hugged our departing cousins and as the car reversed down the driveway, we waved to the departing visitors, sad to see them go.

    We had had much fun with them on this first weekend. It was then that my mother announced that they'd come back for one more visit in three weeks' time and that heartened us. As it was already getting late, we were told to shower and change and then come back outside. We did so quickly and returned outside where the benches were still in a semi-circle. We spent the rest of the afternoon until sunset remembering all that we did during the last two days with the visitors.

    As the darkness started creeping in, we moved into the house to the living room. Roy and Kelvin took to the kitchen as my mother, Radica and my father sat down with us. Not much was said as everyone just relaxed. We got out the compendium and started a game of snakes and ladders and so busied ourselves with our game until supper was ready. As we had a late lunch, Roy and Kelvin made cheese paste sandwiches with hops bread and jugs of tea. We partook of this simple supper and the tea was a welcome change from our usual cocoa. With supper done, we continued with our board games switching to Ludo and Chinese Checkers. But we soon got bored with these games and decided to retire to the bedroom. We each took up our usual spots and pulled the covers. The bedroom door was left open so we could still see and hear the adults in the living room. The light was off in the bedroom but enough light filtered in from the living room. Sherry and Gerry played a game of hand clapping and singing while we snuggled up with each other and reminisced about the past week. It was hard to accept that already one week had gone by and it was fun to try and recollect everything we did since we left Tunapuna. But with four weeks still stretching in front of us, we tried to make plans of things we still had to do. And as the night wore on and the yawns were more frequent, one by one we drifted off into a peaceful slumber and dreamt of that first week in Mayaro.

Chapter 8

The Tropical Storm

The next morning, we awoke to the sound of the radio playing. We knew that Roy was up and going through his morning routine. We were tempted to rouse ourselves but the temptation to stay in bed was greater and we must have drifted back to sleep. I woke with a jump as I felt something cold and wet on my mouth. It was Kelvin and Gerry pasting toothpaste and soap on our mouths. This of course caused a ruckus as we awoke, furious with Kelvin, who was in fits of giggles running around the living room trying to avoid us. Eventually we gave up chasing him and agreed that it was a good prank and we threatened him with getting even. There was no need to go to Mr. James' shop that morning as Jean had supplied us with enough bread. As we would not go for the newspapers, my father tuned the radio to listen to the news. As we did our morning toiletries, breakfast was prepared and the table was laid out as usual. Noting that we were not drinking enough milk, my mother insisted that morning on serving Kellogg's Corn Flakes with milk. We were allowed to sprinkle some sugar with which to sweeten the milk. This was a nice change and we enjoyed the cereal.

    While we were still at the breakfast table delving into sliced oranges, my father bade us hush in a loud voice as he got up and raised the volume on the radio. His tone was very stern and it startled us a bit, but what was to come was even more alarming. The radio station was announcing a weather bulletin from the Meteorological Office. A Tropical Storm watch was in effect for all of Trinidad as a tropical depression about four hundred miles to the east was showing signs of organization and it was expected to develop into a Tropical Storm. This was to be the first storm of the Atlantic Hurricane Season and it was to be named Amber.

Its trek was to the west at about twenty miles per hour. If the present organization and westward track continued, it was expected to make landfall by noon the next day. The bulletin warned that coastal areas on the eastern side of Trinidad could expect high seas and a storm surge that could result in flooding. Residents could expect to lose electricity and water supply and were urged to take all the prescribed precautions. It was expected to make landfall as a Category 1 or Category 2 storm system, and forecasters predicted that the island would experience tropical storm force winds for several hours with several inches of rainfall and strong gusts. The bulletin was repeated in a sinister sounding voice. Needless to say there was a hushed silence around the table as we all let the weather bulletin sink in. As the second repeat of the bulletin was completed, the announcer urged listeners to keep their radios tuned to that station for further updates.

My father, who sat on the sofa next to the radio, rose with a concerned look on his face as he addressed the other adults. There was a decision to be made whether they should try and contact Selwyn and Chestnut to come and pick us up and cut the holiday short; or whether we should stay and try and ride out the storm. We could not believe that a storm could cause our vacation to be interrupted. Surely they were joking. But one glance at the concerned looks on their faces and we knew this was no joking matter. My father came back to the table and told us kids to remain quiet and do not interrupt. No one would dare do so and we listened intently on their discussions.

The reality was that both Selwyn and Chestnut did not have telephones. In addition, there was no telephone at Thackories. My father knew of telephone numbers where he could call and leave messages for them, but the only phone was at Mr. James' shop. We could pay Mr. James to use his phone and get the messages out, but we would have to wait for these messages to be delivered and for Selwyn and Chestnut to return the calls to say yes or no that they could come pick us up. In addition, they also had their own families to see about and would no doubt be busy with their own preparations for the oncoming storm. This was a dilemma and there was a high probability that even if we did get through to them, they would not be able to come and pick us up in time. They discussed the risks associated with staying put and what precautions could be taken. They deliberated thus for a while and it seemed at the end that they had reached a consensus. My father then turned to us and told us that they had decided to stay in Mayaro and ride out the storm. They assured us that the Thackories compound was fairly high and that the building was made of stout concrete and brick. In addition, we were on the ground floor and that there was no risk of losing the roof and being exposed to the wind and rain. He spoke in a kind and gentle voice as much, I suspect, to reassure us kids as to reassure the ladies.

With that decision taken, the next order of business was to start planning for the onset of the storm. We were admonished to not interrupt their discussions but were allowed to remain at the table to listen. Sherry seemed a bit over-awed by the prospect of the storm and began to cry and my mother took her and Gerry into the bedroom to comfort them. With them in the bedroom, the other adults turned their attention back to their planning. Kelvin fetched a notepad and pen with which to write down the checklist of all that had to be done. Among the items that had to be taken care of were filling as much potable water as we could and going shopping to buy batteries, torches, candles, food, canned milk and propane. As they were discussing these checklist items, we heard a shuffle coming up the driveway and looked out to see Lloyd the caretaker.

Lloyd came up and greeted us all and told my father that he had been in contact with the owners. His mission was to determine whether we were staying or leaving. When he found out we were staying, he re-assured everyone that Mayaro had been through storms before and always weathered them. He sounded quite confident when he told us that it was very unlikely that the storm surge would breach the compound wall, but even if it did, there was a six-inch culvert around the side of the house to stop any water from entering. He told us that if we needed anything, we could always look for him in the village later on and with that he bade us goodbye.

As he left, the men sprang into action immediately. First on the list was to get every available water container and thoroughly rinse them clean. We kids were allowed to help forage in the kitchen and bathrooms for the receptacles and help get them cleaned. Thus armed, we made our way to the outside of the house to where the water tanks were situated. My father gave instructions to fill them all with water and take them back to the kitchen. Meanwhile, my mother and Radica had been busy in the kitchen clearing the concrete counter to make place for all the water receptacles. As we put the containers on the counter, they carefully covered them to prevent dust and impurities getting in. This was to be our drinking supply. It took over an hour to accomplish this task and when it was done, we congregated outside. Because the older tanks were made of sturdy galvanize and sat on the ground, we were assured that we could open the top of the tank to get more water should we need it for flushing the toilets. The newer tanks were mounted on concrete pillars above the ground and were made of industrial plastic, so the covers were light.

They decided that we should try and secure the cover of at least one tank with some rope that we had. Kelvin, being of lithe build, armed with a sturdy knife clasped between his teeth, deftly climbed up the pillar and was soon sitting atop the first tank. He used the knife to pierce three holes in the tank's cover and thread the rope through. He pulled on both ends of the rope to tighten and firmly fastened the rope to the concrete pillar. As this tank was above ground, providing the wind did not topple it, and providing the rope held the cover in place, this would be our reserve supply of potable water should we need it. There was a risk that if the sea breached the compound wall and salt water entered the driveway, that the water in the older galvanized tanks could become contaminated with salt water. This would be okay though for flushing the toilets.

With the water tasks completed, my father called out to everyone that we would be going to the village to make our purchases. Normally this announcement would be greeted with much glee and anticipation, but today this was replaced with a feeling of anxiety. We quickly put on our slippers and with the house secured and locked, we all made our way down the driveway into Gill Street. Noting that it was a very quiet group, Kelvin taunted us that we were scared of the storm. That piqued us to counter with clever retorts and pretty soon as we rounded Gill Street into Plaisance Road, it was a more cheerful group.

The first thing we noticed on Plaisance Road was that there was more than the usual activity. There were a lot more people out and about than usual. Some seemed busy, others were just milling around in small groups. We could just catch bits of their conversations and naturally they were all about the storm. I glanced back toward the sea and it was a deep blue against a clear blue cloudless sky with a barely discernable horizon. There was no indication that there was a storm approaching. As we walked past Mr. James' shop we could see that it was filled to overflowing with lots of villagers. No doubt they were making their own purchases. There were lots of people waiting to get into the shop and we wondered why did they not just go to the Mayaro Village Co-operative. Roy explained that these villagers rarely had bank accounts and because of the nature of their living, established a trust relationship with Mr.

James. They would get their goods on trust from Mr. James and would pay him when they sold their catches. This was the custom and was a part of their life. We did not see anyone that we knew and we soon passed the shop.

Soon we came upon the sidewalk on the left side of the road that wound its way up to the village. The Co-op was about half a kilometer away just on the border of the Village Football Field. There was a grove of tall coconut palms and a cluster of almond trees between the sidewalk and the Co-op. The trees cast a cool shadow on the sidewalk and provided a welcome respite from the heat. There was not much conversation as we were all pretty much pre-occupied with our own thoughts. Without the usual dilly-dallying, we soon reached our destination. I had been to the Co-op once before and just barely remembered it. The large doors were made of metal that folded away as they were pulled open. The structure was made of concrete and brick and what was very noticeable was that a lot of open blocks were used in construction. This was of a two-fold purpose: to allow light in and to allow fresh air to circulate. The Co-op was not fancy like the Hi-Lo supermarkets. Rather it was functional. The goods were displayed quite efficiently and there was a noticeable lack of colorful and gaudy advertisements attracting attention to a particular product. Kelvin and Radica secured a cart and allowed Gerry and Sherry turns to push the cart.

We made our way down each aisle whilst the adults consulted their shopping list. Primary on the list were batteries and candles. We found some inexpensive torches and added those to the carts. Hayden noticed that there were no safety matches on the list and those were quickly found and added. With the emergency essentials secured, the next task was to procure the food items. My mother and Radica browsed through the aisles making a selection of canned corned beef, sardines, tuna, and sausages. These were deliberately selected as they did not really require cooking. Next they sought out and found tinned milk. With the prospect of losing electricity they could not buy the normal type of pasteurized milk. Instead they opted for condensed milk and evaporated milk as these would not go bad as quickly. Several loaves of country bread were added as well as flour. They chose flour in case we had to make our own bread should the roads be impassable and delivery from the bakeries cut off. Kelvin, Roy and my father stocked up on their smokes and we were allowed to choose one treat each. When the list was cross checked and all items had been verified as procured, we made our way to the checkout line to pay for the items. While the adults were in the checkout line, Ronald, Hayden and I moved outdoors into the parking lot and conferred with each other on the severity of the storm. We were not far into conversation when the others came out and it was time to head back home.

There were, however, still two stops to make, one at the market and the other at Mr. James for propane. In the interest of saving time, it was decided that Ronald and I would accompany Kelvin to the market while the others took the groceries back home. Roy would then go to Mr. James' shop to get a tank of propane. With that settled, we parted company and Kelvin decided to have a race across the football field to the Junction. It was difficult running with slippers on and the race petered out into a trot. We quickly reached the Junction and carefully crossed the road. It was as busy here as it was in the vicinity of Mr. James' shop. People moved about with an anxious air and everyone seemed to be pre-occupied with their own errands. We entered the market and Kelvin deftly moved about the stalls looking for the produce he was charged with obtaining. We just ambled behind him.

The market provided a myriad of sights and a cacophony of sounds. Vendors were trying to outdo each other to entice buyers to choose their produce and it was interesting to see them jostling with each other for Kelvin's attention. With the purchases made, we tried to tunnel our way out to the exit and onto the sidewalk. As we were preparing to cross the road, Kelvin stopped us and bade us follow him. He approached a doubles vendor whom he was familiar with from the past years. As it was almost noon by this time, he decided to buy doubles for our lunch to take back with us. We negotiated with him to include some saheena and kachourie and he got the vendor to put the pepper sauce in a small cup on the side. The hot doubles smelt savory and we eagerly anticipated lunch. The chores were completed and we set a brisk pace back to the house. As we passed Mr. James' shop, we spied Peter who quickly crossed over to talk with us. All the fishermen were very busy trying to help each other secure their boats and nets before the storm. He told us that all should be well and that he'd look us up the next day after the storm had passed. We bid him good luck and did double time down Gill Street.

  When we arrived at the house, the groceries were already unpacked and stored and Roy had already gotten the extra tank of propane. My mother and Radica were just going to the kitchen to get a quick lunch when Kelvin produced the doubles, saheena and kachourie. These were welcomed with great glee and we all tucked into this lunch. The pepper sauce was tantalizingly hot and we gulped down several glasses of water to cool our tongues. When we finished and cleared up the table, we wandered outside into the driveway to the coconut tree. As I looked out to sea, I could discern a marked change from earlier on. The horizon was visibly darker and the seas were unusually calm. The sun had disappeared and low clouds were gathering. But what was even more remarkable was the absence of any wind. It was like the proverbial calm before the storm. Even the corbeaux perched atop the coconut palms seemed to stare toward the horizon as if in anticipation of the oncoming storm.

  There was not much else for us to do as no one even entertained the thought of a swim. So in our usual gathering spot on the benches, we speculated about the severity of the storm and what destruction it might bring. Ronald conjured up images of immense waves crashing down upon our vacation home and washing us all out to sea. As farfetched as this may have been, it certainly caused alarm for Sherry and Gerry and seeing that they were about to panic and call for the adults, Hayden and I quickly allayed their fears and admonished Ronald accordingly. This seemed to satisfy the younger ones and we resumed the conversation by talking about the oil rigs and AMOCO's installations at Point Galeota. We were not far into this discussion when the bedroom door swung open and my mother and Radica came out to join us.

The chores in the house were completed for the time being and we at once remarked that they had their swimsuits on. Without giving us a chance to ask, Radica told us that we could all go and change into our swimsuits as well. Not needing a second invitation to do so, we sped off to quickly change and within two minutes we were all back outside. The men were already changed into their swimsuits as well when we came back out. My father complimented us all on the orderly and rapid manner with which we accomplished the required preparations for the storm. Now that we had to sit and wait, there was no reason why we could not go for a swim. The tide was out, the sea was flat and calm and the water was sure to be nice and warm. In addition, it would be a few days after the storm had passed before the waters would have settled and before we could venture again for a swim. The compliments were welcomed and the explanations seemed fair to us and with that said, we proceeded down the steps to the beach. No one stayed on the beach; instead, we all went straight into the water. As usual, Kelvin marked the no-pass zone for us and we luxuriated in the warmth of the water. The waves were extremely gentle and rolled rather than crested and broke. We spent the rest of the afternoon swimming, diving and playing in the water. It was almost as if we were trying to do as much to compensate for the upcoming days when we would not be able to enjoy the sea.

At about four in the afternoon, it was time to go in and as we rinsed the sand from our swimsuits, and with the last duck under the water taken, we waded out of the water and made our way up to the house. Instead of bathing with buckets at the low stand pipe outside our house, we decided to use the showers on the concrete deck on the other side of the compound. Rather than taking turns, we all piled into the showers and enjoyed the feeling of the salt being washed off our bodies as the jets of water cascaded down on us. After briskly drying ourselves, with the towels wrapped around us, we made our way back to our apartment where Roy and Kelvin were bringing out two benches into the driveway. They each had a glass with what we assumed to be rum and coke. Even My mother and Radica came out as well and sat in the driveway. Not that we objected to this, but it was a bit out of the ordinary.

My mother explained that we'd soon be cooped up in the house for a long period when the storm finally arrived; why not enjoy a last fling at the fresh air. Hayden and I brought out another bench as my father emerged with a jug of cold Solo soft drink and some cups. Soon we were all holding a glass, or cup, and enjoying the cold drinks. Ever the tormenter, Kelvin teased us to enjoy the ice as there would be none very soon once we would lose electricity. Conversation was easy and the main discussion focused on the remaining preparations. As we sat outside, the music from the radio was audible from inside. As the song finished playing, the announcer stated that there was an updated bulletin from the Meteorological Office on the system. Roy got up and turned up the volume and a hushed silence settled as all ears focused on the radio.

The Meteorological Office update at five p.m. advised that the system had in fact developed into a Tropical Storm and was named Amber. The Tropical Storm Watch was now replaced with a Tropical Storm Warning. It continued its westward trek and was now located approximately two hundred and fifty miles east of Trinidad moving to the west at between fifteen to twenty miles per hour. This speed was unusual but was good news in that the faster it moved the less time it spent over the warm Atlantic to gather strength. All of Trinidad was under a warning and the areas on the East Coast of Trinidad were especially advised to brace for gale force winds, high seas and possible flooding. It was estimated that the storm would make landfall by the next morning but that strong winds and rains would start affecting the island late night into the early morning. The bulletin was repeated and the announcer urged all listeners to take the usual precautions and began to recite off a prepared list. The list was familiar to us all and Roy lowered the volume on the radio. We packed up the benches and took them back inside. It was time to change into dry clothes and complete the final preparations.

During our trip out to the Mayaro Co-operative, the men had purchased a product known as Flashband. Flashband was a broad type of aluminum tape, about three inches wide. Instead of glue at the back, there was a sticky black tar compound. This was useful in repairing holes in galvanized roofs. Before using the Flashband, it was necessary to heat the tar so as to allow it to adhere properly to the surface to which it was applied. We knew what this product was for, but were perplexed as to why we would need it as there was no roof directly above us. Roy explained that it was equally useful in sealing cracks. We followed the three men around the house as they did a walk around and then it clicked. As there was still light outside, with all the doors and windows facing the sea closed shut, we could see the light filtering in through any cracks in the wood. They started in my parents' room. First they lit a candle and placed it on the dresser. Next they unrolled a strip of Flashband and warmed it over the candle. They then cut it into the required size and placed it over the cracks. The windows in the bedrooms were the same as those in the living room. As such, a strip of tape was placed around the base of the window to keep any water out that may be driven by the wind. This was a slow process that required patience. In order to help out, as much as to get us out of the way, my father asked us to go to the other rooms and using a pen, mark out where they needed to put tape. With youthful exuberance we skipped to our assignment pretending that we were fortifying our castle against an invading horde.

By the time they came to our room and the windows were secured, they realized that the door posed another problem. There was a gap of about almost half an inch at the bottom of the door and the floor. Any water in the compound outside would be driven into the bedroom by the wind through this gap. In addition, if there was any flood in the compound, even though there was a six-inch culvert at the side of the house, there was none at the back, and water would surely seep into the bedroom. Collectively the men pondered on this new obstacle and true to the saying that necessity is the mother of invention, they found a solution that they hoped would solve the problem. The idea was simple really. The door, once shut, fit snugly into the doorframe and as such, there was little risk of it rattling.

Roy remembered that Sundar had left the tarpaulin with us and the idea was to use the tarpaulin as a bung under the door. As the tarpaulin was impervious, it would guarantee no water entering the bedroom. The problem was that the tarpaulin was very large. It would need to be cut to make the right sized bung. The men chuckled at the thought of seeing Sundar's face if he knew they were going to cut up his tarpaulin. With the decision taken, the required piece of tarpaulin was measured, cut, folded and rolled. The door was opened, the bung was positioned on the floor and the door was squeezed back into place. It took all three men to get the door closed. But at least it was a good sign that it should be water-tight.

The efforts to make the bedrooms impervious to water exhausted everyone and we gladly sought respite in the living room. There was a small sideboard buffet in the living room next to the face basin. My mother laid out all the candles, matches, torches and batteries on top of the buffet. Small enamel plates were reserved on which to secure the candles to prevent the wax from dripping to the floor. It was already very dark outside though it was only about six in the evening. An appetizing aroma greeted us and reminded us that we were famished. My father made us wash up properly and sit at the table for dinner. Once we lost electricity, no one knew when it would be restored, but with minimal opening and closing of the fridge, it could keep cool for a while. My mother and Radica did an enormous platter of fried fish that could have fed an army. Their rationale for cooking that much was simple. Once cooked, it could serve as leftovers the next day during the storm. Radica made a rice and peas pelau to go with the fish and this also would provision us tomorrow during the storm.

When everyone was seated, we tucked into a hot delicious dinner that drew many compliments to the chefs. Radica jokingly remarked that the bottle of pepper sauce was quickly disappearing. The radio had not been turned off since this morning and the low music in the background during our dinner created a very cozy intimate atmosphere. No one talked about the storm during dinner; rather there were several simultaneous, spontaneous conversations. Sherry and Gerry engaged each other in a contest to see who could finish their meal the first. Hayden, Ronald and I debated who would make the first eleven team for Brooks United when we got back to Tunapuna. And so we engaged each other at the table during a very pleasant dinner.

We would have been content to linger at the table, but my father cut that short when everyone had eaten and tasked each child to take their own plate and cup to the kitchen sink. There was still some work to be done to secure the main living areas and Kelvin's bedroom. Back out came the Flashband and the sequence of unroll, heat, cut and apply was ritually carried out until they were satisfied that all the cracks in the windows were sealed. This completed the list of chores to be done to prepare for the storm. By this time, the wind had picked up and though it was dark outside, we could see the trees swaying in the wind. There was no rain, but the wind was quite strong. We were sitting on the sofas playing a quiz when suddenly there was a huge bang that startled us and made us jump. The main doors to the living room were opened and the bottom portion was propped with the piece of wood that we used for that purpose. However, the wind blowing against the door must have shook it to and fro causing the prop to fall and the door banged in against the doorframe. The top portion was still in place as this was secured with a strong nylon cord to the awning rafter. If this was a sign of things to come it brought us back to the reality of the storm. Thus startled and the quiz interrupted, my mother suggested that we all turn in for the night. There were slight protests as it was not late, but we were ordered to our bedroom. Dejectedly we roused ourselves and went to our bedroom to hunker down for the night. As we were snuggling under the covers, my father came into the room and reasoned with us not to be upset. He assured us that once the storm started we would know and it would probably rouse us from sleep, so it was best to try and get a nap in so that we would not be too tired the next day. Sherry and Gerry asked Ronald to sleep in the bed with them and he willingly agreed. Very soon, they were fast asleep and Hayden and I drifted off as well.

Even though we fell asleep, it was not a deep restful sleep. I was very much aware of the howling wind outside and could hear the rain beating down on the galvanized awning when it started. In that state of in between sleep and wake, with the covers pulled right up to my chin, I dozed restlessly. The darkness of the room and the wind and rain outside seemed to make the room feel cooler than normal and the warm covers were re-assuring. I must have fallen asleep for I felt someone shaking me. I opened my eyes to see Hayden sitting up in the bed. In a hushed whisper, he admitted that he was trying to awaken me. Before I could ask him why, a flash of lightning lit up the entire room and it was quickly followed by a tremendous clap of thunder. Hayden whispered that was the reason as the lightning had just started. Instinctively we both pulled the covers and just lay there waiting on the next burst of lightning and thunder. We did not have to wait long as almost instantly the heavens complied with our anticipation. An even brighter flash was followed by an even louder burst of thunder. It sounded as if the thunder was right outside of the bedroom. That second clap of thunder roused Sherry in alarm and she jumped up crying. We called out to her to be quiet as it was only the thunder. But nothing could calm her down. Her crying awoke Gerry as well and though he did not cry, we could sense that he was scared. All five of us were now up and our voices must have been heard as my mother came into the room and tried to placate Sherry. Noting her efforts were mostly in vain, she offered for Sherry to come to her bed, an offer that was immediately accepted. As Sherry was getting off the bed, she asked Gerry if he would like to go with her also. He said yes and they both took their blanket and made their way with my mother to her room.

The three boys were left alone with two beds. Ronald got up and went out to the living room and told his father, Roy, that there was an empty bed. Roy must have guessed that Ronald may have been a bit uneasy and would have felt more assured if he slept in our room. He agreed to move off the couch and quickly installed himself on the empty bed. Ronald lay down beside him. We did not go back to sleep but rather just laid there listening to the howling wind and the rain. About an hour or so had passed since Roy came in to sleep with us when he suddenly got up from the bed. Ronald asked where he was going. Roy said it was six in the morning and this was the usual time that he always got up. We could not believe it was morning because it was still so very dark. As we got up with him, Roy reminded us to put our slippers on as we made our way out into the living room. He instinctively reached for the light switch to turn on the light, but there was no light. This confirmed that the electricity was out.

Roy stood there for a moment to allow his eyes to become adjusted to the darkness and then made his way to the buffet. He groped around and found the matches and soon he had a candle lit and placed it on the table. With warnings to us to be absolutely quiet, he went to the kitchen and put on a pot of coffee. Instead of sitting at the table, I went back to the bedroom and brought out two blankets and we cuddled up on the sofas. We heard Roy fumbling in the kitchen and supposed that he was looking for the cups. As the coffee came to a boil on the stove, the strong heady aroma permeated the living room and we hoped that he'd pour us some. As we focused our attention on the kitchen, he emerged with four enamel cups and handed each of us one. There was a little coffee with lots of milk and we blew on the hot liquid before we sipped the strong coffee.

As we were indulging in the hot coffee, Roy stopped and stood up. That caught our attention and we wondered what was amiss. As we stood next to him, almost simultaneously, Kelvin and my father emerged from their rooms. The men conferred and then turned to us and told us that the first part of the storm was over. They knew that as the wind had stopped howling and the rain had ceased. The room was a bit brighter and the chaos outside seemed to have abated. Kelvin told us that the eye of the storm was passing over. He explained that the eye was the centre of the storm and that it brought a calm period. To demonstrate, as much as to fulfill everyone's curiosity, Roy opened the top portion of the door and pushed it open. We all crowded around eager to get a glimpse of outside. It was just about the time that the sun should have been up, but there was no sun. However, the sky was a pale blue and there was an eerie calm outside. Roy opened the bottom portion of the door and gingerly made his way outside with Kelvin and my father. We were firmly told to stay inside much to our dismay.

We crowded into the doorway to observe the men and our compound. The first thing we noticed was that there was a lot of water in the compound. The men made a cursory glance around and when they were satisfied that there was no danger, beckoned to us to join them. We did not wait on a second invitation and promptly joined them. We walked to the back of the house and could see that the water was very high. The grey concrete of the building was darkened as it was wet. On the other side of the compound where the three coconut trees were, some of the branches were blown off and were strewed around the compound. Our tree was intact, but several coconuts had been blown free and had fallen to the ground. The adults made their way to the water tanks and were relieved to see that all were intact. With the walk-about completed, we all drifted back to our house and stopped in the driveway in front of our doorway. Kelvin stopped and collected the fallen coconuts while Roy retrieved a jug and the cutlass. My father figured that we would probably have another couple of minutes before the eye passed over and the second part of the storm started. Roy and Kelvin quickly hacked open the coconuts and filled the jug with water and scraped the jelly in as well. As we were finishing up, the wind started blowing again, though gently at first, and we were hustled back into the house and the door properly secured by Roy and my father.

  Kelvin explained that after the eye passed over, the second part was usually the most dangerous part of the storm. The wind blew from the opposite direction and what was weakened in the first part, usually succumbed in the second part. As Kelvin was winding up his explanation, the others were just awakening and making their way to the living room. Sherry and Gerry had slept well once they were on the bed with my mother and my father. Radica lit a few more candles and placed them around the room to give off some more light. The faint candlelight in the still dark room lent a cozy atmosphere and we sat on the sofas listening to the wind pick up speed outside. It was less intimidating this morning than it was last night, especially as we knew it was morning and we had survived the first part of the storm.

  All of a sudden the room darkened and we could hear the rain pelting down hard on the awning. The wind seemed to howl like a banshee and it gave us chills just sitting there. My mother was in the kitchen slicing bread for our breakfast when there was a brilliant flash of lightning. My mother was always superstitious and immediately dropped the knife and left the kitchen. She was taught that whenever there was lightning, one should not use a knife lest the metal attract the lightning. She made Kelvin throw a towel over the mirror at the face basin for the same reason. This bit of eccentricity on my mother's part drew a few smiles from the men, but none dared make fun of her. To finish the task in the kitchen, my father resumed the duty and soon had a platter of bread ready for us. To humor my mother, he put out plastic cutlery with the breakfast. No one bothered with the morning rituals and we settled in at the table for breakfast. We buttered thick slices of bread and added some slices of cheese and avocado. The hot cocoa warmed us inside and gave us some comfort. Hayden and I helped ourselves to a second sandwich. Roy had brewed another pot of coffee for the adults and the men moved off the table to the sofas so that they could have their smoke with their coffee.

We were finished with breakfast and were helping to clear the table when there was a loud high pitched squeaking sound that startled us. The younger ones did not hide their fear and ran to the sofas to be comforted by my father. I must admit that we were also alarmed but tried bravely to hide it. Then there was a loud ripping noise and a tremendous crash could be heard at the back of the house. In a flash, my father called my mother over and had her stay with Sherry and Gerry. The concern on the men's faces caused us much anxiety. They grabbed the torches and made their way to our bedroom in the direction from where the noise came. We were stopped cold in our tracks as we tried to follow them.

The three torches crisscrossed the dark bedroom seeking out any damage. But there was no physical damage to be seen. The windows and doors were intact and there was no sign of water. This was good. They then went to my parents' bedroom and surveyed for any damage. Again, there was a collective sigh of relief at no discovery of damage. They came back to the living room and announced that all seemed to be okay for the time being and there was no need to be afraid. This was easy to say, but even harder to do. Radica fiddled with the radio trying to find a station but there was only static on the airwaves. In a sense, we realized that we were cut off from the rest of the world while the vicious storm raged outside. There was nothing else to do but wait until it was over and that would not be for another few hours.

My mother took the younger ones into their bedroom and cozied up under the covers with them. I could hear her telling them a story. That was a good move on her part as this would comfort them and take their focus away from the storm. The men and Radica got out a pack of cards and started a game at the table whilst enjoying another pot of coffee. Hayden, Ronald and I did likewise and started our own game of go-to-pack. This took our minds off the storm as well but every so often we jumped at an extremely savage clap of thunder. Though we were engrossed in our card game, it was difficult to ignore the storm. It seemed as if the storm was competing for our attention for just as we were immersed in our game, the wind would hiss loudly and cause something or the other outside to crash or bang. It seemed as if the storm was reminding us that it was still there. And so we passed the next few hours.

Gradually as the morning wore on, we could hear soft snoring from the bedroom where my mother and the younger ones had fallen asleep. No one knew what time it was and we could only hazard a guess. Hayden enquired and we discovered that it was almost eleven in the morning. The wind was still blowing very strong and we could hear the occasional gusts. The rain, however, seemed to be lessening. We realized that Radica was no longer at the table and I found her in the kitchen. She was preparing the left over fish from the previous night's supper. I asked her if she needed some help and she gladly accepted. She asked me if I was afraid of using the knife and I proudly said no. However, she switched tasks and she chopped the onions and chives while I continued stripping the fish being careful to not get any bones. While we prepared the fish and other ingredients, we chatted about the storm and what possible damage may have been done outside.

When we were done, she mixed the chopped onions, chives and the flaked fish together in a bowl. She was preparing to make fish pies for lunch. I helped her with the small balls of dough. With both of us working, we quickly had about four dozen pies ready for the hot oil. She took over that responsibility and thanked me for the help. As I walked out to the living room to wash up, I noticed that the room was much brighter and that the rain was barely discernable. The wind was still blowing but the audible fury was quite less. The lightning and thunder had stopped and it seemed as if the storm was playing out its last legs. My silent observations were confirmed as Roy made the same remarks to the others at the table.

The card game was abandoned as Roy and my father grabbed hold of the door and gingerly drew back the bolts while keeping a firm hold on it lest the wind should whip it open. The wind was steady but not strong and slowly they guided the top portion of the door into its open position. We all crowded in the doorway eager to look outside. The rain was just a steady drizzle and the wind was light. An exclamation from Kelvin drew our attention to where he was pointing. Towards the back of the house, we could see that the galvanized awning from the apartment upstairs had been blown off and had fallen down. It was partly resting on top of the awning at the back of our bedroom and partly resting on the ground. At once we knew this was the loud crash we had heard. The downed awning partially obstructed our view of the sea but we could see that a part of the fence was broken as well. A cursory glance in the opposite direction confirmed that the electrical wires on the poles in Gill Street were still intact and that they were not blown down. These observations took a split second and we withdrew from the doorway as the men felt it was safe enough to open a few of the windows. We had been cooped up in the house since the previous night and as the windows near the sofas were opened, a refreshing breeze swept through the house. It immediately blew out the candles, but there was no need for them anymore as there was enough natural light to brighten the place. The noises awoke my mother and the younger ones and they excitedly joined us at the windows to stare out into the driveway. The sky was still grey and the clouds were still very low and angry looking, but there was light. The storm was over.

Chapter 9

Galeota with My Cousins

Radica called us away from the windows as lunch was ready. The fish pies smelt heavenly and we saw a mug of grapefruit juice on the table. It seemed that the end of the storm opened our appetites and we delved into the hot pies and tamarind chutney that she provided. My mother thanked her for taking care of lunch and we all tucked in. We were allowed some liberty at the table and there was a cacophony of noise with everyone trying to carry on several conversations. It was a noisy but carefree meal and before we had finished, my mother bade us all be quiet and she led us in a prayer. She thanked God for having watched over us and for keeping us all safe and sound during the storm. She also asked God to watch over those who were less fortunate than us and to show us ways in which we could help them. After a meaningful Amen, we cleared the table and readied ourselves for a jaunt outside the house.

The first order of business was to survey the compound for any damage. While we thought that we would be part of the exploration party, my father would have none of it and admonished us to stay put at the house. Seeing our dejected faces, he compromised and allowed the three boys to accompany the men on the condition that we stay with them. The storm had not done much damage to the Thackories compound. The water tanks were all intact. The improvised lashings to the plastic water tank covers had held and the store of water was preserved. The doors and windows to all the apartments were intact and not compromised. The front gate was still on its hinges. It seemed that the only damage was to the awning that had been blown off. We rounded the compound and approached from the right side. The three coconut trees had a few branches blown off and were strewed along the ground. From this approach, we could see that the awning had fallen on top of our awning. Ours was still in place though the galvanize was dented from the impact of the other one crashing on top of it. Part of the fence that was joined to the brick wall was ripped from the cement and a section about four feet long was dangling and flapping in the wind.

Apart from that, there was no other damage to the compound and we were eager to report the good news to the others. Before we returned home though, Roy and My father went back to the water tanks and closed off the valves. They then went into the house and turned the taps on. As was expected, there was no water. He tested the light switches and confirmed that the electricity was also still out. He called the family together and told us that even though the water tanks were full, it was uncertain when the water supply would return to normal and he urged us all to practice economy. There was a good stock of candles and batteries to serve us as well until the electricity was restored.

With the compound inspection completed, we were eager to walk out to Gill Street and Plaisance Road to see the effects the storm had on these places. However, even though the light poles were intact, no one was certain what the state was further up the street. If there were downed poles, the electrical wires may have still been live. It was decided that the three men would venture out alone to make certain it was safe and they promised that if it was, they'd come back and get us. With our fingers crossed, we watched them leave the driveway and turn right onto Gill Street. We kept watch at the windows and it seemed like an eternity before we saw Kelvin trotting back up the driveway. He beckoned to us to come and reminded us to put on our sneakers. We had our slippers on, but were made to change into our sneakers. He helped my mother and Radica close the windows and shut the door and the rest of the family accompanied him at a quick pace.

As we turned into Gill Street, there was no visible damage. The first building we passed was Nadens and all seemed to be okay there. There was no sign of damage, though Sherry remarked that a couple of the plant pots had been blown down and were broken. To our right was Assee's Flats with its bold green façade. It too seemed unscathed. Thackories, Nadens and Assee's made up the three main buildings on Gill Street. These three were built of solid concrete and brick and it would have taken a mightier blow to render significant damage to them. As we passed Assee's, we came upon the almond grove to the right and the small wooden shack that served as the bakery. The almond trees were also intact though the ground was littered with almond pods and leaves. But there were no broken branches. The bakery also was not affected by the storm. At the back of the bakery there was a large high wall that separated the bakery from the house at the corner of Gill Street and Plaisance Road. The bakery was also in line with the grove of almond trees. We reasoned that the almond trees braced the onslaught of the wind coming in from the sea and protected the front of the bakery; and in the same way, the high wall at the back did the same when the eye passed and the wind blew from the opposite direction. We were very glad that the bakery was okay and that we could look forward to more treats from its ovens.

As we passed the bakery, we neared the corner of Gill Street and Plaisance Road. We quickened the pace as we saw my father and Roy waiting for us at the corner. As we regrouped, we could see Plaisance Road teeming with activity. It seemed that just about everyone was out. We turned left and slowly walked toward Mr. James' shop. We were eager to see if his shop was affected by the storm, but our attention was diverted to the group of old wooden shacks on the other side of the road opposite the shop. Many fishermen and their families lived here and at once we could see there was significant damage done by the storm. Several of the buildings were totally destroyed. There were zinc sheets everywhere. Where the buildings had collapsed, we could see beds and sheets soaked from the rain. In total, we counted five completely destroyed homes. There were another four with roofs completely blown off and other various degrees of destruction.

At once we thought of Peter and his brothers and we looked around to see if we could make him out among all the folks. Roy spotted him and imitated his whistle to attract his attention. Peter heard the whistle and turned in the direction of the sound. He saw us and came over, but his usually cheerful face told a different story. His home was one of those where the roof was completely blown off. The intense rain had soaked all his belongings and the water caused damage to his stove. Kenny's home was not affected and they had decided that Peter could move in with him until he could get his roof replaced and repaired.

He recounted to us that he was asleep when the ripping sound of the roof woke him. He had just enough time to jump out of bed and make for cover as the wind plucked the roof from the rafters and blew it off. After recounting his tale to us, he seemed to cheer up a bit and enquired how we had fared. Compared to his experience, we were very lucky. The villagers already had a meeting among themselves and they were resolved to rebuild the damage quickly. Fortunately, there was a village fund that was available to lend them the financial assistance. Apparently all the fishermen paid an installment into this fund for the proverbial rainy day. And in this disaster, they had provided for themselves. This was their insurance plan, crude as it may seem.

As we bid Peter goodbye, my father lingered back with him and after a short conversation, rejoined us to continue our walk. Mr. James' shop was the next object of our scrutiny. The two storey building had seen better times but it stood intact as a testimony to solid construction. There were lots of people in and around the shop, just as before the storm, and as we did not need anything, we did not linger. We did not bother to go any further up towards the Junction for we thought that if there was to be any significant damage, it would have been closer to the sea than further inland. We decided to return home and urged the adults to take the way home via the beach.

Turning to the beach, we saw that the boats were safely moored high up on the shore and were not damaged by the high storm surge. As we got to the beach, we noticed that the waves were enormous and that the tide was alarmingly high. Kelvin explained that it was not the tide, but rather the storm surge. Waves crashed and ran almost up to where we were standing. A glance down the beach confirmed that the water ran all the way up to the walls of the buildings, including ours, so this route was not an option. We stood there a few moments longer looking at the waves crash and then, urged by my mother, turned back into Gill Street to return home. The sun which peeked out every now and then from behind the still heavy clouds, seemed to have retreated totally and the sky was now a dull grey. The dark clouds seem to bring a cooler air with them and we hurried our footsteps back to the house.

While my father unlocked the door, my mother told us that there were two buckets in her bathroom and asked us to get them, fill them with water and take them back to the bathroom. This was for the girls to have a bath inside the house. The boys were told to don their swim trunks and were allowed one bucket of water each with which to bathe in our usual place outside the house. This was a welcome diversion as we splashed each other. We had to caution Ronald not to use too much soap as there would not be enough water for him to rinse properly. As we toweled dry, a cool breeze blew and caused goose pimples to appear on our skin. I think I actually heard Ronald's teeth chatter. By the time we had changed into our dry clothes, two candles were lit, one in the kitchen and one in the living room. It seemed odd sitting at the table with only one candle. The room felt darker and cooler than usual and Roy explained that was because there was no electricity in the village and the usual glow from the street lights was no longer there. He said it was a pity that it was cloudy outside for if it was cloudless, we could have gone outside and would have seen millions of stars. Roy could sense that we were restless and decided to tell ghost stories.

The solitary candle provided only a dim light and the flickering flame produced dancing shadows on the walls. Roy told us a tale of the la diablesse and the lagahou and swore that it was a true recount of his experience growing up and playing in the canefields at dusk. We were wide-eyed with wonder at the story though we did have a doubt about the bravado he described. As we were absorbed with the story, suddenly, there was a shrill scream from Sherry and a frightened howl from Gerry. Kelvin, sitting next to them, his movements camouflaged by the dark, moved his hands behind them and gently brushed his fingers on their necks. This of course would have startled anyone and he was rolling with laughter at frightening them. When they realized what he had done, they pounced on him and pummeled him with their tiny fists. They engaged in a mock fight and brought a sideshow spectacle to the onlookers. The ladies were just about finished laying the table for supper and they called us to be seated. A simple but hearty supper of macaroni and corned beef with jugs of hot tea satisfied our ravenous appetites. The meal was pleasant with several conversations ongoing. The ambience was all the more cozy because of the candle-light. Radica was in the process of slicing a fruit cake, when we heard the crunch of pebbles and a car engine coming up the driveway. The headlights soon came into view through the open windows and door and we recognized Uncle Latiff's car.

Latiff was my father's elder brother and apparently he was paying us a surprise visit judging from the surprised but delighted look on my father's face. The car came to a stop and out jumped my cousins Kevin and Colin. Our family was a matriarchal family and therefore we gravitated toward my maternal uncles, aunts and cousins. I never really grew up or spent any significant time with Latiff's children or Latiff for that matter. But when we did meet, usually at my paternal grandmother's house, we usually had a good time and got along well. So it was a surprise to see Colin, Kevin and Latiff's grinning faces. After the greetings were called out, Latiff explained that he was on his way to Point Galeota to the AMOCO installations for two nights. Latiff worked with the Customs and Excise Department and would be posted to Galeota for a few days every so often to inspect the tankers that were scheduled to dock and to leave. Apparently this was one such time. He knew we were in Mayaro and decided to stop in and pay us a visit and see how we had feared after the storm. We made place for our three visitors at the table as they sat down to have something to eat.

Colin and Kevin were excited about going to Galeota with their father because they would have the house to themselves for the whole day while he was at work. They started telling us of their plans to go fishing and to try out Colin's new spear gun. This made us a bit envious of the two. It was then that Latiff sprang his second surprise. He asked my father if he'd allow me to accompany his two boys. Kevin and I were the same age and Colin was one year older. I was overjoyed and looked beseechingly at my father and mother hoping that they'd approve. I sensed hesitation on my mother's face and pleaded with my father. He questioned Latiff about safety and once reassured, he gave his approval for me to go with them for two days. Then suddenly it struck me that Hayden and Ronald would be staying back in Mayaro. I turned to Latiff and asked about my two cousins, whether they could come as well. With a laugh, he said yes and that made five boys extremely happy. We had to be excused from the table as we could hardly contain ourselves.

We moved to the couches and began discussing plans for what we'd do in Galeota. Our discussions were interrupted by Latiff stating that he wanted to get to Galeota that same night before it was too late. Hardly believing our luck that the unexpected trip was going to start immediately, we were told to go and pack a few clothes so that we could be underway within the hour. Not needing a second invitation to do so, we scurried to the bedroom and with the aid of a flashlight, we selected a few shorts, jerseys and underwear and quickly put our bags together. My mother reminded us to pack our toothbrushes and gave us a family size pack of corn curls for a snack. Latiff had re-assured her that he had a house-keeper coming in to prepare meals and that there were workmen at the house doing some renovations who would keep an eye on us. As we came back into the living room with our bags, we saw Sherry and Gerry pleading with my father to allow them to go with us. Needless to say, they were too young and my father had to be quite firm with his no. This made them sulk and they retreated to the couch pouting. Oh well, they'd get over it. We boys had more important things to focus on and an adventure was beckoning to us.

Latiff finished off his second cup of coffee and told us it was time to hit the road. We bade goodbye to our folks and my mother hugged and kissed us and made us promise to be safe and careful. We climbed into Latiff's Rambler. Colin and Hayden sat in the front and the rest of us shared the back seat. With a toot of the horn, Latiff reversed down the driveway and eased into Gill Street. A last honk and a wave goodbye and we were off. We took Gill Street to Plaisance Road and then up to the Junction. At the Junction we turned left onto the Guayaguayare Road and followed it all the way to Galeota. Latiff estimated that it would take us about half an hour to get to the house in Galeota. We had the windows down and the salty night air refreshed us. It was pitch black outside as the electricity was still out after the storm. We commented on how dark it was and Latiff brought the car to a slow stop. He then told us to observe as he switched off the headlights. There was total darkness around us. It seemed to envelop us and it certainly was eerie. With a laugh he put the lights back on and we continued our journey.

There was not much to see as it was so dark and we settled back on the car seat and allowed the breeze to lull us to sleep. It wasn't a sound sleep as it did not take any effort for Hayden and Colin to rouse us. As we opened our eyes, we saw light and they explained that we were in Galeota and passing the AMOCO compound. There was a generator on site and this provided the backup emergency power for the installations. Latiff explained that our house would also have power as it was fed off the same grid. It was another ten minutes before we arrived at Latiff's house. It wasn't his personal house, but rather a house allocated for use by the Customs officials to stay during their assignment at Galeota. Because there was staff rotation, a housekeeper was employed by the Customs division to keep the premises tidy and clean. The house was typical of the type of construction in Trinidad. It was a two-storied building with the living areas on the second floor and open space underneath. Latiff parked the car under the house and we clambered out and followed him up the stairs. There were three bedrooms and we quickly bagged our rooms. It was already decided that Hayden and Colin would share one room; Ronald, Kevin and I would share the next and Latiff would have his master-bedroom. The living room led out onto a huge porch which overlooked the road and in the distance, we could make out the sea. We stayed on the porch talking until Latiff bade us go to bed. Reluctantly we turned in and in half a wink we were fast asleep.

The sun filtered through the Venetian blinds and danced on our eyelids causing us to blink. We awoke with a start and rushed out to the living room. Latiff was finishing his coffee and preparing to leave for work. The housekeeper, Ms. Gaitree was already there and busying herself in the kitchen. Latiff introduced her to us and admonished us to listen to and obey her instructions. But he also told her that he'd allow us to go wandering as far as the bridge on our own. We saw him off from upstairs on the porch. As we sat there in the early morning, the air felt slightly chilly and we hugged our knees to our chests to keep warm. We could see past the road, over the grove of trees, and in the distance could make out a narrow ribbon of blue sea. The road wound for about one mile and at the end of the road, there was a rusty old bridge that spanned a narrow river. That would be the object of our jaunt for today.

Soon Ms. Gaitree called us in for breakfast and we tucked into sada roti with fried eggs and country chocolate. It was delicious and we ate ravenously. After breakfast, we changed into our day clothes and donned our sneakers. We had planned on exploring the local area as far as the bridge and were eager to get going. We informed Ms. Gaitree of our plans and in response to her question, said that we'd be back by lunch time. Before taking her leave, we asked her for any odd scraps of raw meat or fish that she may have had in the fridge as we wanted to try out some fishing and needed bait. She nodded and produced a small plastic container with chicken scraps left over from her preparation of the midday meal. We thanked her as Kevin and Colin retrieved their nylon fishing reels and hooks.

The road was coarse and the asphalt rough. I guess at one time it might have been smooth after being paved, but the salt blast from the sea over time must have caused its deterioration. I could not imagine riding a bicycle on this road and having a fall. The road went straight on up at a slight incline and eventually we came to a fork. Continuing straight would have led us to the bridge we had passed the previous night, which was the objective of our morning jaunt. But being boys, our curiosity got the better of us and we paused to deliberate where the other road to the right would lead to. This road was narrower that the main one and it wound for about fifty yards before disappearing around a bend. Colin, who had been to Galeota once before, though he had never explored on his own, surmised that based on the general direction, this other road must lead down to the sea. With a quick affirmative vote taken, we agreed to postpone the trip to the bridge and explore down this narrow road to see where it would lead.

Needless to say, this area was very rural and there was no traffic on these roads. This area contained about ten houses all belonging to the government for their visiting officers. Usually not more than one or two were occupied at a time and there were no cars on these roads. Nevertheless, we walked two abreast with Colin leading the way. Both sides of the road were lined with dongs trees and they were laden with ripe fruit. We resisted the temptation to stop and pick the fruit preferring instead to press on to see where the road led to. The road wound several times for about half a mile before we saw the vegetation change. The rows of dongs trees gave way to coconut palms and we had a feeling that Colin's hunch was correct.

As we turned what was the last corner, we came upon a small whitish-brown sandy beach that led down to the sea. We quickened our pace and broke into a run to get to the beach. Colin felt elated that his hunch was correct as all five of us stood on the beach taking in the vista. It was not a large beach, only about five hundred feet long. The tide was out and it took about forty steps to get to the edge of the water. The water was a deep blue and was surprisingly clear. The beach was littered with old coconut branches and odd flotsam washed up by the tide. But what caught our attention was a small river to our left that flowed out to meet the sea. Instinctively we all turned toward the river and made our way over to it to explore the banks. Colin said that he was sure that this was the same river that ran under the bridge that we were going to originally. It made sense as it was the only river in the area and it had to wind its way out somewhere. So we agreed that it was one and the same. It did not seem to be very deep, but we were not about to find out.

The water was a brown color but quite clear. It may have taken on the brown color from the brown sandy bottom. It cut a narrow shallow channel through the beach in order to flow out to meet the sea. We walked along the right bank to where the water flowed through the channel and was only ankle deep. It felt warm and ticklish as it flowed about our ankles. Ronald wanted to have a swim in the sea and voiced his desire, echoing our collective thoughts. However, Colin cautioned against this as there were no other persons about and especially no lifeguards. He had no idea how deep the water was or if there was a steep drop off at the edge of the water. He wanted to be safe and responsible feeling that he was so entrusted by his father. Reluctantly we agreed with him and settled instead to sit on the sand at the water's edge where the waves ebbed and flowed around us.

We sat there digging our heels into the sand and lapping up water with our hands to refresh our flushed faces. We must have sat there talking about cricket and football for an hour or so when Kevin started getting bored and wanted to go fishing. He was right as this was a small beach and, as we could not go swimming, there was not much more to do here. Colin agreed and we tried to wash the sand from our pants' bottoms and with a last look around, we made our way back to the coconut lined road. This time, we stopped to pick dongs. The trees were low and the purple berries were easily reached without having to climb. We ate our fill of the sweet fruit and then continued our walk back to the main road. When we got to the fork in the road, because neither of us had a watch, we could not gauge the time. We did not want to be rushed in our fishing quest remembering our promise to Ms. Gaitree to be back by lunch time. So rather than get into trouble, Colin suggested we go back to the house and play small goal football until lunch was ready. It made sense and we turned in the direction of the house for the short walk back.

Colin's hunch, for the second time for the morning was right. It was near eleven thirty when we got back to the house. We called out to Ms. Gaitree that we were back and she hollered back that lunch would soon be ready. Kevin retrieved the football and we erected the stones for the goal posts and divided ourselves into two teams. Colin and Hayden were on one team with Kevin, Ronald and I on the other. The heat radiating from the asphalt was intense and we soon grew hot and sweaty. With the score two-two after a while, we called it quits and retreated to the shade under the house. There was a standpipe outside next to the steps and we took turns rinsing our feet, hands and flushed faces. The steps of the stairs became our seats and we lolled back recovering from our hot exertions. Presently Ms. Gaitree called out that we could come for our lunch and we clambered up the staircase to the back door and the kitchen.

Ms. Gaitree had made a chicken pelau for our lunch with a bowl of cold cucumbers sliced and seasoned with a squeeze of lime juice, salt and pepper. This would hit the spot perfectly and we gratefully accepted our plates. Ms. Gaitree told us that we could eat on the porch or on the steps if we liked. We opted for the stairs and with our plates and enamel cups of freshly squeezed orange juice, we settled into the shade on the steps to devour our lunch. As we ate, Ms. Gaitree came out to chat with us. Between mouthfuls of her delicious pelau, we answered her questions and got a lot of information from her about the area.

We told her about the small beach that we had discovered and she told us that it was wise not to have ventured into the water. Apparently about six feet into the water, the sand dropped off steeply for ten feet and the water was deep. She congratulated us on our prudence and as she was in a good mood, we told her that we'd be going fishing right after lunch. She had no objections and that was settled. As we finished our lunch she took our plates from us and told us we could go on about our fishing business. We did not need a second invitation so we hastily washed up, grabbed our nylon fishing lines and bait and made our way back to the road.

We did not dawdle this time as we wanted to get to the bridge quickly. It took us about fifteen minutes at a quick pace to get to the old rusty bridge. It was made out of iron and had rusted to a reddish-brown color because of exposure to the elements. It was a narrow bridge that could accommodate only one vehicle at a time. Though the bridge supports and laterals were made of iron, the path on the bridge was made of stout wooden planks laid compactly and showed little sign of wear. To each side of the bridge, there was a narrow pedestrian walkway separated on either side by a four-foot latticed iron railing. We climbed onto the left walkway and stopped midway on the bridge. We looked down at the water and gauged that it was quite deep. It flowed very slowly and was a deep brown in color. Unlike the mouth of the river that flowed out to our little beach, the water here was not clear. Colin and Kevin had three nylon lines between them, but there were five of us. We agreed for Colin and Kevin to have the first turns as it was their equipment. The rest of us played eenie-meenie-minie-mo to decide who would have the third line first. Ronald won and Hayden and I resolved to watch on as they fished. They deftly baited their hooks with the chicken scraps and with a careful distance between each other, twirled their lines and tossed them into the river. About ten feet up the line from the hook, there were red and white floats. We looked on patiently at the floats looking for any sign of a nibble.

The three fishermen held the lines in their left hands and used their right index fingers on the lead part of the lines to feel for any sign of a nibble. It seemed like an eternity had passed before Ronald's float bobbed below the water and he exclaimed that he had a bite. He rose from his sitting position and stood to manage the line carefully lest he tug too hard and the fish got loose. He was sure that it was a big one as he was getting a good fight on the end of the line. Gradually he pulled and eased the line up to the bridge and once he was sure that the fish was securely caught on the hook, he quickly pulled the lineup. It was a good catch. It writhed and dangled on the end of the hook as Ronald deftly pulled it over the iron railing and onto the walkway. It was about a foot long and brownish-slivery in color. We did not know what species it was. Ronald expertly grabbed hold of it around the head and gills and proceeded to extract the hook from its mouth. Meanwhile, Hayden had scooted over to the roadway to the bushes and stripped a coconut branch to make a string onto which to thread our first fish. As he had caught the first one, Ronald gave up his line to me as it was my turn next.

We passed the afternoon taking turns fishing going on the principle that once you caught a fish, you gave a turn to the next person waiting. We had about six good sized prizes on the string and Colin had the good sense to place them out of the sun into a shady spot in a bucket of water that we had brought for this purpose. We did not realize how much time had passed until we heard a car horn sound and looked up to see Latiff's car coming toward the bridge. He stopped and parked the car at the side of the road and came over to see what we were doing. He was impressed with the catch and told us that the fish were guabins. They were fresh water fish as the sea did not make its way into the river. We had caught guabins at the Caura River with Roy before, but they were small and we had never seen them this size. Latiff promised to have Ms. Gaitree fix up a good fish fry for us with our catch. Then he made an announcement that had us all screaming with excitement. He had left work early to come home for a nap as he had to go back to work that night as there was a tanker leaving. He told us that he would take us to the AMOCO installations with him and that once the tanker left, we could go to the jetty and see what we could snag with the spear gun. As it was near to four o'clock, we gladly hopped into the car with him and drove back to the house. He gave us orders to have a shower and change and get some rest. We willingly followed his instructions and pretty soon we were lounging on the sofas in the living room.

It had been a long day spent in the sun and our energy levels were depleted. We were quite content to have a nap on the sofas to recoup. About six o'clock, Ms. Gaitree woke us up for dinner. She had prepared our catch and an appetizing aroma of fried fish permeated the air. She warned us about the fine bones in guabin and we duly took note of her caution. It was delicious made even more so by the fact that we had caught it ourselves. As we finished up and cleared away the table, Latiff checked the spear gun and pretty soon we were on our way out to the AMOCO compound. It was a short drive of fifteen minutes to the AMOCO security gate. Latiff checked in with the guards and once cleared, we drove over to the Customs sheds. Latiff took us to his office and admonished us to remain there until he was done. There was nothing to do in his office but wait. So to pass the time, we found some blank sheets of paper and pencils and played a game of paper cricket. This was played by writing lots of numbers from one to six all over the sheet randomly as well as the words "bowled," "caught," "lbw," "stumped," and "runout." The "batsman" would take a pencil, place it on the paper and with the index finger on top of the eraser, and flick the pencil to make a streak mark. If that mark hit one of the numbers, that was your score. The batsman continued until he struck one of the outs. That occupied us for a while and the time passed quickly.

About two hours later, Latiff came back and announced that the tanker had departed and that we could proceed to the jetty. The jetty was adjacent to the Customs sheds and we went to the car to retrieve the spear gun and some flashlights. The spear gun belonged to Colin so he had the first try. Latiff explained that once the tanker was anchored, lots of fish came around to the surface looking for food. Once it left its anchorage and made its way out of the harbor, the propellers churned up the water and this attracted lots more fish to the surface looking for food. He was right for as we neared the edge of the jetty and we peered into the water, there were lots of fish to be seen moving about close to the surface. We settled on a spot where it seemed the fish were most abundant.

The distance from the jetty to the water was about twenty feet straight down so we were careful about getting too close to the edge. Colin stretched the rubber coil and anchored it against the catapult on the trigger. He surveyed the water and chose a target and fired off a shot. He had aimed at a large fish, what he thought to be a kingfish. But he had missed. He recoiled the lead line and Latiff carefully installed the spear on the gun once more. We had decided on turns prior to this based on our cricket game scores. Ronald was next, followed by Kevin, me and then Hayden. Ronald scanned the water, found his target and fired his shot. He also missed his target. Kevin fared just as badly as the two previous marksmen.

When it was my turn, Colin called out loudly that there was a shark fin on the water. I turned in the direction he was pointing and saw that there was indeed a small shark swimming right at the surface. I took careful aim and fired my shot. Wham! I struck him and the spear went through this side. I anticipated the fight and cradled the gun butt under my armpit and held on firmly to the shaft to allow the shark to reel off the line. Colin came to my assistance and together we let the line out, stopped and then reeled in. It took about ten minutes to drag our victim close to the jetty as he gave a good fight though he was wounded. Five willing pairs of hands helped to haul the load on the line up and with a jerk, we pulled it onto the jetty. It was about three feet long and Latiff told us he was a sand shark. Carefully, Colin and Latiff removed the spear and we dropped the shark into a plastic bag.

After that excitement of the first catch, Hayden, who was to go last, was eager to get his own shot on target. And so he did. Wham! His shot found its target and as we reeled in the catch, it was a red snapper, about six pounds and a good size. Latiff decided that Kevin, Colin and Ronald would have one more shot each to see if they could shoot something and then we would head for home. Unfortunately, their shots missed again and they were disappointed. But Hayden and I were elated at having snagged our prizes. I claimed the bragging rights for my shark. Reluctantly we left the jetty and made our way to the car. We stowed the plastic bag in the trunk and washed our hands to rid ourselves of the fishy smell. Then we climbed into the car and made our way home. We wanted to clean the fish then and there but Latiff would have none of it. He stored the two fish in the refrigerator and said that Ms. Gaitree would take care of it in the morning. With a reluctant goodnight, we made our way to our beds and fell fast asleep. It had been a terrific day.

The next morning, we awoke to the sound of rushing water coming from the kitchen. It was Ms. Gaitree. She was already there and was almost done cleaning the snapper. Her next task was to clean and skin the shark. Breakfast was already prepared and covered on the table. We feasted on eggs, bacon and country bread and butter. As Latiff's work was done and the two nights completed, we would be leaving Galeota this morning. Latiff would drop us off in Mayaro and he and his boys would continue back to Tunapuna. They were to leave for vacation to Canada in three days' time and needed to prepare. Ms. Gaitree told him that she was making roast coconut bake and fried shark for us to take back with us and that we had to wait. He agreed and we spent the morning on the front porch talking. I was glad that my two sets of cousins got along well with each other and I was silently grateful for Latiff's invitation to spend time with his boys.

At about ten o'clock, Ms. Gaitree had finished her culinary delights and wrapped the bake in a cloth to keep it warm. She packed up everything in a basket and we were ready for our departure. Latiff had a few private words with Ms. Gaitree and then it was our turn to thank her for her generosity. She laughed loudly and hugged us all and bade us be good boys. We retrieved our bags from the bedrooms and trudged down the stairs to the car. Ms. Gaitree was staying back to clean up and prepare for the next officer coming on the next rotation. We waved cheerily to her and with a last glance at the house, we focused on the road ahead back to Mayaro.

The trip back to Mayaro was very pleasant. The sun shone brilliantly and there were a lot of sights that we had missed when we drove at night on the way down two days ago. Latiff drove at a leisurely pace and within thirty minutes, we were turning into Gill Street and our driveway. It was just after eleven in the morning and we found the rest of my family on the beach playing cricket. Upon seeing us, they abandoned the game and came up to our apartment. The galvanized awning that had fallen was nowhere in sight and we guessed that Lloyd and the owners would have come and removed it and repaired any damage done by the storm. My mother hugged us and my father and Latiff exchanged pleasantries. Latiff declined staying for lunch with us as he had to be back in Tunapuna early with the boys and had to report for work at the Piarco airport by four in the afternoon. He gave the roast bake and fried shark to my mother which she gratefully accepted. Hayden, Ronald and I thanked him for the trip to Galeota and we hugged Colin and Kevin as they got into the car. Pretty soon the car disappeared down the driveway and we turned excitedly to recount our trip to Galeota to the rest of the family.

Chapter 10

Day Trip to Tunapuna

Ronald and I awoke the next morning to the familiar sound of Roy moving about in the living room getting his coffee ready. We rousted Hayden and joined him for our now familiar morning routine. Electricity had been restored and the kitchen light was on. As had become our morning routine, we made our way outside in anticipation of the sunrise. One by one the others awoke and joined us outside for the morning ritual. As we sat there looking at the sun peeking over the horizon, my father told us that my mother needed to go back to Tunapuna to keep an appointment with her doctor that had been booked a few weeks ago. It was her annual checkup and she could not afford to miss the appointment. It was scheduled for eleven o'clock the next day. Usually he would have accompanied her to the doctor's office, but because of the timing this year during the vacation, they had decided that one of us would accompany her by taxi back to Tunapuna for the day and then back to Mayaro.

With that said, he turned to me and told me that he'd like me to go with her. I had no problem with that and readily agreed. Ronald piped up and volunteered to accompany us. Both Roy and my father agreed and that was settled. Now we had something else to look forward to. We had traveled by taxi before but only between Tunapuna and Port-of-Spain. This was a different matter altogether. This was a great distance involving changing several taxis. But we were confident that all would go without a hitch.

The rest of the day passed in the familiar way we had become accustomed to over the past two weeks. There was the usual morning walk for the newspapers and bread, followed by breakfast, a game on the beach and lots of swimming. But each day brought with it a new sense of anticipation and excitement, after all, we were in Mayaro and on holiday away from home. There was less pressure from the adults with restrictive rules. That did not mean that we were angels by any means. Being kids, we did have our moments, but there was a tendency by the adults to allow us a bit more freedom and to be less constraining.

When evening had rolled around and we had showered and changed, my father and Roy sat with mummy, Ronald and I and wrote down all instructions on a piece of paper. They told us precisely where to find the taxi stands, which taxis to take, where to get off and the estimated time for each sector of the trip to and back. We would start off early the next morning at six a.m. from the Mayaro Junction on the first sector to Sangre Grande. From there we would change and take another taxi to Valencia. From Valencia we would change again and take a taxi to Arima. From Arima, we would get our last taxi to Tunapuna. They gave us landmarks to look for to pinpoint where we would find the taxi stands. We would follow the same route in reverse on the way back. They estimated a total travel time of about three hours from Mayaro to Tunapuna which would have given my mother enough time to get ready for her appointment at the doctor.

We were roused from our slumber at five a.m. the next morning and hastily executed our toiletries and changed our clothes. Radica was already up and had made us some hot tea and cheese sandwiches. She also made up a packet of sandwiches for us to take with us as well as a bottle of water and a bottle of juice. At five-forty-five, we set off from the house accompanied by my father and briskly made our way up to the junction. It was not yet dawn and it was still pretty dark outside. Faint lights shone from a few houses. The air was cool and we pulled our collars up on our necks. As we crested the hill past the Police Station, we could make out two taxis sitting in the taxi stand. As we approached, we could see that one driver was snoozing and the other was listening to the radio. Both taxis were empty. The driver listening to the radio saw us and got up out of the car. "Grande" he called out to us and my parents nodded. Each taxi could seat up to five persons and this meant that we would have to wait until two more people showed up. Ronald and I climbed into the back seat while my parents chatted outside. We observed them talking with the driver and then my father shook the driver's hand. He called us out and told us that the driver had agreed to take us all the way to Tunapuna directly.

In essence, my father had hired the taxi for the day. He told us that the driver had agreed to wait for us and bring us back directly to Mayaro later that evening. As it turned out, the driver had family in Curepe with whom he would visit while waiting on us. While this was a good turn of events, Ronald and I were somewhat disappointed as we were looking forward to the adventure of traveling and changing taxis along the way. My father saw our faces and bid us look on the bright side, that we would have more time in Tunapuna with our cousins. As usual, his words cheered us up and we all climbed aboard. We waved to my father as the driver carefully pulled out of the taxi stand.

His name was Jagdeo and he was indeed a chatterbox. No sooner had we left the taxi stand, he started talking. He delved into his family history and traced his beginnings in Curepe and recounted to us how he ended up living in Mayaro. His story took us as far as Manzanilla. The windows were rolled down and the early morning breeze lulled us to sleep. The car rolled along on the bumpy roads and it was not until we felt the car slow down did we awake. We wiped the sleep from our eyes and tried to focus on where we were. My mother told us that we were approaching Valencia. Aghast that we had slept through Sangre Grande and the Stretch, all energies were refocused on the journey that still lay ahead.

The hills of the Northern Range were clearly visible directly in front of us and as we turned the bend, we recognized the Valencia Junction. There was not much traffic on the road and, as we approached the highway, Jagdeo accelerated and went at a fair clip. Ronald had the left rear window and I had the right. As we passed the Piarco roundabout, our excitement grew for Tunapuna was only a few minutes away. We saw the Consol Buildings and the driver got into the right lane to turn into Macoya Road. Constantine Park came into view and soon we turned left onto the Eastern Main Road into the heart of Tunapuna. My mother pointed out Cemetery Street to the driver and he made the left turn to bring us to our destination. At seven forty-five in the morning, we stopped at my grandmother's house. We were more than one hour ahead of schedule. We alighted from the vehicle and thanked Jagdeo for the safe drive. My father had already paid him so there was no need for my mother to pay. Jagdeo and my mother chatted and agreed on the time for him to come back and fetch us for the return trip to Mayaro. With that settled he honked his horn and pulled away for his trip to Curepe to see his family.

My grandmother's house on Cemetery Street was not fenced and the yard was open to the road. The two-storey house was open to one side underneath to the left. The right side contained an apartment where my Aunt Jean and her family lived. There were red concrete stairs to the front of the house that led to the second floor. In front, there was a good sized covered porch or gallery and as we looked up, we saw our grandmother sitting in her usual chair sipping her cup of tea. We waved to her and were about to go to the back of the house when my mother chided us to greet our grandmother first. We skipped up the stairs two at a time and hugged Ma. After the greetings, my mother told us that her appointment with the doctor was at eleven o'clock and that she would take a taxi the short distance to the office.

She also told us that there was no need to accompany her to the doctor's office and that we could stay in Cemetery Street until she came back and it was time to return to Mayaro. She had made arrangements with Jagdeo to pick us up at three o'clock which would also have given her some time to spend with Ma.

Delighted at this news, we stormed into the house and sought our other cousins. There were three rooms upstairs in addition to the living room and kitchen. Roy and his family lived in one room; my other Uncle, Gordon and his family lived in another room. Ma had the third room. It was cramped for space and full of people, but this living arrangement was typical of the East Indian community in that era. There were a total of twelve persons living upstairs and four downstairs. The thinking was that one should save their money instead of renting so that one day they could build their own house.

We barged into the living room and heard voices coming from the kitchen. The kitchen was on the second floor to the back of the house. The usual morning routine, familiar to us all, unfolded. Anthony, Derek, Ernest, Rosemary and Michelle were there and in some varying degree of brushing their teeth. There was no face basin. Rather, this task was accomplished using an enamel cup of water with which to rinse. Upon seeing us, they finished up and loudly hailed to us. Breakfast was just put out on the table for them and we joined the table for a hot cup of cocoa. My mother came into the kitchen and greeted everyone. She produced the packet of sandwiches that Radica had prepared. We had forgotten about those and willingly exchanged them for a piece of hot sada roti and fried aloo. It was a noisy breakfast table with everyone trying to get the most recent news about Tunapuna and about Mayaro. We were so noisy in fact that my grandmother had to call out to us to make less noise. I guess that the noise must have carried because Steve came bounding into the kitchen from downstairs and told us that he had heard our voices. He squeezed in between Ronald and I and we resumed the cacophony though we tried to keep our voices down. As we finished our breakfast and cleared the table, the older boys, Anthony and Ernest, bade the girls play by themselves and the boys headed downstairs to play.

The first order of business for us was to go to Pa's old wooden shed at the front of the house. My grandfather used to sell newspapers out of this old shed. Since he had passed away, the shed all but fell into ruins, but it was a sanctuary for us to hang out. As we installed ourselves around the shed, we fired of a salvo of questions to the boys begging for news, paramount of which, was about the football team. They had confirmed to us on their last visit to Mayaro that that the team had been formed, that Mr. Brooks had agreed to sponsor the team and it was to be called "Brooks United." Since then, without Hayden, Ronald and I, they had played a practice match against a team from Archibald Street called Young Gifted and Black or YGB. They had a decent first game even though they lost 2-1. They reckoned that when Hayden came back, he would re-enforce the defense, and I would be another option to Pudden in goal. We begged them to tell us the highlights of the match and as Ernest summarized, we laughed out loudly at the tales of Glen's antics on the field.

We in turn told them about what we did since their last visit. They were particularly interested in hearing about the storm. We tried to recount every detail as best as we could remember and got a few oohs and aahs when we came to the part about the awning crashing down. They in turn told us that the chennette tree at the back of ma's house was swaying dangerously and the branches were actually brushing against the roof. But it was a large sturdy tree and offered some degree of protection from the wind.

As we sat there talking, a light breeze blew and kicked up a fine cloud of dust from the dry earth. The shed was in the shadow of the ancient avocado tree and the pomerac tree that grew majestically in the front yard. The sun, to the east, had risen sufficiently high to send golden rays filtering through the leaves. As I gazed at the light, I suddenly felt very peaceful and very calm within. Maybe it was the surreal effect of the light and the coolness of the shade that inspired this feeling. I don't know, but I do remember feeling very much at peace.

As I sat there, half listening to the boys' conversation around me, the other half of my attention was drawn to the sprawling cherry tree that grew against the wall separating Ma's yard from Chachee's yard. For some reason the cherry tree caught my attention and I focused on it. Then I realized that it was abundantly laden with deep crimson fruit. I snapped out of my trance-like state and called this out to the boys. Ronald was also taken aback at the abundance of ripe fruit. Two weeks ago before we had left for Mayaro, it was sparse. He immediately wanted to attack the cherry tree but was halted in his tracks by Ernest. Rather, the older boys pointed to the tip top of the pomerac tree. We had to follow their pointed fingers. Nestled at the top was a sight to behold. Some of the largest, reddish-purple specimens that we had ever seen were clustered there. Anthony explained that they had been eyeing these pomerac for two weeks now and they wanted to wait until they were at their sweetest before picking them. Of course we thought that now was the opportune time, but the others defended their turf collectively. Reluctantly we turned our gaze away from the tree and walked back under the house.

The table tennis board was set up, we assumed, from the previous day, and it invited us to grab the rackets and start a game of winner stay on the board. We so occupied ourselves for about an hour or so unable to defeat Ernest. It was Steve who suggested that we play something else. Rather bored with the same daily routine of cricket, football, tennis, marbles, Anthony proposed that we take a walk down to the cemetery and hang out on the old train-line. This was met with a chorus of approval and we put the rackets and ball away. As we strolled out into the street, we stopped in front of Chachee's house and whistled for Vernon. His whistled reply came immediately. We walked ten yards and stopped at the next house and called out to Glen a few times but there was no reply. While calling to Glen, Vernon appeared and jumped over the low wall and joined us. Next stop was at the corner of Kewley Street to hail out Andrew. He was in the front yard pulling out weeds in the garden and abruptly stopped his exertions and joined us. The group had now grown in size to eight and we trekked the few yards to the entrance to the cemetery. Rather than go directly into the cemetery, we took the track to the left of the entrance next to Arthur's house that led straight up to the old train-line overpass.

The trains had stopped running in Trinidad several years before and the old iron tracks were rusted a coppery red. There were a lot of overgrown bushes on the track but they quickly gave way as we got to the top. The sun was high in the heavens and the heat was intense. Rather than try and sit on the hot iron tracks out in the intense heat, we picked our way and negotiated the tracks across the overpass to a little spot that we had carved out for ourselves a while aback. It was a little grotto-like enclave made out of growing vines that crept up the side of an old tree stump and two large trees. It was a perfect retreat out of the sun while still enjoying the breeze. It also afforded us a view of the entire cemetery and if we stood up, allowed us a view over the boundary wall to see the Lever Brothers Sports Grounds. We jostled for space and eventually sat down, most of us clasping our hands around our knees. Several simultaneous conversations took place often involving more than one group. We tried to follow our own conversations while trying to listen in to the others around us. One question was certainly common to all, what were we going to do with the rest of the morning. Tired of playing the same games day after day, we needed something different to avert boredom. Ernest suggested picking cashews from the trees that grew at the fringe perimeters of the cemetery and doing a cashew nut roast. It was a good idea and we would have voted for it had Vernon not come up with a brainwave.

From where we were sitting on the old train-line, we followed his outstretched finger pointing the way down the road that ran along the middle of the cemetery, past Eddie's house, to the side of the Canning's factory, to the highway. He explained that all we needed to do was to follow the indicated path to the highway, cross the highway and get to the south side of Pasea where there was a lovely shallow river that flowed under the shade of bamboos on one bank and vegetable gardens on the other. This was indeed a grand idea, but did we dare? We did a lot of daring deeds, foolhardy at times, and mostly without parental consent. But crossing the highway was one of those taboo boundaries that neither of us had ever dreamt of breaching. Vernon rationalized that it was a weekday and mid-morning so the traffic would be very light. Besides which, the highway was only about twenty feet across.

We all turned to Anthony and Ernest, the eldest among us. They were as eager as the rest of us and we saw the gleam in their eyes that would lead to their approval of the plan. As we all jumped up from our sitting positions, they gruffly admonished us to keep this a secret and never to blurt this out to the adults. They also paired up one younger boy with an older boy with instructions to hold hands when it came time to cross the highway. I got paired up with Vernon. With a brisk trot, we set off down the path from the old train-line. Normally we would dawdle in the cemetery and make spooky noises, but today the primary objective was more appealing than trying to scare each other about the dead.

As we approached Eddie's house, we saw him fixing his bicycle in the back yard. Eddie was Anthony's friend and he came from a rather large family. We all felt that Anthony, although Eddie's friend, was also interested in one of Eddie's sisters. We used to poke fun at him about that relationship, but he was always very private and never divulged anything to us. Though we didn't know it at the time, Eddie's family would eventually become linked to our family through Eddie's eldest brother, also named Anthony, who would marry Angela, Steve's sister. We hailed out to Eddie who looked surprised to see such a large group. We quickly told him of our plans and he at once joined the team. We stayed on the worn dirt track that ran along the western wall of the Canning's factory and soon we were on the gravel shoulder of the north side of the highway. There was no traffic and we bounded across the roadway in a flash and ran down the embankment on the south side of the highway. I felt an adrenaline rush in anticipation of our adventure. Vernon led the way across the vegetable gardens and we were careful not to tread on the young plants. Within five minutes or so, we came to the western bank of the river.

The river was not deep; in fact, it was quite shallow reaching only up to our knees. It was more a stream than a river, and the water looked crystal clear and cool. All along the eastern bank, there were groves of bamboos. The bamboos were not thick groves, but were set in a linear fashion all along the bank. The eastern breeze caused them to sway gently and the leaves rustled in cadence. The bed of the channel was stony and the water rippled as it flowed along. I stood there marveling at the sight around me just as a gentle breeze wafted the scent of burnt cane from the Orange Grove Estate and tickled my nostrils. The sun was fierce and almost directly overhead and my skin felt scorched. I was abruptly awoken out of my reverie by a splash of cold water on my face, Ronald having grown tired of me just standing there and not responding to his several shouts to me. Smiling, I took off my sneakers and jersey and plunged right in with the others.

The water was deliciously cool and immediately refreshed our bodies and spirits. It was so shallow that we could not swim. Rather, we just sort of sat in the water and reclined on our elbows to allow the water to flow over most of our bodies. Every so often, we would duck our heads under the water to wet our hair and complete the feeling of refreshment. There were no watches or clocks on a day like this. Time stood still and was idyllic as we made the most of our youthful innocence and exuberance. But our stomachs played us a different tune. One by one we confessed that we were hungry but acknowledged that we were a fair clip away from home. By the height of the sun, Andrew surmised that it must have been close to noon or just past. Eddie laughed at us mockingly and pointed out the nearby vegetable gardens. This area south of the highway was predominantly under vegetable cultivation. His logic was simple and he saw no difference from raiding fruit trees in our neighbors' yards. Yet this one did not sit right with us.

For some reason, we felt that taking vegetables from these gardens was tantamount to stealing. Several of our schoolmates from Tunapuna Hindu had parents who worked or owned these gardens and who depended on them for their livelihood. In a way, it was like stealing money from our classmates. There was a decided unease at the suggestion and though it was tempting, we decided unanimously not to raid these vegetable gardens. With that settled we agreed to continue bathing a while longer and put off our hunger for later. It is so amazing when you're young how quickly one can refocus. One moment we were hungry; the next we forgot about our hunger and refocused on our furtive romp in the river. About fifteen minutes has passed when we heard a loud voice calling out my name. Collectively and in unison we all turned in the direction of the voice. I could make out Mohan, one of my class mates.

Mohan was clad in shorts and wore rubber Wellingtons and was drenched in sweat. Ronald and I skipped out of the water and ran up to meet Mohan. He was helping out his family in the garden and was just coming to the river for a quick splash to cool down. Like many of our other friends from school, Mohan's family cultivated these lands and grew crops which they sold at the weekly market in Tunapuna for their livelihood. At once I was relieved that we had not acceded to Eddie's suggestion to raid the gardens as Mohan was a good friend of mine. We chatted with Mohan on what we were doing. He then asked us what time we were going to return home and if we had eaten as yet? This was such a coincidence. He told us that just about a quarter mile from the river, he was roasting some breadfruit and invited us to share it with him. I quickly shouted the invitation to the others who quickly scampered out of the water and came up to hail out and thank Mohan for the invite. I was very proud that my friend was offering all of us something to eat when we were really hungry. In no time at all we saw the smoke from the pit where the breadfruit was roasting.

There was a sunken hearth lined with stones that looked to have been used often. Mohan explained that his family had made this fireplace so that they could either cook or re-heat food while they were in the fields. Using 2 wooden tongs, Mohan and Vernon deftly removed 2 charred breadfruit from the ashes and laid them out on a banana leaf. They then cut rectangles from another banana leaf and handed to each of us to use as plates. A small pot that sat on the embers was retrieved and laid next to the breadfruit. Mohan then deftly pulled out the stalk from each breadfruit, and with his knife, cut and divided it up among us. He then opened the small pot to reveal some tomato choka to accompany the roast breadfruit. This was heaven. Such a simple meal made all the more sumptuous because of where it was eaten and that it was generously shared by a genuine friend. This was indeed living off the land!

Mohan pointed to the breadfruit tree where he picked the breadfruit and indicated another area where he harvested the tomatoes, chives and peppers for the choka. Anthony fished out his ubiquitous packet of salt from his pocket and we sprinkled a bit on the sweet breadfruit. The smokiness from the roasting process and the natural sugars combined for a wonderful creamy taste and texture and when mixed with the choka, was absolutely divine. We ate every scrap and profusely thanked Mohan for a wonderful meal. He beamed from ear to ear and responded that he was only too glad to share the food from his family's land with us. We gathered up the scraps and placed them in a nearby oil drum which served as a garbage bin. When the bin was full, they would fire it up to incinerate the garbage. We thanked Mohan and decided that we'd better set off back to Ma's house lest we be late and get into trouble. With a final wave goodbye, we set off toward the highway. This was indeed a very eventful day back in Tunapuna.

It was just about coming up to two o'clock in the afternoon when we crossed the highway and made our way back through the cemetery to Ma's house. The sun had dried us and our clothes bore no telltale sign of our excursion. Normally our parents would leave us to our own exertions and would seldom be concerned about our whereabouts before dusk. By the time we got back to Cemetery Street, we discovered my mother and Ma sitting and chatting in the living room. We declined lunch saying that we had already eaten and instead took up positions on the back stairs. The sun was making its way to the west and was shining on Pa's old shed making it too hot to sit there. The back stairs were in the shade of the chennette and plum trees and we bagged our usual places and rested a while. The taxi was coming for us at three o'clock and we were pretty contented to sit on the stairs and just chat.

Suddenly Ronald interrupted the conversation and reminded everyone about the bunch of pomerac. I could see the other boys zealously wanting to protect their horde, so I reminded them of how willingly Mohan shared his food with us. That might have done the trick, for they reluctantly agreed to climb the tree one more time to double check ripeness. Ronald and Anthony were selected as climbers and when they reached the top, there was a squeal from Ronald. We were admonished to carefully catch the fruit as it was picked and gently thrown to us. The harvest yielded twenty-four of the largest, reddish-purple specimens that we had ever seen. Anthony quickly descended the tree and divided the fruit. We each got two and the remainder was taken upstairs to Ma. We washed the pomerac under the sink and bit into the juiciest, sweetest pomerac that we had ever tasted. We were quietly munching our fruit when my mother looked out from the back door and told us to come inside and say our goodbyes. It was nearing the time for Jagdeo to come pick us up for the return trip to Mayaro. We hugged and kissed our grandmother and bade our goodbye to our aunts. Jagdeo had arrived and was waiting for us. We bade our cousins goodbye and they in turn reminded us that they'd be back to visit us one more time in Mayaro before the vacation was finished. With a honk of the horn after reversing into Archibald Street, Jagdeo made a left turn onto Cemetery Street and we were once more on our way back to Mayaro after a pleasant day trip back to Tunapuna.

It was three fifteen in the afternoon and the sun was immensely hot. We rolled down the windows in the taxi and lay back on the seats. A cooling breeze infiltrated the car and must have lulled us off to sleep. We unconsciously felt the rattle and bumps as the car rolled over the potholes and bumpy roads causing our heads to bob against the back seat. We were roused from our nap by an intense heat that seemed to stifle us. My mother must have heard us stirring in the back seat and called out to us that we were stuck in a traffic jam on the highway near to Santa Rosa. We had been going at a decent clip from Tunapuna, but as soon as we passed the Airport roundabout, the traffic slowed to a crawl and was not moving. Jagdeo surmised that there must have been an accident further up to cause the standstill. There was nothing we could do but exercise patience in this situation. The opposite lane on the highway was free and devoid of cars.

After what felt like an eternity, we saw an approaching car. Several drivers including Jagdeo were outside of their cars and hailed the approaching driver to stop. He obliged and explained that just after the stone pillars at the entry to Wallerfield, there was an accident involving a truck and a car and two persons were seriously injured. The driver said no one was killed, which was a relief to all, but he explained further that the ambulance and fire tenders were on the scene still trying to get the injured persons out of the wrecks and attended to. He explained that the police were letting vehicles through one by one and that he did not think it would be much longer before traffic started rolling again from what he had seen. It was a relief to know what exactly had caused the traffic jam and a further relief to learn that no one was killed. Even though it taxed our patience to the limit, we waited patiently while listening to the radio. We were delighted when at last we saw the cars in front of us starting to slowly move. Jagdeo put the car into gear and we started to move slowly forward.

By my calculations, it took us forty minutes further to slowly roll past the stone pillars at Wallerfield. We could see the flashing lights from the police cars and the officers allowing cars one by one to pass the accident scene. The injured persons were long removed and transported by ambulance to the hospital in Arima. But the wrecked vehicles still partly obstructed the roadway. Once we got past the wreck site, Jagdeo accelerated and we were once more on our way. As we pulled away, my mother spoke to Jagdeo and estimated that we had lost nearly two hours in the traffic jam and that we would be really late getting back to Mayaro. Her estimations were correct and instead of getting to Mayaro at about five o'clock, we would be there sometime after seven in the evening. There was a roti shop in Valencia that Jagdeo knew of and he asked my mother if she would like to stop there to get something to eat. He said it was okay with him if we ate in the car while he drove. She turned to us and asked a rhetorical question as we gave a resounding yes to his suggestion.

With that decided, Jagdeo navigated his way to a roti shop two doors down from the Ponderosa. He told us to come out of the car and stretch our legs a bit as it would take about fifteen minutes for the rotis to be ready. My mother placed the order and we chose our cold drinks. When the rotis were ready, my mother paid for them and we clambered back into Jagdeo's taxi to continue the trip back to Mayaro. Ronald and I each had a beef roti with slight pepper and my mother had a chicken roti with no pepper. We all opted for

Apple J as our choice of cold drink. The roti was hot and we cushioned the heat with the paper napkins. It was fun sitting in the back seat of the car eating. We hardly noticed that we were on the Valencia Stretch and that it was dusk. By the time we were aware of our surroundings, night had fallen and we were in Sangre Grande. We had just finished our food and we sat up alert at the sights and sounds at night in Grande.

There seemed to be lights of every color everywhere. People were milling about in small groups, walking and talking. Some were seated at tables on an outdoor patio in front of a bar from where loud calypso music was blasting. There were cars everywhere. We could smell the bread from the bakery and the gasoline from the service station. It was a cornucopia of sights, sounds and smells as we wound our way through the main street in Sangre Grande. And just as suddenly as it came into view, the town disappeared as we turned a bend and left the bright lights behind. The shimmering light yielded to the darkness of the cocoa estates as we started this section of the trip. We had never been this way at night and it was a novel experience for us. For one thing, the night was more pronounced and seemed darker.

The faint outlines of the cocoa trees seemed to dance in a blur as we sped past, barely able to focus on any one spot for long. It all seemed quite eerie and we imagined all sorts of perils that we could face if we were stranded in these fields all alone at night. We conjured up all sorts of fantastic beasts and animal-human forms putting peril in our way. Unconsciously, Ronald and I both turned up our windows and turned to each other at exactly the same time, probably seeking reassurance from our nocturnal fantasies. We just grinned at each other and settled back on the seat facing forward. It's not that we were scared or anything, but this made us feel better. In any case, there was still a way to go before we got to Manzanilla. Without the daylight to show us our well-known markers along the way, it was impossible to tell exactly where we were. It was not until we were ten feet away that we realized that we were just passing First and Last Grocery and Bar. Manzanilla was the next phase and we craned our necks to try and catch a glimpse of the sea in the dark night. Then all of a sudden we saw the bright moon high in the night sky and a long silvery finger reflecting on the dark surface of the ocean. We were in Manzanilla proper and we at once rolled down our windows.

    It was a cloudless night and the moon was nearly full. But the canopy of overhead coconut branches and the density of the grove of trunks prevented the full illumination of the moonlight. We were, however, able to catch glimpses of it through gaps in the trees and it was a beautiful sight. We asked Jagdeo to slow down a bit and my mother said okay. He brought the car to a stop, and just as Latiff had done a few days ago, he switched off his lights. At once the darkness enveloped us but within a few seconds, as our eyes adjusted to the dark, we realized how bright the night actually was. Despite the dense trees, the moonlight still filtered through the branches and did illuminate part of the roadway. The breeze, as usual, carried a salty heady aroma from the ocean and we sniffed at the familiar scent. Jagdeo only stopped for about a minute or so and soon we were moving again. With closed eyes and hands clasped together, Ronald and I leaned forward to hold onto my mother's shoulder as we slowly rolled over the dreaded Spring Bridge. We counted to ten and the bridge was out of the way. Relieved, we sank back into the seat with the windows down and the wind on our faces. I asked my mother to let us know when we got to the Junction.

    Ronald and I sat silently in the back seat, each with our own thoughts. I reflected on the past day and marveled that time and distance was all relative. Only this morning I bade goodbye to my father and within a few minutes again, in the same day, I would be reunited with him. Tunapuna seemed so far away and a distant memory the same as was Mayaro this morning when we were swimming in the river over the highway. As I tried to grapple with time and distance, I smiled to myself with the knowledge that all I did today would be locked away in some memory vault to be retrieved in detail one day in the future. My reverie was brought to a halt as my mother announced that we were approaching the Junction. It seemed that the car could not go fast enough to make it to Gill Street and our driveway, and when Jagdeo stopped in front of the apartment, finally we were back in Mayaro reunited with my family. It was a quarter past seven when we got back to Mayaro much to the relief of the rest of the family. They were worried as we were expected back since five. They did speculate but were relieved to see us home safely. My father and my mother finalized matters with Jagdeo and thanked him again. He cheerily bade us goodbye, reversed down the driveway and with a honk, pulled out of sight.

      Everyone was eager for our news from Tunapuna when we gathered around the table. As we had eaten in the car, we weren't hungry but did have a cup of tea. My mother said that she had a good report from Dr. Procope and that her yearly checkup was a success. While she chatted with the grownups about Tunapuna and the traffic jam, the children had our own side conversation. Ronald and I recounted our adventure across the highway to swim in the river and our meal with Mohan. In turn, the other told us about their day without us. It was like any other except that their numbers were diminished. They swam for the most part and did practically little else. We spent about another hour at the table talking about our day before everyone decided to call it a night and we got ready for bed. The boys helped Roy to close the windows and secure the doors. Pretty soon we hunkered down on the soft mattresses and in a flash, drifted off to blissful sleep.

Chapter 11

Fishing with Mr. LeeHa

We must have been very tired from the previous day's exertions because when we finally awoke the next morning, the sun was already very bright. With a laugh at seeing our disoriented faces, my mother told us that it was past nine o'clock and that she did not want to wake us up before. My father had done the morning routine for bread and newspapers and the adults already had their breakfast. Ours was covered on the table and we could have it as soon as we did our toiletries. One by one we accomplished this and sat down at the table. As we slowly ate, my father sprang some news that perked us up at once. On his way to Mr. James' shop this morning, he ran into Mr. LeeHa. Mr. LeeHa was a mathematics teacher at Fatima College and was a friend of the family. My parents had hoped that when I did my Common Entrance Exam in two years' time that I would pass for Fatima which they had selected as my first choice (I eventually did). Mr. LeeHa was also a fisherman in his spare time on weekends and he had a boat of his own. This news excited us immensely.

Mr. LeeHa's family owned a beach front property further down the beach near to Church Road. Alloy, this was his first name, would be based there for two days and would be taking the boat out fishing. He had extended an invitation for us to come visit him at the house and maybe would take us out for a boat ride. My father, I think to placate my mother, immediately added a condition that the sea was not rough and choppy and that the adults accompany us kids. That seemed to be good enough for my mother did not protest and we exclaimed in delight. With that settled, we wanted to set off right away, but my father laughingly dismissed that idea and said that we could do so later that afternoon. We had to give Alloy some time to get settled. This made sense, but like the traffic jam yesterday, this was going to tax our patience again.

It would be a few hours before we could go walking down the beach to Church Road, so we donned our swimsuits and persuaded the adults to go for a swim instead. Even though we went to a river yesterday, we missed the sea and were eager for a good swim. The sun shone brilliantly and the tide was out. A wide swath of beach was left which would have been perfect for a ball game. But the water was too inviting and like a magnet, pulled us to it. The water was crystal clear and there was a gentle breeze. The waves were more like ripples and we splashed about gleefully. Gerry and Sherry had a small pail and chased the young moonshine fish in a vain attempt to catch them. There were not many other people on the beach and it seemed like we were the only ones about. In the distance we could make out small groups of people, probably like ourselves, either on the sand or in the water, probably doing exactly as we were.

I bent and hugged my knees so that the water could reach my chin and cover my shoulders. I was aware of everyone around me and could pick up bits and pieces of conversations, but I was content with my own thoughts. I let go of my knees and spread my arms and reclined my back to a semi-floating position. The sun shone brightly, almost directly overhead, causing me to squint. I rotated my position so that my eyes were away from the direct sunlight. The salty water felt warm and luxurious as gentle waves cascaded over me. I was content to just laze about in the water. There was no need or desire this morning for vigorous water activities. Time certainly crept slowly as we enjoyed the water, but hunger brought an abrupt end to that. As we had a late breakfast, lunch was impromptu and improvised. Cheese and avocado sandwiches and grapefruit juice were quickly put together and we were delighted that we would eat our lunch on our walk to Church Street.

We each accepted a sandwich and a drink as we hit the beach and started off towards Alloy's place. The tide was still out and we walked almost abreast of each other. The informality of the lunch made its simplicity even more delicious as we savored each bite. This was probably the first time that the entire group of holiday-makers were venturing out together. Usually it would be the children and an adult or two. Today it was everyone. We were eager to point out to my mother and Radica some of our spots where were pulled seine, where we fished for crabs and other markers along the beach. Church Street was about two kilometers away and we quickly closed the distance in about twenty minutes. We saw the familiar spire from the Church and hastened our pace for another two hundred yards in the direction of the boat that was leaning to its side. This was Alloy's boat and we saw him puttering about in the yard.

Alloy's family had three houses on the beach front that was accessed from the main Guayaguayare Road via LeeHa's Private Road. His mother lived in Mayaro and occupied one of the houses. The other two were usually rented out to holiday-makers like ourselves. Today, however, they were empty but two families were expected that coming weekend. Alloy cheerfully greeted us as he called out to his mother. The adults exchanged greetings while we explored the boat. From all appearances, it seemed ready to venture out on the sea. The blackish green seine nets were neatly piled in the middle of the boat with the corks on one side and the sinkers on the other. The weight of the nets in the middle would allow a good trim of the boat. The fuel bowser was stashed under the seat at the stern near to the engine throttle. The oars were laid along the sides. The anchor was secured on the prow.

With our initial inspection over, we refocused on the adults in eager anticipation. Alloy saw our looks and laughingly invited us to sit in the boat for instructions. We all clambered in and secured our spots. Hayden and I helped my mother and Radica into the boat and when all were seated, Alloy started his safety instructions. We were told where to sit, how to sit, where to hold onto, what to expect and what to do if there was an emergency. We could see my mother's expression growing anxious and worried but Alloy reassured her that the trip would be uneventful. He pointed out to her, indicating with his finger, that the sea was very calm that day and because of the gentle breeze, the water was almost flat. He did, however, caution that when we stopped and dropped anchor to fish, the boat would rock to and fro on the water's surface and that we might feel queasy. He produced a bag of red sweet and sour hard candies that he told us would help with queasiness. With the safety briefing completed, he told the ladies they could sit in the boat but asked the rest of us to alight and to help drag the boat to the water. We were ready to go fishing.

Eight pairs of hands joined Alloy in pulling the boat to the water's edge. We were familiar with this routine and soon we were all piled in with Alloy at the throttle. The breakers were easily negotiated and Alloy opened the engine pointing the prow in a south easterly direction. He intended to fish at a spot where he had previously caught a lot of red snapper. He would not be using the seine nets on this trip, but rather pointed out an assortment of white plastic bottles around which were wound fishing nylon with hooks and sinkers. There was a small worn cooler near to the fuel bowser that held the bait. The boat made steady progress with just the occasional spurt of white foam splashing into the boat. Hayden, Ronald and I, slyly let our hands droop to the side of the boat and delighted when the water struck them. My mother handled the boat trip quite well even though we could see her knuckles firmly grasping the edge of the plank that served as the seat. My father sat beside her with one arm around her as much to steady her as for re-assurance.

Alloy pointed out various markers along the shoreline which by this time, as we glanced back, seemed far off in the distance. He reckoned that we had gone out about one kilometer with a short distance more to go before he reached the spot he was targeting. The wind whipped through our hair and cooled our faces. With the prow at a slightly upward angle, the horizon was not discernable; rather the clear blue vault of the heavens provided the foreground to our journey. Soon Alloy eased up on the throttle and the prow lowered as he reduced speed. The boat slowed and Alloy maneuvered the tiller to steer to the spot he wanted and just like that, he cut the engines. We were there and the fishing could start.

First order of business was to drop the anchor. Alloy allowed the current to play with the boat until we felt a slight shudder and stop as the anchor fixed itself to the ocean floor. The boat stopped drifting and bobbed up and down in the rippling water. He retrieved the bait box and cut up the herring into one inch square pieces. Roy handed him the fishing lines and the two of them fixed the bait onto the hooks. The procedure for us was simple: just lower the line and unravel the nylon for about twenty to thirty feet and wait for a nibble. Alloy and Roy made their way to the prow and standing with legs askew, they let out some line and then, with the plastic bottle in their left hand and the other end of the line in their right between thumb and forefinger, they twirled the line using the momentum of the lead to gain acceleration, and cast off in the distance. Everyone had a line and we patiently waited to see who would catch the first fish.

It was rather hot, but there was a steady gentle breeze that kept us from getting too warm. It seemed that Alloy had chosen the right spot for within five minutes or so, he had the first bite. We focused our attention on his action to see how he would reel the prize in. Again this was a simple procedure. Grasping the plastic bottle by the neck in his left hand, right hand guiding the line, it was a circular left wrist motion to wrap the line around the bottle and pull up the catch. From the tautness of the line, it looked to be a big one. Alloy then dropped the bottle and used both hands to haul in the nylon line. Then there was a splash as the fish on the other end jumped up in its struggle to free itself from the hook. But he was caught and Alloy expertly and patiently hauled him onto the deck of the prow. It was a magnificent red snapper, about eight pounds, just about two feet in length. The scales glistened as Alloy held it down and deftly removed the hook. He held it up for us to see and we all agreed that it was beautiful. Hayden remarked that it would taste even better when fried with bake which made us all laugh.

That first fish was all the incentive we needed. Everyone focused on their own line hoping to have as good a catch. My mother was the next to taste success as she let out a shrill scream and called for help. Laughingly Roy went to her assistance and showed her how to manage the catch and to reel the fish in. He let her play with the line and haul the catch nearer the surface. She begged Roy to take over the line and he obliged. Her catch was a six pound carite marked by the yellow spots along the median of the body. We could see how proud she was of her prize. Ronald yelled that he had snagged one and we watched as he very competently pulled in his catch. His was a cavalli, about five pounds and nicely dense with very pronounced characteristic yellow tint on the tail and fins. We continued in this manner for the better part of two hours and had all, with the exception of Sherry, grown oblivious to the pitch of the boat in the swells. Her face had a green tinge and we knew she was feeling nausea coming on. Alloy opened a bottle of club soda and gave her a drink and one of the hard candies to suck on. He moved her to the back of the boat were the pitch was less discernable. The rest of us refreshed ourselves with some oranges that Alloy had brought and each accepted the offered hard candy.

My father estimated that it was closing in on late afternoon and we took stock of our catch. Everyone except Sherry had a catch. Alloy and Kelvin had caught the most and we counted six red snappers, eight carite, one cavalli and two kingfish. Not a bad haul for a short fishing trip. Alloy was pleased and remarked that sometime it took the fishermen all night banking on the sea to come up with a haul like this. He admitted that he kept this particular spot a secret to himself but knew that it was only a matter of time before other boats found this spot. With that, the men hauled up the anchor and stowed it as Alloy brought the engine to life. The fish was stored on ice in an old blue cooler that was secured in the cargo area of the prow. We were a bit drained from the sun and even though we enjoyed the fishing trip, were glad when Alloy opened the throttle and we sped back towards the shoreline.

Fifteen minutes later, he eased the throttle and slowed the boat to a gentle chug. We could see the spire of the church as he maneuvered the boat past the breakers. The boys were waiting on this part and as he gave the sign, we jumped out of the boat and jockeyed for positions on either side to guide the boat to shore. By this time, the engine was shut down and the tide helped us to ease the boat to the shore. The keel stuck firm and the boat lilted to the left and came to rest. It took us another fifteen minutes to "jock" the boat up into position on the sand. All hands helped clear the boat of the items that needed to be secured and the men lifted the engine and stowed it in the shed and padlocked it. Alloy then insisted that we take all the fish, but my father protested that it was too much. They laughingly agreed on us taking two snappers and the two kingfish. Alloy would take the rest for his family in Arima.

Alloy's mother or "mums" as she was affectionately known, came out to see the catch and was surprised at the haul. Seeing my mother and my father starting to thank Alloy for the fishing trip, she admonished them that surely we were not about to leave to go back home. In her usual jovial way, she told them that she had prepared dinner and that we were all expected to come to the table. This was not a lady to be argued with and my father graciously accepted the invite. And what a spread it was! There was corn soup with salted pigtail and dumplings, roasted coconut bake, fried fish and cold coconut water. Her house was small but had an open floor plan and the dining table occupied centre place. There were large wooden shutters propped open to let the breeze and light in. Once seated at the table, there was a magnificent view of the shore and sea and the picture windows were framed by the coconut trees on the fringes of the yard. Mums told us to help ourselves and my mother and Radica dished out for us.

Table conversation was varied and eventually came to rest on Alloy questioning us kids on our school progress. He jokingly laughed that if I passed for Fatima, he would take a special interest in my mathematics development. While I laughed along, I felt a bit of dread at the pit of my stomach for mathematics was my worst subject. He regaled us with stories of the Fatima boys' successes and mis-adventures and how he dealt with them. At the back of my mind, I knew that going from primary to high school would be an adjustment and his stories reinforced the trepidation that I felt. Ronald and Hayden were not as concerned with these stories as I, for their school choices were primarily set for the secondary schools in and around Tunapuna. I on the other hand, was targeted for Fatima or St. Mary's College. Sensing my discomfort, Alloy changed the topic and engaged everyone on their first fishing experience out on a boat. Feeling relieved at the attention being diverted away, I relaxed a bit and joined in the casual banter. The sun had set and mums lit the kerosene lamps as this house did not have electricity. The lamps gave off a warm glow from the sooty lamp shade. We stayed a bit longer for the men to have a neat shot of grog and then my father gave the sign for us to leave. We all thanked Alloy and mums for their hospitality and wished Alloy a safe journey back to Arima the next day. We then set off along the beach back to our beach house.

It was seven o'clock in the evening when we left and the tide was out. There was a wide swath of beach and the moon cast a long silver finger on the water. The sky was clear of clouds and without any direct lighting to obscure our vision, the heavens revealed thousands of stars. My father stopped and pointed to a formation that he said was the Big Dipper. It took a while for us to follow where his finger pointed to, but as he described the formation and we more closely followed his extended index finger, we fixed upon the constellation. We could make out the distinct shape of a ladle that gave its name to the stellar body. Soon the heady musky aroma of the old mangrove tree tickled our noses and we skirted the beached behemoth.

Gerry complained about being tired and Roy lifted him onto his back in a jockey position as the adults beckoned us to quicken the pace. As we entered our beach house compound, my father tinkered with the key to open the door and soon we all flopped down on the sofas after the lights had been turned on. My mother chased us to brush our teeth, rinse the sand from our feet and get changed for bed. It wasn't long before we all changed into our sleeping attire and with a goodnight to the adults, we gratefully sought our beds. It was a long tiring day and soon we drifted off to sleep to dream about our first boat fishing trip.

I was the first to awake the next morning and the house seemed eerily quiet. I tiptoed out of the bedroom into the living room and saw Roy still asleep on the sofa. Not wanting to awaken him, I silently slunk to the kitchen to get a drink of cold water. Maybe it was the creaking of the rusted hinges on the fridge, but Hayden and Ronald awoke and whispered to me about going outside to sit. We very slowly tugged at the door latch until the bolt slid back. Hayden held the top half firmly lest it was windy and be whipped open with a loud bang. He eased it back into an open position and we opened the bottom half with the same diligence. Glancing back, we saw that Roy was still asleep and that the light was not disturbing him. The ground felt cool under our bare feet as we make our way to the back of the house to our favorite spot on the bench.

It was a typical Mayaro morning. The sun was already halfway up and we could feel the warmth of its rays. The coconut tree in our yard gently swayed in the breeze coming off the sea and the salty air was delicious. We chatted about the previous day's fishing trip and wondered when next we would be able to set out in a boat to go fishing. The past few days were very busy and even though we were on vacation, we agreed that it would be nice to just laze around and swim and do nothing. As we sat there talking, Kelvin rounded the corner and cheekily interrogated us as to what we were doing up so early. He joined us on the bench and surmised that it was probably getting on eight o'clock in the morning. I guess our mutterings may have carried into the house as Sherry and Gerry came out to join us, still rubbing the sleep from their eyes. The sound of the bolts being drawn back on the bedroom door soon revealed my father's grinning face.

The small party had more than doubled when Roy also joined us outside. Kelvin went in to prepare coffee and we hoped there would be also something hot for us. Pretty soon the adults had their enamel cups of steaming coffee and we had cups of cocoa. The warm liquid felt exquisite on my tongue and I could feel the warmth coursing down my throat and warming up my insides. I sat there silent with my own thoughts, occasionally catching a snippet of conversation here and there. I would have been content to just laze there but my mother's voice called us in to breakfast. That jogged me out of my reverie as we raced to the table to secure our usual spots.

Radica and my mother were already at the table and had laid out a simple breakfast. Everyone served themselves and we tucked into large piles of country bread and butter. Fried Vienna Sausages with onions and ketchup complimented the delicious bread and the ubiquitous mugs of tea and cocoa were quickly depleted. Casual conversations abounded around the table. One piece that caught my attention was a comment from my mother that we were just at the halfway point in the vacation. I questioned here if she was sure and, with a laugh, she replied yes. There was a comment about looking at the glass half full and not half empty. No one was in a rush to do anything and the adults spent a leisurely time around the table while we adjourned to the sofas, but not before being admonished to clear away our plates and cups.

Sherry and Gerry retrieved a pail of sea shells that they had been collecting and set about to sort them out. I pulled out the deck of cards and the boys started a game of go-to-pack. My father and Kelvin busied themselves cleaning the house while my mother and Radica took an opportunity to lounge outside on two chairs they placed under the coconut tree. I observed these goings-on and enquired about Roy. He was nowhere to be seen. It seemed a mystery as the others also looked puzzled at my enquiry. Kelvin commented that he must have gone off on his own and we should not be too concerned. While that may have satisfied some of the others I still felt uneasy, and I knew Ronald probably did also as his eyes caught mine and I could see his anxiety. I tried to imagine where he may have gone to and tried to put some of the conjured up images out of my mind. Roy was a simple man, but he was also an adventurer. He was known to tempt fate at time and some said he was foolhardy. But he was my uncle Roy and I was concerned not knowing where he had gone to. The lack of an answer from the adults reinforced the feeling of dread in the pit of my stomach. But I said nothing more, keeping these thoughts concealed to myself.

When the household chores were done, my father and Kelvin joined the ladies under the shade of the coconut tree. The bedroom windows and back door were open. I left the card game and retired to the bedroom. I laid down on the bed using 2 pillows to prop my head and just closed my eyes a bit. A thousand thoughts ran through my head among which were the upcoming new school year, my cousins back in Tunapuna, the football team, and a myriad of fleeting thoughts. They were soon punctuated though by the boisterous antics of Hayden and Ronald who dived onto the bed bringing me out of my reverie. It was quite pleasant just lying on the bed and we did not feel the need to get up and do anything. It was that kind of lazy morning. But I still felt uneasy about Roy. I sensed the same from Ronald who had not said anything as yet. I turned to him and asked him if he knew where his father may have gone. He simply shrugged and I could see that he was a bit worried. At that point I made up my mind and got up off the bed and made my way to my father outside. I interrupted their conversation and asked pointedly if they knew where Roy was. He was there a while ago when we woke up from sleep, but now he was nowhere to be found, and we were a bit worried as no one knew where he went to. Just as my father was about to speak, we all heard a whistle, a very familiar whistle, and I was immediately relieved. It was Roy's whistle and as we turned in the direction of the sound, we saw him sauntering up the driveway with a parcel in his hand.

    Ronald was the first out of the bedroom but he did not run to his father. However, I could tell from the look on his face that he was relieved. In typical fashion Roy simply made his way towards us with a cheeky look on his face. Before he could speak my mother intonated her disapproval of his wandering off without letting anyone know. Sheepishly he accepted the admonishment, and just as quickly called everyone over. Curiosity and anticipation led us to gather around him. His eyes twinkled as he brought the parcel up and handed it to Radica and my mother. Needless to say they were very surprised as they took it from his hands. He was smiling broadly and urged them to hurry up and open it. The parcel was a simple brown bag that was folded over into a square with the flap tucked underneath. There was a bit of tape that held it close. With my mother holding it, Radica undid the tape, opened it, reached inside and pulled out two identical shawls. Their puzzled eyes and open-mouthed expressions asked the questions, why, what was this for? With a laugh, Roy told them that he had heard them talking the previous week about the chill in the evening air. He had gone to Mr. James' shop last week and asked Mr. James to get him two shawls. Mr. James' wife had travelled to San Fernando on a visit to her sister and she got the shawls there and brought them back to Mayaro. Roy had gotten a message that Mr. James wanted to see him and that's why he left quietly this morning without telling anyone anything. Now that the shawls were here, he asked if they liked them. They both hugged him, draped the shawls over their shoulders to show their appreciation, as they thanked him. This was so like Roy. Always thinking of others and doing things for others. Such a simple thoughtful gesture that with the explanation, forgave the anxiety he caused us that morning with his disappearance.

Chapter 12

Curried Duck Lime with Selwyn and Gatch

The next two days were spent doing pretty much the same: morning stroll for newspapers and bread, pulling seine, playing cricket and football on the beach, swimming in the ocean, evening strolls out to the village, seeing after the meals, spending quiet evenings playing cards and board games, sitting outside and talking. Time moved slowly and no one complained. Everyone was totally at peace, totally relaxed. My father's beard had grown and he refused to shave touting it as his badge of relaxation. This was the way he enjoyed his time away from work. For him it was total relaxation, with no cares in the world save for his family. It gave us the needed time to reconnect as a family and as an extended family. We were sitting around the breakfast table sipping on hot cocoa and planning the rest of the day when Kelvin told us that we were going to have visitors for two days. He wanted to prolong the agony by not telling us who was coming, but we wrestled it out of him eventually. Selwyn was coming to visit and coming with him would be Gatch and Jeanne.

Selwyn was a friend of the entire family. He lived on our street, Hackett Lane, in Tunapuna. He worked at the County Council with Radica and Kelvin. He and my father had a penchant for horse racing and he spent a lot of time at our home with my father checking the horses. They were very close indeed. Gatch was Selwyn's friend who became our friend as well.

Gatch used to play music at parties in his spare time and we had him play at several at our home. This was indeed a surprise and we were anxious to know when they would be coming. With our questions answered, my mother gave us specific chores to set about to accommodate our pending visitors. With visitors coming, we needed to prepare once again to accommodate everyone. This meant that the sleeping arrangements would again be redone. After a quick recap of the assignments, we set about our chores to prepare for the new visitors, just as we had done a few weeks ago when Jean and Sundar visited.

Mummy and Radica took charge of the 3 bedrooms. The three boys had to sweep and tidy up the main living areas. Sherry and Gerry were excused and allowed to play in the driveway. My father went outside to inspect the levels in the water tanks. Roy and Kelvin retrieved the old fiber mattress that was rolled up and stored under the slanted staircase. We occupied ourselves with these activities for the better part of an hour. When we were done, we surveyed the fruits of our efforts and were satisfied that all was ready. Kelvin and Roy had taken the mattress outside and beat it with a stick to get some of the dust off. They then brought it inside and Radica put a clean tuck-in sheet on it. But instead of laying it on the ground, they rolled it back up and set it upright against the wall next to the face basin. They would only put it out when we were ready for sleep at night as there would be much activity in the apartment during the day. My father reported that the water tanks were full and that there was a water supply on the main. My mother then went over the sleeping arrangements: Gerry would sleep with mum and dad; Sherry would be with Kelvin and Radica; Gatch and Jeanne would have one bed in our room; Selwyn and Roy would have the other bed; the three boys would bunk on the mattress on the floor of the living room. We looked forward to this as it felt almost like camping out.

With the chores done, we changed into our bathing suits and were just about to go to the beach when we heard the cars coming up the driveway.

Selwyn's light blue Vauxhall made its way up to the door and came to a stop. Gatch was the first one out and in his loud raspy voice, he called out greetings to everyone. Selwyn and Jeanne joined him and exchanged hugs with everyone. It was a beautiful sunny day and it would be perfect for our visitors. We helped them get their bags out from the trunk of the car, into the house and showed them where to put their things. Jeanne brought a basket covered with a white linen cloth and handed it to my mother. Eager and curious to see what was inside, we crowded around to get a peek. Our visitors had brought some fresh hops bread in Sangre Grande. To go with the bread, they also brought a generous portion of char siu pork from the old Wing Sue restaurant in Tunapuna. There was also a huge bag of crimson red, almost purple, ripe pomerac. This would be our lunch and we could not wait to tuck in. But it was not yet lunch time so the ladies stowed the basket in the kitchen. Jeanne, Gatch and Selwyn already had their bathing suits on under their clothes and did not need a second invitation to the beach. We each grabbed a ripe pomerac and munching on our fruit, we went down to the beach. The visitors could not wait to hit the water and voiced their eager anticipation of the salty brine. It was a bright sunny day. The tide was out and the water was crystal clear. Everyone dived into the water and luxuriated in the surf.

  Eager to hear news from home, we all huddled around in a circle as the gentle waves rolled over us at a leisurely cadence. With the conversation mainly about politics and horses, we kids engaged in our own conversation and paid less attention to the adults. Our ears though caught a snippet of conversation about a party, and that gained our full attention. Selwyn lived on his own having been divorced many years ago. He lived on our street and had a very nice home there. At least once a month, Selwyn would have a Friday evening lime at his place. That usually involved a lot of cooking and good food, lots of music and dancing, and lots of drinks. Even though we children were too young to attend the parties, we were allowed to go early enough, before the party really got into full swing, and have something to eat. Gatch was always at all of Selwyn's parties and both of them were fantastic cooks. Naturally when they started talking about a party here in Mayaro, we were excited. The first question came from Sherry and she asked whether the children would be able to attend. Selwyn laughed and told her that tonight's party was going to be a family party for everyone. That elicited loud cheers from all the children.

    Jeanne and Radica slipped out of the water unnoticed by us until we heard them call to us from the beach. They had gone back to the house to get a picnic lunch for us. We raced out of the water and rinsed our hands at the water's edge. The basket was opened and char siu pork sandwiches were handed out to everyone. My father and Selwyn poured cold juice into disposable cups and passed the drinks around. The sand was dry and we installed ourselves there and delved into our lunch. Gatch had a small container of soy sauce mixed with pepper and ketchup which he offered as a condiment for our sandwiches. We drizzled a bit onto our sandwiches but Sherry and Gerry did not. It was a delicious meal and a taste that we had not had in a long time.

    As we sat eating, Hayden, also a budding DJ, enquired about details for the party and we were delighted to learn that Gatch did have a collection of music cassettes with him for tonight. He had prepared a few cassettes with a mix of music since he could not bring his turntables and speakers. With the entertainment part taken care of, the conversation next moved to the topic of food. That night there would be curried duck, dhal and rice. Gatch had purchased two drakes that had been cleaned, the skin roasted, cut up and seasoned. It was just a matter of building a fireside to cook out in the open night air. That sounded like a capital idea to us and we were excited to help. With the sandwiches devoured, another bag appeared from within the basket and currants rolls were broken in halves and shared. After lunch, we stayed on the beach and in the water until the tide started turning. At about four in the afternoon, it was time to get ready and we all made our way back to the house to shower and change.

There was no dawdling over showers this afternoon as we wanted to get ready to help. My mother remarked at our speed and haste with a laugh as she saw us emerge from the bedroom already showered and changed. Now it was time to help. The men had set up a few stones in a circle and were trying to level it. The pot would sit on the edge of the stones with the fire beneath, so it was very important that the pot was stable and not rock. We crouched on our haunches and tried to eyeball if it was level. Roy used a piece of wood to help gauge. With a few adjustments to the stones, they thought they had it right.

With five men who each prided himself on being the best cook, we knew there would be a certain amount of posturing and picong. As to who would end up being the main chef, we placed bets. We listened in amusement to each of their claims of culinary superiority, but in the end it was Gatch who received the apron. His argument was simply that it was he who bought and seasoned the ducks, that Selwyn always used too much salt, that Kelvin was too young to know how to cook duck, that Roy was a terrible cook, that my father was the host, and the host should relax and have his meal prepared for him. By this time, the men had brought out a bottle of grog and they took a drink with that settled. All during this posturing, the amused ladies stood by and then good-naturedly jeered them to get a move on for if it took them that long to decide who will cook, how much longer it will take them to decide who will light the fire.

In order to complete the set up for the outdoor evening party, we needed to bring the tables and seats from inside to outside. We manoeuvred the heavy wooden table through the doorway bringing it at an angle with the legs first, then straightening it and then reversing the angle for the next set of legs to get clear. After that it was easy to bring the benches outside. We placed the table in the middle of the driveway and arranged the seating around it. The plastic tablecloth had to be secured to prevent it flying away in the wind. To do this we got some tape, folded the four edges under the table and taped the plastic to the wood. Ronald and Sherry helped to bring out the plates and cutlery and they set the table. With the uneven asphalt of the driveway, the table rocked a bit. To remedy this Hayden set out and found some flattish stones which he used as shims under the table legs to render the table even and stop the rocking.

Satisfied with our efforts to set up the table and seating, we next turned our attention to the side board or buffet. We would need this for Gatch to set up the music. Eager hands took hold of it as we brought it outside and set it up against the bedroom wall. Gatch and Selwyn then brought out the small speaker, amplifier and cassette deck, connected everything in a flash and ran the extension cord to the nearest outlet. Gatch had a microphone and as he powered everything on, he did a quick sound check and all was fine. He plunked in a cassette and immediately the strains of The Mighty Shadow's "Bassman" filled the air. Gatch adjusted the volume so that it was not too loud, and we had music. Hayden and I brought out the cooler and laid out a few bottles of soft drinks on the table. Preparation was completed and we turned our attention to the fireside.

The rice and dhal was being cooked on the stove inside the apartment. The main dish, the curried duck, was being cooked on the fire outside. By this time, the fire had been lit, the pot was on and the chefs were just about to start. Gatch had a bowl with onions, garlic, hot pepper, chandon beni and pimentos. The oil was hot and he measured out and poured in the curry powder and quickly stirred it into the oil. As the curry started to cook, he added the aromatics and there was a whoosh as the cool ingredients hit the hot oil. He stirred and let it cook for about 2 minutes then added a bit of water. There was another whoosh this time with a cloud of steam as evaporation set in as the water hit the hot pot. He then stirred the pot as the curry had to cook a bit before he would add the duck. Satisfied that the curry was cooked as evidenced by the nice thick paste inside the pot, Kelvin handed him the basin with the seasoned duck and he added it all at once. A sturdy cloth was nearby for him to hold the pot as he stirred the meat in to coat it with the curry. Once that was done, he covered the pot, adjusted the burning wood and looked around and smiled at everyone, proud of his efforts. He announced that his efforts called for a drink and the men poured a long one and sipped.

The heady aroma filled the air and tantalized our nostrils making us salivate as we waited impatiently for dinner to be ready. But it would be a while yet before the duck was cooked, so we found a tin of Elmer's Chee Wees and greedily delved in to partially sate our appetites. By this time, the rice and the dhal were done and covered in the kitchen awaiting the main attraction to be served. Roy and Kelvin peeled several large cucumbers and a medium onion and cut them into very thin slices. Then they added some salt and pepper and squeezed a juicy lime and left it to pickle. Satisfied that all was in place and ready, the ladies came outside, took a seat and relaxed with a cup of tea. As I sat there looking on at the various activities, I felt a warmth inside of me that grew and radiated outward.

I loved my family very much and this time with them was so precious. As a ten-year-old standing there looking on, I only knew that I felt happy. I was content to sit there and absorb everything around me when I was abruptly brought out of my reverie by Ronald poking me. I heard his voice prodding me to come and help stir and turn the pot. Gatch had just taken the cover off the pot and was going to turn the duck, when Ronald asked if we could do it. Gatch took the two cloths that he had nearby to hold the pot steady and we each took turns to stir the pot under the watchful eye of my father. Of course whenever you turned the pot, you had to test it. My father took the spoon and scooped up a bit of the sauce, blew it to cool it down and then poured a bit into each of our cupped palms. We tasted the curry sauce and it was just right. Just enough salt and pepper to taste but not to overwhelm. The men tested a piece of the meat to see if it was done and announced just about ten more minutes.

  I heard my mother calling to Hayden and I and we went inside the house to see what she wanted. She handed us four large eggplant on a tray and another tray with about a dozen large tomatoes and told us to take it to my father. With the pot coming off the fire soon, and with the wood fire still very hot, she decided to get the eggplant and tomato onto the fire and roast them. There would be baigan and tomato choka for breakfast tomorrow. That was fine with us as that would mean there would be sada roti to go with the choka. Another treat to look forward to tomorrow. We took the trays to my father. Kelvin had retrieved the piece of wire mesh from on top of the water tanks and when Roy and Gatch lifted the pot off the fire, he placed the wire on top of the stones. My father arranged the eggplant and tomatoes on the wire and then stepped back to allow the fire to do its magic. The wooden soft drink cases were turned upside down and stacked to make a level stand to rest the hot pot on. The rice and dhal were brought out and put on the table and we eagerly lined up with our plates for the ladies to dish out for us. With a warning to hold our plates carefully, we found our seats around the table, in the open evening air, and settled down for a delicious dinner.

  The sun had already gone below the horizon and the lights outside the apartment were switched on. Roy lit the two flambeau that he made and placed them near the outer wall. A kerosene lamp was also lit and placed on the table. It was a clear night sky and the temperature had dropped just a few degrees. But it was cozy. The mosquitoes were repelled by the wood fire and flambeau, but Radica still lit a few mosquito coils and placed them around the al fresco dining area. Roy saw to the drinks and made sure everyone had a cup or glass in front of them. Then we all sat down to enjoy the wonderful repast. But before we tucked in, my mother asked Gatch to stop the music for a moment. She wanted to say grace. Asking us all to join hands, she led us in a prayer of thanks for the bounties that we had, for the friends and loved ones around us, and to remember those less fortunate than us. It seemed fitting that she would lead the prayer as she was the one who looked after our Catholic and religious upbringing and her simple words seemed to echo in my mind as they were etched into my memory. After we all said Amen, it was time to relax and eat. Gatch turned back on the music and replaced the calypso cassette with one that had popular and classic songs from the 60s.

The food was delicious. There was a smokiness to the duck that came from the wood fire that was indescribable. Lots of compliments were paid to the chefs as the conversations drifted around the table. When we could eat no more, we cleared away the dishes and returned outside. At the parties at Selwyn's house, we would stay on the porch at our house and would hear the strains of a sing along. We wanted to do the same tonight if this was to be a party that the children could finally attend. Gatch laughed loudly and asked what our choice was. Hayden, Ronald and I all chorused calypso with a bottle and spoon. They knew exactly what we wanted. It was a good choice as even my mother smiled as she sat at the table tapping her hands on the table in a pseudo drum like beat. Gatch found the cassette, inserted it into the player and turned the volume up just a tad. For this session we needed the music as background accompaniment only. The lusty singing voices of the participants would be central. As the music started, we knew the sequence of the medley of songs and we strained to catch the cue to start. As we heard the pause in the melody, most of us who knew the lyrics chimed in almost simultaneously with the immortal words of the Mighty Sparrow, "Jean and Dinah, Rosita and Clementina, 'round the corner posing, bet your life is something they selling."

And so we carried on singing tune after tune, belting out the words that we knew and encouraging the others to join in.

Hayden had an ardent love for music and would grasp at any chance to take the controls at the turntable and amplifier. He hung around Gatch almost all night and Gatch eventually gave him the headphones and told him to take over. With a huge grin on his face, Hayden took over and immersed himself in selecting and playing the tunes that would keep us partying until late. The fire was rekindled with more wood and it crackled and burned brightly providing us with light and warmth and warded off the chill of the night air. As the flames danced in the gentle breeze, it cast wobbly shadows of the partying dancers against the wall and lent a coziness to the atmosphere.

As an adult looking back and remembering these moments, I can still feel the warmth of the fire and the tingle of belonging. No one paid attention to the time as the night wore on. It was not until my mother looked around for Gerry and found him asleep on the couch that we noticed the time. It was past 2 o'clock in the morning. Though no one wanted to end the party, we knew we had to eventually and we set about clearing up and taking the furniture back into the house. Many hands certainly made light work and in no time we had packed away everything. The boys tried to slink away into our bed, but my mother caught us and made us brush our teeth before turning in. As soon as the light was switched off, we fell fast asleep dreaming of calypso rhythms.

The next morning was a lazy one. After the late night, everyone slept later than usual. One by one we rousted ourselves and lazily made our way to the common living area. Those that were still asleep were allowed to continue their slumber. By the time everyone was awake, a very late breakfast, or rather, brunch, was being prepared. Simple but satisfying, it brought us together once more before Selwyn and Gatch would leave. There was tomato and baigan choka which had been roasted on the fire the previous evening. To go with it, there was hot sada roti. This was a real treat as my mother did not make sada roti very often. After everyone had eaten, it was time to bid our visitors goodbye. We helped them load the car and thanked them for a memorable weekend. Selwyn reminded us that he would be back in a few weeks to take us home, and with a honk of his horn, we watched them pull out of the driveway and disappear onto Gill Street back to Tunapuna.

Chapter 13

Errol, Leon and the Trip to Rio Claro

My father worked all his life with the airline and had three very close friends. My godfather Cecil Gomes, my sister's godfather Tony Chung, and my brother's godfather Errol Pena. Even though he was close with all three friends, I think he had a closer relationship with Errol. Errol and Cecil worked in Flight Watch as it was called back then. My father worked in Traffic. Errol and my father eventually worked in the same department. Errol's family, Janet his common law wife and his two boys Larry and Robert, were also very close to us. Long before we started going to Mayaro as a family, there was Manzanilla with Errol and his family.

    I would have been about six years old when my father and Errol used to rent a beach house named "Coconut Sands" in Manzanilla. There, with the two families, we would spend a few weeks together at the beach. I vividly recall Suzy the Alsatian dog romping about with us and licking Sherry on her nose. I remember changing our clothes in the evening and driving out to the First and Last Bar and Grocery to get bread. On these trips, my father and Errol always got a cold Carib Lager Beer which they would bring back to the house. When they got back home, we would all sit on the low brick wall facing the road while they drank their beer and chatted. They would always leave a drop in the bottle for both Robert and I. There was one particular evening I remember when both Errol and my father had a few drinks well and were pretty well oiled. My father, in an alcoholically merry state, held my mother and said to her: "J, I love you like hog loves mud…you are my Rose of Tralee." My father used to call my mother "J" as he shortened it from the spelling of Jemma, even though she spelt it Gemma. Little did he know that years later, that phrase would be one of his famous, or notorious, quotations which everyone in the airline came to know about. When I myself worked in the airline, Errol was one of my supervisors. It was a phrase that epitomized their relationship in the earlier days. Against this background and their common love for the beach, it was not surprising that we would meet Errol and his family on this holiday in Mayaro.

We were having a leisurely breakfast at the table when we heard the sound of a car coming up the driveway. Curiosity made us leap up to the windows to see who it was. There were two cars. It was Errol and his friend Leon. In his typical deep voice, Errol alighted and jokingly boomed out to my father an admonition about even though he was not invited to Mayaro, he nevertheless invited himself. It was a noisy reunion as Errol, Janet, Robert, Leon and his wife came in and sat down. Eager to discover the reason for the visit, we listened intently to the snippets of conversation. Errol and Leon were here in Mayaro for just one night and were staying with Leon's brother in a house about a few hundred yards from where Peter lived. As Errol knew where my father was in Mayaro, they popped in to see us. That answered their sudden appearance. But there was another surprise and one which would delight us no end.

Errol and Leon had a hankering to place some bets on a major horse race in England. Leon had received a tip and he must have had some inspirational sign on the drive to Mayaro that the tip was a good one. That convinced him to want to go to Rio Claro to place the bets. Knowing quite well that my father could weigh in on the tip, they came over to see what he thought and if he'd like to go to Rio Claro as well to place his own bets. My father sat down with them and they poured over the English horse paper for a while. Convinced that it was a good tip, they decided to make the trip to Rio Claro. The ladies however, had no desire to go to Rio Claro and they declined. Sherry and Gerry also did not want to go, but the boys did. With five men and four boys, it would be too tight a squeeze in one car so they decided that both cars would make the trip. When we awoke that morning, we had no idea that we would be making a day trip to Rio Claro. This was certainly unexpected but immensely exciting.

  Within fifteen minutes, after having bid the others goodbye until later, we were on our way out of Gill Street and turning right onto the Naparima Mayaro Road. It would take about forty-five minutes to get there. It was a beautiful morning and as the cars sped on, a lovely cooling breeze came through the open windows. We looked forward to this drive as it would take us through a part of Trinidad that we had never been. We had never driven through the south from east to west. We had been to San Fernando, but that was the furthest south we had gone. Never to Rio Claro and never via the roads in the south. So as the cars drove on, we sat and gazed at the countryside that rolled by, observing everything that sailed past the windows. It was a fairly straight drive all the way from Mayaro to Ecclesville. Beyond that, there were a few turns as we neared Rio Claro. The road was dotted with Hindu temples, Christian churches and Muslim mosques. Several small agricultural villages lay interspersed. We wondered what we would do when we got there. We knew they were going to the Racing Pool to place their bets and then probably wait for the race and the results. We did not have to wait long to find out.

  As we arrived into Rio Claro, we drove past a large mosque which dominated the entrance to the town from the east. It seemed that we were suddenly thrust from a sleepy forested place into a busy and bustling hub. Rio Claro was very busy. Before stopping though, Leon and Errol drove on to the outskirts to the west. They wanted to show us two magnificent sights and we were not disappointed. As they turned into a street and made an about turn and entered Rio Claro from the west, we passed between a magnificent pink and blue Catholic Church and an equally magnificent white Hindu Temple with a gold and blue dome. We drank in the splendor of these two buildings for a few moments and marveled at the splendor of the main markers at the entrances from the east and from the west. We then came upon the town centre and main junction with all the bustling stalls, taxis and the four-armed signpost pointing to all corners of Trinidad. Errol and Leon found two parking spots and we alighted from the vehicles eager to go have a walk around.

They estimated it would be just over an hour to place their bets and listen to the race. They got their bearings and we set off for the Racing Pool. It was fairly crowded inside with hopeful punters. The floor was littered with old discarded pari and forecast tickets that probably once held some hope of a big win. Errol got the racing program and some betting sheets. They already knew the horses they were going to bet on so it did not take them long to write their bets, line up at the cashier and place the bets. The race would be in thirty minutes so there was some time yet. There was a parlour adjacent to the Racing Pool so we went in to get some refreshments. There was a glass case on the countertop and a delicious aroma of corn and beef arepas tantalized our nostrils. After purchasing a bagful of arepas and nine cold RC colas, we walked out onto the street munching away on the hot pies. We saw the church and temple in the distance off the main street and decided to take a quick walk to have a closer look. The buildings were truly magnificent. As we had food with us, we did not enter but instead admired from the outside. Errol glanced at his watch and decided that we should head back to the betting shop to listen to the race. It was being broadcast live from England.

They had agreed that the tip was a good one and after having checked the form of the horses, they all placed bets on the same horses. As we entered the Racing Pool, there was a renewed sense of excitement with a heightened buzz all around. It was just a few minutes to post time so we found a corner table to ourselves and awaited the broadcast. The very distinct English accent of the BBC broadcaster boomed over the speakers. My father had a racing program and we used our fingers to follow along as he read the starters and jockeys. The horses had entered the starting gates and over the thousands of miles, over the wires that connected the wireless set, we heard the bell ring and they were off. The announcer was animated and called the race as it progressed. The noise level in the Racing Pool increased exponentially as everyone was excitedly urging on the horse that they bet on. I had been to the races with my father before and I knew his animations so as they turned into the home stretch, it was no surprise that he started air whipping his horse as he heard his bet in third place. It may have been the positive vibes that he sent over the Atlantic, but his horse accelerated and pushed hard and pipped the leader at the wire by a nose to win the race.

Jubilation and cheers erupted all around the Racing Pool. All the adults in our party had bet on the same horse. All their bets had won. They were elated as were we. They had to wait until the race was declared official before they could cash in their bets. Roy decided to stand in the cashier's line to be first to the window. They all passed their bet slips to him as we waited. It was not long before the race was official and Roy presented the bet slips to the cashier and collected our winnings.

The winning horse was the second favourite in the race and came in at 3:1 odds. The payout was decent for the pari tickets. They had all placed bets to win, so they almost tripled their bets. It was a great windfall since earlier in the morning they had not even intended to play the horses. Now it was time to go home back to Mayaro. But first, on the way out, we would stop off at the Royal Castle outlet and pick up Chicken and Chips and Devil Dogs for everyone as a treat. It took another twenty minutes for our order to be ready and we piled into the cars for the drive back. The aroma of the hot chicken and chips was too much to bear and we were allowed to eat as the cars drove on. We had dressed the boxes with ketchup, mustard and the famous Royal Castle pepper sauce and it was simply delicious. As usual the way back seemed to take less time and we were soon pulling into the driveway on Gill Street.

Sherry and Gerry excitedly rushed out to greet us anxious to see if there were any treats. They were simply delighted with their chicken and chips and devil dogs and promptly sat at the table to devour their treats. The ladies heard of the luck with the horses and everyone was in a good mood. Errol and Leon called for a drink to celebrate the win and Roy and Kelvin poured out rum and coke. As they were sipping their drinks, Errol and Leon invited us all over to Leon's brother's house that evening for a lime. Leon's brother was also on vacation and his house was located about half a mile from ours. We knew exactly where it was located as we would see it often from the beach as we walked by to go to the seines pulled on the north side of Gill Street. With preparations of their own to tend to, Errol and Leon took their leave of us. There was still time to go for a swim, but no one seemed interested. Mummy and Radica left for the kitchen as they were going to make a dessert to take to the party that night. Daddy and the other men took the benches at the back of the unit and sat there chatting. So we decided to take a stroll out to the top of Gill Street to see what was happening there.

As we strolled past the old bakery, we could see a good sized crowd gathered in front the verandah of the old shop that directly faced Gill Street. Curiosity emerged and we hastened our steps to investigate. We discerned the hum of voices with some shrill and some louder than others. As we approached the scene and manoeuvred our way around to get a good vantage view, we saw the object of their attentions. It was an enormous snake, an anaconda. It was about fifteen feet in length and its girth was huge. It lay still and we assumed it was dead. As we listened to the voices of the locals, we quickly learned that it was one of the fishermen who found it. He had returned from his boat and was going to his shack. The door was slightly ajar and he cautiously opened it expecting the worst. As he opened the door, he saw a slithering movement and realized it was the snake. In a flash, he ran outside in the year and looked for a weapon. He saw a stout plank of wood and he grabbed hold of this. Thus armed, he ran back to his shack to take care of the intruder. Upon hearing the sound of the human, the snake tried to slither under the bed, but the man grabbed hold of it by the tail and dragged it out of the shack onto the sandy yard. The reptile then reared its huge head and coiled and lunged at the man. As it did so, the man dived to the side, recovered, and struck four or five mighty blows to the head of the snake. The blows were effective and they stunned the monster. It was not dead, but dazed and immobile. By that time, a few villages were on the scene and together they held the reptile down while others got some strong cords and they bound the head and mouth. They then dragged the beast out to where it lay.

      The commotion attracted lots of onlookers, among them Mr. James. He had a telephone at his house and he had called the police to help deal with the reptile. The call had already been made and soon the police jeep arrived on the scene. The sergeant took charge of the proceedings and then informed everyone that they had telephoned to the SPCA to come and get the snake. It was alive, but stunned, but bound and no immediate danger to anyone. The SPCA would take the snake to the Zoo and see if they would take it into the Reptile House. It was the first time that we had seen an anaconda and we were fascinated by its size. Someone guessed that it probably weighed about three hundred pounds. We would have stayed there to await the removal of the snake, but Hayden reminded us that we should get going as we had to shower and change for the party at Leon's place. With a last look at the anaconda, we turned and retraced our step back to our home to get ready.

As we got back to the apartment, Gerry raced ahead excitedly eager to tell everyone about the anaconda. He blurted out the recount and marveled at how big it was. When he got to the part about it not being dead, I think he freaked out my mother for she launched into a tirade about danger and what if the snake came back to life. Her admonitions were maternal and natural, so my father intervened and said that we were smart and would not have put ourselves in danger. To placate her even more, he hustled us off to get showered and to change our clothes, as much to get us going as to get us out of the way and to calm her. It didn't take us long to shower and change and in half an hour everyone was ready. We locked up the apartment and started our stroll over to Leon's house. It was still light out as the sun had not as yet set, but there were long shadows cast from the west. We made our way past the old shop as Gerry pointed out where the anaconda had laid upon the sand, and directed our steps through the small thicket of almond trees until we came upon the house where Leon and his family were staying.

We walked along the side of the house to the front porch that faced the ocean. The party was in full swing as we heard lots of talking, laughing and music. As we approached from the side, Leon's brother Charles, loudly hailed out my father and came out to embrace him and my mother. Introductions to the rest of the adults and the children were made and we were invited to join them on the porch. At the front of their house, there was a huge yard with coconut trees and a short picket fence all around. In the middle of the yard there was a circular concrete table with concrete benches set around it. As the party was mainly on the porch, the children set up ourselves at the concrete table. The sun had started to set and the light was dimmer. Leon came out and brought 2 small galvanize buckets with citronella oil and lit those around the table. He had similarly lit a few around the porch. Then Roy and Charles came out with armfuls of bottles which we made out to be flambeaux. They placed the flambeaux randomly around the walkway and the yard.

Suddenly the placed seemed much brighter and the scent of the citronella oil lent a very cozy atmosphere. Some of the flambeaux were near enough to us so that we felt some of the warmth emanating from the flame that felt good in the open evening air.

To pass the time, we had brought our cards and we started a game of go-to-pack which Sherry and Gerry could play as well. Mummy brought out a plate of saltfish accra and a bowl of channa for us to nibble on. As night fell, we grew bored of the card game and got up from the table. I walked to the fence at the bottom of the yard. There was a gate which opened to the beach. I leaned on the fence, looked upwards and was amazed at the sight in the heavens. As we had left the light of the flambeaux, we were in the dark of the night and as it was a clear cloudless night, millions of stars were visible. This never ceased to fascinate me. I was joined by the other boys who told me that Sherry and Gerry had gone into the house. As our eyes had grown accustomed to the dark by now, we surveyed the wide vista before us. The heavens, the stars, the gentle waves, the hissing of the foam, the dull lights of the oil platforms that lit the horizon and the utter peace of the moment lulled me into silence. I was snapped out of my reverie my Ronald chattering away on my right about being hungry and wondering when we would eat. He had two handfuls of channa with him which he shared with us. The peppery channa brought me back to reality and accentuated my own hunger. As if on cue, we heard my father calling to us to come inside. It was time to eat.

Without hesitation, we scampered back to the house hoping for a wonderful repast. We were not disappointed. Charles and his wife had prepared a lavish spread. For the main feature, there was breadfruit oil down with saltfish and pigtail steamed in coconut milk and covered with young dasheen leaves. There was also a huge platter of fried fish with bake. This was going to be a treat. The good thing about still being a child was that we were served first. We lined up with our plates and Charles dished out generous helpings of oil down. After I was served the oil down, I made my way to the buffet, took a piece of fried fish and bake, added some pepper sauce and ketchup, and then made my way back out to the concrete table outside. All the porch lights were on by this time and the flambeaux added to the ambience. Sherry and Gerry stayed inside at the dining table. Kelvin and Radica joined the three boys outside. It was a delicious savoury meal.

When we had finished eating and had returned the dishes to the kitchen, we were about to decide what to do to pass the time when we heard loud guffaws of laughter coming from the porch and Errol's raised voice. There was the sound of a shac-shac or otherwise known as maracas. In glee we rushed to the porch to discover that there was about to be a sing along. Leon and Charles had a cuatro and shac-shacs, Errol had a wooden toc-toc instrument. This was going to be fantastic. I loved these sing alongs and I knew almost all the words to most of the calypsoes and songs that they usually belted out. On cue to Errol's beat, the cuatro started to strum and we started with Sparrow's classic "Jean and Dinah." Everyone from inside the house came out to the porch and we all squeezed in and around the musicians. This sing along was usually a medley of calypsoes from years gone by that had become classics.

As we got to the end of *Jean and Dinah* they flowed into *Melda, My pussin, Ah woman in jail, Chicken Chest, Fire Fire, Ah Going Dong San Fernando* and others. To end off the medley, the classic *Last Train to San Fernando* was belted out and everyone lustily lent their voices to the chorus. Applause erupted at the end of the set and every face bore a broad groin and smile. Neighbours, friends and families all here together, enjoying good food, good company with pure joy in the moment of time. To end off the night, Errol and Leon started a *Santimanitay* extempo. The more lyrically minded were encouraged to take the floor and extemporize to the well-known strains of the beat. Hayden was the first on the floor and he sang about a "fella named

Kelvin Ramdass." As soon as he started with that, huge laughter erupted. Hayden's rhymes and extempo were brilliant and we clapped him on his back when he was done.

After the last set, it was time to go home and reluctantly we bid everyone goodbye, thanked our hosts, hugged Errol and Janet and started to make our way back to our place. Roy and Kelvin had torches so that we could see the path through the track. As we walked, Roy was apparently still in a jolly mood and he started to sing *The Big Bamboo*. At once I chimed in and we had a fun roving band of impromptu minstrels making our way back home. I parked this night into my memory and felt a warmth envelop me as I looked around at my family and loved ones. As we turned into our driveway and opened the apartment, I could not help smiling and feeling contented. As we prepared for bed and before turning in, I went to my mother and father and hugged them tightly, kissed their cheeks and went to bed.

Chapter 14

The Final Week: A Bittersweet Departure

The next few days brought with them the reality that soon our holidays would come to an end and it would be time to pack and return to Tunapuna. After breakfast one morning, we were just lazing around the table not doing anything in particular. I still had my cup of cocoa and took it with me outside and sat on the bench. The others, Hayden and Ronald, followed me and wondered if I was alright. I just smiled and said yes. But there was something I wanted to share with them. Looking around and satisfied that no one else was about, I told them that while I felt happy, there was a sadness in the pit of my stomach that I could not properly explain. I tried to explain that to me the pending return home would mean that this time would be over and that I would never be able to recapture it. In my youthful innocence, that was the only way I could explain it. Maybe inside of me there was a subcutaneous romantic budding, and it would be a feeling that would always linger with me for the rest of my life.

With the final week of holidays already counting down, I had an urge to do everything that we could possibly do and not waste a moment of the day. Somehow I felt that I had to create memories and make them last. I think it was at this time of my life that I started to take note of minute details of events around me, process them and store them away. I never knew back then that one day I would be able to unlock that vault and call upon these archives with such vivid recollection. To me back then, it was about making the most of each day and doing everything with gusto.

The morning ritual of going to Mr. James' shop for bread and newspapers took on a renewed sense of deliberation. From the tactile sensations of the fine sand and prickly coconut flowers on the warm asphalt to the olfactory sensations tantalized by the muskiness of the almond trees, mixed with the discernable salty air, the walk to the shop had a new perspective. I felt that I needed to observe everything, remember everything and recollect everything. I touched the bags of sugar and flour stacked on the ground in the shop and felt the coarse fibres of the crocus bags. The cacophony of sounds was harmonious to my ear as I heard Mr. James' voice with its pleasant lilt taking orders, the raspy bark of a fisherman ordering his breakfast, the shrill laughter of a woman exchanging gossip with another, the sound of the glass case being knocked accidentally by an enthusiastic boy. I sniffed the air and smelled the aroma of strong coffee and salami, of beer and rum coming from the other side of the shop.

Mr. James snapped me out of my reverie as he smiled and called to me asking if I wanted the usual. That made me smile. Mr. James knew what my usual was. As insignificant as that may seem, somehow it had a profound impression on me. I was someone and Mr. James knew me and he knew what I wanted. I smiled back, nodded and paid for my purchases. As I was about to turn to leave, he stopped me and told me I could take something from one of the candy jars. I reached in and took a choco-mint, thanked him and walked out. I looked at the sand in front of the shop strewn with old crown corks pressed into the compact sand from the thousands of feet that trampled them and I smiled as I made my way back to Gill Street.

As I approached the apartment, I could see everything going on inside as the shutters were propped open. The table had been laid and a tantalizing aroma emanated from the kitchen. I handed the bread to my mother and the newspapers to my father. As I passed the table to go outside to wait until breakfast was ready, I stopped and looked at the orange and green jugs on the table. I reached my hand out and touched them and felt the heat from the hot beverages they held. I marveled at how long these jugs had been in the family and how many meals they served us. They were part of these trips and these memories and any other jugs would have seemed out of place. They were familiar and somehow that made me feel good. We did not have to wait much longer as breakfast was ready and we were called to the table. Fried fish and buttered slices of bread were in abundance on the table accompanied by steaming hot cocoa and tea. As I served myself I could not help but remark aloud about the miracle of the loaves and fishes and drew an analogy to my parents providing sustenance and nourishment for our bodies just as the miracle provided nourishment for our souls. I must have struck a chord with that observation as my mother looked at me with piercing eyes and she smiled at me. It was a private moment between she and I and I knew that one day I would call upon the memory of that smile to sustain me.

The daily routines of swimming, playing cricket and football, going for walks along the beach and exploring our surroundings took on a new perspective and importance. Usually while walking along the beach to get to the seine, I used to jump into and splash the shallow pools left behind by the receding tide. But now as we walked along the beach, I looked at these shallow pools differently and they revealed a new marvel to me. I watched as the little fish darted around these tiny pools and the way the sun caused the ripples to reflect on the sandy bottom caught my attention with a pronounced curiosity. I touched the sand and the water was amazingly warm to the skin. I stared as a chip chip burrowed its way into the sand with one air bubble left to pop as it submerged itself into the safety of the brown sand. I found myself taking time to notice little things that I had taken for granted before. I gently picked up a fragile sand dollar and felt the smooth but yet coarse shell then gently placed it back into the pool. As we walked at the water's edge, when I stepped forward, I noticed how the sand yielded to the pressure of my weight and pressed the water away from my footstep, but as I glanced back to where I had stepped before, I saw my footprint and that the water had flowed back and settled into the imprint on the sand that I had left. As I look back on that I cannot help but draw an analogy to our own footsteps that we take in life with each imprint that we leave being an impression on something or someone.

As I looked upon the coordinated precise actions of pulling the seine, it metamorphosed into a living organism, a community. The leader provided the guidance to the others. The workers knew the objective and goal. The fish was ancillary to the process. The unison with which they worked, the taut muscles that hauled the nets, the cadence with which they moved, each knowing what part they played in the process, these all brought the seine to life for me. The fish was the prize and even then as I held a carite in my hand, looking at it wriggling, the dominion of Man over the Earth came to the fore as I recollected my Sunday School teachings. The nets and ropes that had been hauled to the beach lay like an extended lazy serpent. The discarded sapatay fish still glistened with moisture that attracted the intent gaze of the corbeaux perched atop the coconut trees waiting for the humans to disperse before they would swoop down to commence their feast. The fish vendors who had come to purchase the catch had gone and the only evidence of their presence were the tire tracks of their vans that left a deep imprint on the sand from where they had driven off. As I left the seine and we made our way home, I glanced back to look at it one more time and locked that memory away.

The next few days went by and we found ourselves doing much the same that we had been doing all holiday long. But the repetition was not monotonous for each brought some new perspective for me. Catching crabs at the river was one of the most indelible memories I kept. It was not just about the crab, but the location and the setting. That old coconut tree that leaned and curved over the water was iconic. I can close my eyes and remember the colour of the water, the feel of the sand on the bank, the crackle of the dried coconut branches as we walked over them, the warmth of the river water, the channel that the water cut through the sand as it flowed out to the sea, and it seems that I was just there.

On one of our walks along the beach, I stopped to touch the old tree that had been washed up on the sand for what must have been years. I never knew the origin of that tree, but we all guessed that it came from Venezuela carried on the tides by the mighty Orinoco and the current of the Atlantic and finally brought to rest on our beach. The wood was bleached by the sun, but there was still a heady scent around it. As I touched the wood, I noticed tiny holes or pores that must have been caused by insects that once lived in the bark. I pressed my nose to the wood and inhaled and was marveled at the mild musky scent. Perhaps I expected it to be stronger. As I looked at and touched the tree, I imagined it being tossed on the waves on the turbulent passage between the mainland and its final resting place. I climbed onto it, held onto one of the broken roots that jutted out, rubbed my sandy feet against the wood, and then I clambered down. I glanced at it again as we walked home and wished that I had a camera to capture it.

One afternoon we decided to take our last walk out to the Junction. It was not that we needed anything in particular, but moreso for the social and recollective opportunity to do this as a family before we left. Over the past few weeks, we had rediscovered the simple pleasure of leisurely walks. As we set out, I focused on the journey rather than the destination. Every landmark along the way was looked upon with captive eyes, from the Co-operative, the bar, the football field, the police station, the junction and the market. Kelvin pointed out the bench at the hospital where he sat while Radica was being attending to a few weeks ago when she was stung by the jellyfish. I pointed out the taxi stand where we had met Jagdeo who drove us to and from

Tunapuna for my mother's doctor's appointment. The rusted ice bin outside the Chinese shop for some reason caught my eye and I went up to it and pressed a rusty spot that had started to flake. I rubbed the small fragments between my fingers and was surprised at how easily it disintegrated. Even metal was not indestructible. I dusted the fragments from my fingers and brought them to my nose and sniffed at the ferrous scent left there. Meanwhile my father had gone across the road to where a vendor had a fairly large stall set up. It was a lady selling roti.

    She was new to the area as we had never seen her there before on our previous trips to the Junction. Just like back in St. James in Port-of-Spain, she had her stall fully set up to make fresh hot roti. There was goat, beef, chicken and conch. My father asked a redundant question if we wanted roti for dinner as we all chimed yes in unison. The lady was happy as this was going to be a big sale for her as she took the orders for the ten roti. I wanted to try the conch roti as I had never had it before. With a warning that it will take her a while to prepare all the roti, she set about her task. To pass the time, Roy offered us dessert before dinner, much to the chagrin of my mother who eventually conceded to him. We crossed over the road to the shop and he purchased Mr. Big and Screwball ice cream for everyone. I peeled back my cone and dived into the nuts and chocolate at the top. Every bite and lick was savoured as we sat on the concrete steps eating our treat. The sun was lower in the sky and we knew that in about half hour it would set. But there was no anxiety to get back home. Another twenty-five minutes and the lady called to us that the food was ready. She had put each order in its own brown bag with a paper napkin and the order written on the bag. I looked at mine that said conch slight pepper, brought it up to my nose and sniffed in delight at the savoury odour. We thanked her and set off for home as the last rays of the sun disappeared.

    The street lights along the Plaisance Road had come on and they lit our way along the sidewalk. As we came upon the row of houses after the Co-operative, we saw lights on in all of them and we could see people moving and going about their business. I heard a familiar sound and knew instantly that someone was cooking curry as the wind carried the tantalizing aroma of the spices that hit our noses. In another house, a family sat on the front porch with a radio playing some music. As we passed them, they waved and called out goodnight to us. We cheerily waved back to them even though we did not know them. Pretty soon we came upon Mr. James' shop and saw that it was crowded as usual. I glanced to my left and saw a light on in Peter's hovel and wondered what he might be doing. Before turning onto Gill Street, I stopped at the intersection with Plaisance Road and looked out at the ocean. I stood there for a moment, closed my eyes, then turned around and looked back in the direction of the Junction from where we had come. I could make out the crown of the hill. I smiled to myself and turned to join the others. Very soon we were home and after washing our hands, we all sat around the table and opened up our brown bags and delved into our roti for our dinner. I was glad that I tried something new by ordering the conch. It was delicious. We finished our meal, spent the rest of the evening outside on the benches with the lit flambeaux, and then turned in for the night.

  The next few days seemed to go by in a blur. Time always seemed to speed up at the end of the holidays, just when you wanted it to slow down. We went to the seine every morning, not so much for the fish, but moreso for the experience and to etch them into memory. We visited all the old places we had been accustomed to. We even went back for another visit to the Moore house. This time it did not hold as much trepidation for us as before. Somehow the light seemed to penetrate the trees a bit more and the light seemed to dissipate the aura of mystery about it. But for the most part, we spent most of our time in the water swimming. It was as if we needed to swim and splash in the salty brine to store up the feeling for the next year until we would be back. The weather was beautiful each day with blue skies dotted with small white puffy clouds and the sun drenching us with its warmth. The water felt heavenly as it cooled us. I looked at my father as he floated in the water and I thanked him in my mind for choosing Mayaro as the place for our annual vacation these past few years. I felt so happy when I was here. I was close to my family, but on these holidays, it seemed to bring us closer. I did not say it to him, I only thought about it.

As we sat at the breakfast table the penultimate morning, there was a silence and gloom in the air. Always the one to sense our feelings, Radica sat with us and asked us why we were so glum. The departure and the end of the holidays was our response. Then she too said that she felt the same way, and that all the adults also felt the same way. It was always sad to leave a place and time where one was happy. But all good things did come to an end. However, if we held on to the memories, we would keep them alive with us regardless of where we were and how much time had passed. She added that it was true not only for the memories of our holidays, but also of all whom we loved. I did not know why at the time, but those words from Radica stayed with me all my life. Sensing our gloom as well, my mother came over to the table and spoke to us. She told us that we still had almost two full days and that we would make the most of them. But first she wanted us to organize our things, pack our bags and leave out just what we needed until the next day, and the quicker we got that done, the more time we could spend outdoors on the beach and in the water.

In no time at all, we accomplished packing and sorting out our belongings. Changed into our beach wear, we took the cricket and football gear and went down to the beach. Gerry had a pail and shovel and said he was going to build the biggest sandcastle ever. The tide was out and a wide swath of beach was left behind. I saw Gerry start to dig a hole and asked him if that was where he was going to build it. When he said yes, I told him it was too near the water's edge for when the tide turned, it would destroy the sandcastle.

He looked puzzled so I showed him a spot higher up on the beach and explained that eventually the water would get to the castle, but if he did it here, it would last longer. He looked up at me and said he wanted to build a really big sandcastle and asked if I would help him. I wanted to play cricket with Hayden and Ronald, but I looked at him and thought that he too, by building this sandcastle, was probably building his own memories and that maybe he wanted me to be a part of it. I looked at him and said that I would help. I called to the others and told them to come and help Gerry build his sandcastle.

At first they did not want to, but I begged them to come and help. Eventually they gave in and came over. We all agreed that it was a good spot. I saw them about to take over the project, so I stopped them and asked Gerry how did he want to build it. He explained and tried to draw his idea on the sand. Hayden caught on to what I was doing and piped in with an idea of his own and asked Gerry what he thought. Gerry smiled and said yes. I felt warm, this was good, I was helping my brother to make his own memory and we would all be a part of it.

We had to go back to the apartment to get two proper buckets to bring water and wet sand so that we could mold and shape the castle. Sherry set about with Ronald looking for green branches, sea balls, old sticks, shells and any interesting flotsam that they could use to decorate the castle. Hayden helped Gerry to fill the larger bucket with moist sand, pack it tightly in and then invert the bucket, tap it and remove it to leave behind castle structures. Using the smaller pail, they added levels to the structures and soon the castle took shape. We used the bucket of water to moisten the structure and thereby further compact the sand and strengthen it. Using our hands, we cupped handfuls of water to do so and to smooth out the rough patches. We used an old stick to carve out the turrets. Gerry took some of the shells and placed them for windows. A strip of coconut branch was placed at the top for a flag. A moat was dug around the castle and a series of sticks placed together built a bridge over the moat. We compacted the moat and brought buckets of water to fill it. When the sand was saturated, it started to fill up. Gerry was delighted with his sandcastle and called to everyone to come and see it. I remember the sheer joy in his voice and the sparkle in his eyes as he proudly showed off his sandcastle to the adults. He was so happy that day.

The effort to build the sandcastle had left us hot so we eagerly took to the water to cool off. Our skin seemed to sizzle as our hot bodies hit the cool water of the Atlantic Ocean. The water was clear and felt heavenly. We must have swum for about two hours when my parents made their way back to the beach carrying a tray. It was a picnic lunch with cold drinks. They had made corned beef sandwiches and there was ice cold orange juice. They made us rinse the sand of our hands and shake them dry. We sat under the shade of some coconut trees as they passed out the sandwiches and cups of juice. The picnic was delicious. There were two large bars of Cadbury chocolates which my mother broke and shared among everyone. It was the one with fruit and nuts which I loved. I held the last piece between my fingers to let it melt and then sucked the chocolate in delight from my fingers.

After lunch we had to take a short rest to relax and allow the food to digest before we went back into the water. I found a nice sandy spot against an old tree and lay back to rest a bit. The canopy of coconut branches overhead blocked the direct sun from my eyes and I closed them for a bit. I did not sleep, but rather rested them and listened to the sounds around me. From the murmur of conversations by the others, to the hiss of the foam, the breaking of the waves, the rustle of the branches, the call of a seagull, the gentle wind blowing, I listened with my eyes closed, and I smiled.

We spent the rest of that day in the water and on the beach until it was almost sunset. This was our last evening in Mayaro and we wanted it to last. As we traced our steps back to the apartment, we made our way to the concrete deck and the outdoor showers. The cool fresh water cascaded over my head and erased the salt from my lips. The trees around us rustled in the breeze. When I was finished with my shower, I stood on the deck with my towel wrapped around me and with one sweeping glance, I took a snapshot of everything in my periphery. Slowly I returned to the apartment and quickly changed into my dry things. When I had changed, I joined the rest of the kids at the table. They had started a game of dominoes and I waited to join in. Roy had lit the mosquito coils and placed them around the room. I can sit here now and remember how comforted I felt by the aroma of those smouldering coils.

There was a familiar odour coming from the kitchen and we looked forward to dinner. Mummy and Radica prepared fried fish for dinner, and it should not have been otherwise. An enormous platter of fried fish was put onto the table alongside a platter of bread and butter. It was simple but so delicious. I thought to myself that our first dinner when we arrived five weeks ago was the same dinner that we were having on our last night five weeks later. That made me smile. After the meal, in almost a ritualistic way, we all made our way to the back of the bedrooms and sat on the benches outside. The flambeaux were again lit for the last time and we enjoyed the night air and salty breeze coming off the ocean. We must have stayed there until just past midnight as we prolonged our last night in Mayaro.

The next morning, my father roused us from our sleep telling us that we did not want to dawdle on our last day. He urged us to get a move on with our toiletries as we had just a few hours until departure. As I heard that word, I felt a pit in my stomach and a feeling of anxiety overcame me. I did not want to leave, not yet. I had been so happy these past five weeks, with my parents, my siblings and my family, and I did not want this to end. I my mind I knew that we always got along and that returning to Tunapuna would not change our relationships, but here in Mayaro, it was different, it was special. I had observed my father and my mother these past few weeks and I saw them like I had never seen them before. They were at peace, they were relaxed, and they were content. As I sit here, I wish that I could recapture that feeling that they had during that time, that I could find that formula and apply it to my own life. As we went about our chores packing up all our belongings and securing all the boxes, I found out that Selwyn and Chestnut would be here by eleven o'clock and the plan was to get going by two o'clock. A two-hour journey should get us home by four in the afternoon with enough time to get unpacked before dusk. There would be time for one more swim in the ocean.

Punctual as ever, Selwyn rolled into the driveway and honked his horn just as we had finished arranging the boxes and bags into a neat pile near the doorway. A few minutes later, Chestnut arrived and brought out a small box for my mother. His wife sent aloo pies, saheena and kachourie for our lunch. This apparently had been pre-arranged. Both Selwyn and Chestnut wanted to take a dip in the ocean and we all changed and went down to the beach. Perhaps Mother Nature knew we were leaving and in her way of bidding us farewell, bestowed a beautiful blue sky, warm crystal clear water and gentle waves. It was perfect and I thought to myself what an appropriate way to say goodbye to Mayaro.

I stood up in the water, looked down the beach and took in all the vistas. The long line of brown trunks and green canopies of the coconut trees stretched all the way to the horizon to my left. At the end of that view, would be Point Galeota. I looked to my right and followed the shoreline all the way to Point Radix and could just about make out some spray from waves that crashed upon the rocks there. Most of the boats had already been back from the seines and I saw Peter's boat safely upon the shore. I was snapped out of my reverie by a call from my father that we had to get rinsed and changed. I closed my eyes for a moment, ducked under a lumbering wave, felt it break and cascade over me as if to wash me one last time, and I made my way out of the water. A quick shower and change and we were once again at the table.

Lloyd was there when I came out of the room. He had come to check on the apartment before we left. As he was chatting with my parents, Peter's whistle came to our ears and we jumped up to greet him. He had brought a parcel with him and handed it to my mother. It was his way of saying goodbye, with fish. Mummy bade everyone find a seat as she and Radica opened the box sent by Chestnut's wife and served a quick lunch. The Indian delicacies were very savoury and delicious. While we were eating, my mother called for everyone's attention as she wanted to say something. We were curious and sat in anticipation. She announced that she and my father had extended an invitation to Peter to come and spend Christmas holidays in Tunapuna with us and that Peter had accepted. What fantastic news this was. The anxiety of our pending departure was replaced by sheer delight. Peter smiled and said that he very much looked forward to being with us. At once he was bombarded with offers to take him to a parang, to midnight mass, to meeting our family. He would come and spend two weeks with us and would be there the day school closed for the Christmas holidays. Now we had something else to look forward to. That news put everyone in a good mood and in a way it made the anxiety of leaving Mayaro less sad.

Pretty soon we loaded up the cars and it was time to say goodbye to Lloyd and Peter. Lloyd shook hands with the adults and patted each of us on our backs with a warning to pay attention in school and to study hard. My father handed him a small envelope which contained some cash, a small token from our family, for him having taken care of us yet another year. Peter hugged everyone and his raspy voice sounded happy when he said he will see us in December. I noticed that his eyes glistened with moisture and guessed that he was also overcome with emotion. We climbed aboard the cars and with what seemed like an anti-climatic honk of the horns, we pulled out of the driveway onto Gill Street and we said goodbye to the beach house. Slowly we lumbered out of Gill Street and turned left onto Plaisance Road. With a final glance at Mr. James' shop, the cars picked up speed as we motored towards the junction. As we passed the football field and the junction came closer, I glanced back one last time down Plaisance road and kept my gaze there until the black asphalt that met the brown sand and the blue ocean disappeared from my view and I silently said goodbye to Mayaro.

    The journey home was silent. I guess everyone was deep in their own thoughts. The windows of the car were open and there was a cooling breeze coming in. I sat back on the seat and closed my eyes. Ronald called to me to look at the ocean and the coconut trees before we left Manzanilla and before it disappeared from view. But I smiled and said no thanks. As we made our way back to Tunapuna, I sat back on my seat with the breeze hitting my face and the car rumbling on. With my eyes closed I pressed the play button in my mind and replayed the last five weeks in Mayaro in my mind and I smiled as I fell asleep.

Chapter 15

Going Back as an Adult

I must have dozed off amid the images of the blue waters of the Atlantic Ocean, the long brown stretches of sandy beaches, the coconut fringed shoreline and the smell of the salty air. I was roused out of my sleep as I heard the voice over the loudspeaker announce Exhibition as our next stop as the GO Train out of Toronto slowed at its first stop before my destination at Oakville. Satisfied it was not my stop, I closed my eyes once more, left my new home in Canada, felt the rumble and shake of the wheels of the train over the tracks, and drifted back to sleep again to continue my time in Mayaro.

      I felt another rumble and shake, but this time it was my car that hit a pothole as the shocks of the car tried to absorb the impact. The roads in Curepe were terrible and badly in need of repair. We were on our way to my mother-in-law's house in Ramgoolie Street to plan our trip to Mayaro. I had been married to Vashti in nineteen ninety-five and three years later, after jobs in Dominica, Nevis and Montego Bay, she and I had decided to migrate to Canada. It was a sad decision for both families and we knew it would be especially difficult for them. My brother-in-law Ahamad and I had a close relationship and we talked about doing something special before Vashti and I left Trinidad for Canada. Vashti's eldest sister was Kamini and Ahamad was her husband. Without hesitation, I told Ahamad that I would dearly love to go to Mayaro to spend a few days there as it always held a special place in my heart and my memories. Ahamad set about it immediately and used his contacts to find a few houses in Mayaro. We would be going to Mayaro for five days and I was thrilled.

  I had not been to Mayaro to spend time in a beach house since I was a child. The last time I was there was back in nineteen seventy-five. Twenty years later, here I was, planning a trip once more, but this time, I was no longer a child. I was a man, I was married and I was part of a new family with my in-laws. My parents and family had continued going to Mayaro over the years, but without me. I studied at a university abroad and then worked overseas and so I missed several years with them. I asked my parents to come with us on this trip to Mayaro with my in-laws. My father and mother sat with me and told me that it was now my turn as an adult to make my own memories with my new family. It was sad for me to hear this from my parents, but I understood what they meant. In a way, they were preparing themselves for my eventual departure from Trinidad and I knew they were torn inside. With a heavy heart, I accepted their decision and turned to planning the trip with Ahamad.

  It had been so many years since I had been to Mayaro and I knew Ahamad was equally excited about it. He called me and told me that he wanted us to take a drive down to Mayaro to see a house in Church Road. Without hesitating, I agreed and he picked me up and we set off. The trip was just as I had remembered. Most of the familiar landmarks were still there. We stopped at the Ponderosa and this time, instead of a coke, I had a beer, and then we set off down the Stretch. I was happy to see the old and the familiar and recognized some of the changes along the way. The Seaway Bakery was still there and as we neared Manzanilla, I secretly hoped nothing else would have changed. We came upon First and Last and I smiled as it was just as I had remembered it. I wanted to stop there for a moment so Ahamad obliged. We got out of the vehicle and I walked around and went into the shop for a moment. As I came out, I looked around and in my mind I saw Errol Pena's old Vauxhall with my father, Robert and I getting bread and going back to the car to head back to Coconut Sands. I smiled again. I told Ahamad thank you for stopping and we continued our journey. As we pulled out, I glanced back in the side mirror as First and Last receded from view and I could see the dwarf of a boy that I was back then, standing and looking out towards the ocean.

I felt transported back into time, as though the years had been stripped away and I was a mere lad once more as the Atlantic Ocean came into view. Even though I was sitting next to Ahamad in the vehicle, I was riding in Selwyn Tinto's car with my siblings, my cousins and my uncle Kelvin. At the sight of the Atlantic Ocean and Manzanilla Bay, I felt the same joyful leap of my heart that I felt back then as a boy and it lifted my spirit one more time. I was silently grateful that Ahamad was not chatty as I relived this moment privately in my mind. I guess that he too may have been reliving his own memories as well. As we drove through The Coconut, I noticed that there was a lot more sunlight and suddenly I realized that it had changed. The vaulted arch of the coconut trees that I remembered was no longer there. A few rows of trees on either side of the road had been cut and removed so the previous canopy of green leaves was gone. I was disappointed in this new vista as I remembered the cool shade of the brown and green tunnel of my childhood when last I was here. I made a remark to Ahamad and he confessed that he too was annoyed that the beauty of the drive was spoilt.

As we drove on, I asked him to slow down as we approached where I remembered the Coconut Sands beach house to be. But it was no longer there. It had been neglected and had fallen into ruins with only an old column remaining. I was silent. A bit further on, we came upon the Spring Bridge and there was a pleasant surprise. I guess that because my memory of the Spring Bridge was one of trepidation, the sight of a shiny new sturdy metal bridge was a relief. As we drove into Mayaro, I looked at the time and asked Ahamad if we could make a slight detour to Plaisance Village before we went to Church Road. He agreed and as we came to the Junction and made the slight left turn, I saw the black asphalt road run straight down and stop at the brown of the sand that fringed the blue of the Ocean. It was as I had remembered and I was glad.

The football field and pavilion was still there. There were more houses, and they seemed bigger and grander than I remembered. My pulse raced a bit as we drove down the road and I saw up ahead on the right the old green building that was Mr. James' shop. It was open and there was a buzz of activity there. To the left where Peter's old shack was, there now stood several small concrete houses. The old Chinese shop was gone, totally demolished, with a vacant piece of land there. I glanced to my right and saw the sign for Gill Street against the familiar green and white background. We turned into Gill Street and I asked Ahamad to stop. It had changed. The old grey Thackories Beach House was no longer there. The green Assee's flats were no longer there. The grove of almond trees had also disappeared. I drank this view in from the top of Gill Street and I could go no further. I asked Ahamad to turn around and we left for Church Road. The changes had been too much for me. I can't say if I expected everything to have been untouched by the years, but it was not as I had remembered and I did not want the present reality to ruin the precious memories of my childhood past.

Ahamad sensed that I was disappointed and I was thankful that he did not talk about it. Not wanting my disappointment to ruin the trip for us and our upcoming vacation, I turned my attention back to the approaching Junction as we drove up Plaisance Road. The Junction brought a smile to my face and changed my mood. There was change here, but for the most part, it was just as I remembered. The market took centre stage. With this fleeting glance as we drove by and turned onto the Guayaguayare Road, I was buoyed and knew that soon I would be here, walking about in the market and retracing my childhood steps. We drove past Lee Ha's Private Road and I wondered if Alloy's family was still there. Things had changed in Mayaro from when we vacationed there as a child. I was disappointed, but I accepted it and I was grateful for the memories that I had. Now I had a new life and a new extended family. I silently thanked my parents for creating those memories, to enable me to glance back and remember with fondness. But now it was time to look forward and I set my eyes on the road ahead as we approached Church Road and my new destination in Mayaro.

    We turned into Church Road and were driving along when I spotted a gentleman walking along the road. It was Joseph Philbert. I was secretly hoping that I would see him as I knew he lived on Church Road. Philbert was one of my crew when we worked together in French Guiana building the launch complex for the Ariane 5 Rockets used by the European Space Agency. I hailed out Philbert as Ahamad stopped the vehicle. I jumped out and Philbert and I hugged each other in a genuine embrace. It had been a few years since our project together in South America and the last time I saw him was on the Methanol Plant that we were building in Point Lisas. We quickly caught up on the gap in time and Philbert pointed out his house to me as he made me promise to come see him when we came down with the family. We shook hands as he departed and Ahamad and I continued the short drive to the house we had come to see. We passed the old Church on the right and turned into the private road on the left that led to the house.

    It was a huge two storey house. On the lower level, there was a sitting and dining room, a big kitchen, washrooms and a smaller porch facing the ocean. On the upper level, there were five bedrooms, a smaller kitchen with a microwave, another sitting area and an enormous porch also facing the ocean. As Ahamad and I walked around, we both said it was perfect. It was clean, well-appointed and would easily hold the twenty odd persons expected for the trip. Our mission was accomplished and we felt elated as we spoke to the agent who was there to show us around. With so many people coming to spend the short holiday, Ahamad and I thought that it would be a good idea to have someone come and help with cooking and cleaning. We spoke to the agent who said he had someone that he would highly recommend and we agreed then and there to hire that person. It was going to be a five-day holiday starting on the Friday one week away. Time could not come fast enough and the wait would be interminable. With all the arrangements made, the date set, the help hired and the deposit paid, we made our way back to the car for the drive back to Curepe. Eager faces awaited our arrival, anxious to know if we had found a house. Our thumbs up sign caused quite a few squeals of excitement. We had under a week to complete the preparation for our sojourn out to the East Coast and the embrace of Mayaro.

My sister-in-law Kamini and I sat down and started to plan out the logistics. We started with the headcount to finalize the number of people. We then allocated families to the five bedrooms. Next we made a list of the items we would need to take with us. Feeding twenty odd people three meals plus snacks and drinks per day for five days required the skill of a quartermaster. We planned out the main menus for lunch and dinner and then made out a shopping list for the grocery and market. My brothers-in-law, Raj and Rennie were drafted to do the shopping over the next few days. Each family was charged with the responsibility for their own transport, linens and toiletries. The helper we had hired was named Ms. Dorothy. Ahamad chimed in that he would invite his handyman Franklin with us as he could also help Ms. Dorothy with the daily tasks of looking after the kitchen and the house. Over a cup of coffee, I told Kamini that the agent who we had met told us that there were seines but the bounty was less and almost everything was sold to the restaurants and hotels. As such, that left very little for foraging like in the old days as I remembered. I was adamant though that our first breakfast should be fried fish. So to ensure that we had what I desired, we agreed to purchase some before we left Curepe. I smiled at the irony in buying fish in the Tunapuna market that probably came from Mayaro, to take to Mayaro with us so that we could have breakfast in Mayaro on our first morning. But better safe than sorry.

Vashti and I tried once more to convince my parents to come with us, but it was in vain. We sat on the porch at my house with them and I told them about my recent trip with Ahamad and about the changes I had seen especially on Gill Street. My father told me that he too saw the gradual changes over the years each time he went there, but it was inevitable. Maybe my memories of Mayaro vacations as a child were so innocent and pure that it was the ideal and I could picture it no other way. I did not invite Sherry and Gerry to go with us. Gerry and his wife Alicia had just been blessed with a baby girl, Gerarda, and I knew they would not go. Sherry and her husband Rudy were flying out to St. Lucia that same weekend. As we sat talking with my parents, I looked upon their faces and I saw sadness etched in their brows. I knew this was hard for them. After high school, I left Trinidad for three years to attend the University of The West Indies at the Cavehill Campus in Barbados and I spent five years working overseas. So there was a gap of eight years that we missed with each other. That gap could never be recovered and with my pending permanent departure from Trinidad for Canada, it was tearing us up inside. My mother sensed my angst, buried her own, and told me to take the memories that we had made together and use it to build my own family. I knew it took all her strength to say those words to me and I will always remember them.

Friday morning soon came and it was the day of departure for our trip to Mayaro. I wanted to set out early before sunrise so that we could drive through The Coconut in the early morning, but most of the others had to work and would be coming later in the evening. As it turned out, Kamini, Ahamad and their family would leave with Vashti and I in the early afternoon and get there ahead of the rest. Ahamad had a huge all-wheel drive jeep with lots of cargo space at the back. He and I agreed that I would leave my car at home and take the jeep instead as it would take a lot of the load we were carrying with us. I was up early and had coffee with my parents sitting in the gallery. It was a beautiful morning and the hills of the Northern Range in the backdrop were brilliantly verdant against the clear blue sky and I could see the buildings of the Abbey at Mount Saint Benedict. A kiskedee flew down, perched on the electrical wire and whistled his song.

It was still cool in the morning air and my mother pulled her robe closer for warmth. Vashti was up and made grilled cheese sandwiches which she brought out in the gallery and we had breakfast there. As we ate, we chatted about the trip later that day. I told my parents about the plans and my father joked about the huge number of people going. When we used to go, there would be ten of us for five weeks. This time it would be twenty odd people for five days. We spent the rest of the morning sipping coffee and reminiscing fondly about our past holidays. I tried once more to get them to go with us but to no avail. I accepted that this was now my time and they were letting me go. As we packed the vehicle with our stuff, my mother brought a fruit cake packed in an old cookie tin and told me to give it to Ahamad. She and my father came downstairs to see us off. We hugged, said our goodbyes and waved to them as we set off for Curepe.

Before going to Curepe, I made a detour to the Tunapuna market as I had to stop at our fishmonger, Baito, to pick up six baichine that I had ordered and had asked him to filet for me. I smiled again at the irony of buying fish in the Tunapuna market that had been caught in Mayaro to take with us to Mayaro. I parked the car opposite F&R Haddeed's store and we walked the short distance to the market. It was a Friday and lots of vendors were setting up stalls and bringing in produce for the weekend. Vashti and I weaved our way about a hundred yards or so and arrived at Baito's stall. He hollered out a huge greeting to me and politely said "ma'am" to Vashti. He had already prepared the fish as I had ordered and he showed me the filets. They were fresh and he wrapped them up in newspaper and put them into a plastic bag for us. I paid him, thanked him and promised to give his regards to my father. As we did not need anything else, we made our way back out to the car park. I dropped the fish into a cooler with ice to keep it cool and fresh, backed out onto the Eastern Main Road and set off for Curepe.

    Kamini was already there at the house with her twin girls, Anika and Farhanna, when we arrived in Curepe. She was going to take her mother and father in her car. There were more bags and boxes to be packed into the jeep which Franklin and I loaded. Kamini and I cross checked our list and verified that we had not forgotten anything. Satisfied that all was in order, she placed a few phone calls to Ahamad to find out where he was. As we had to wait for him to arrive, I called and ordered pizza for our lunch. While we waited, we phoned each of the other families and reconfirmed the time they were leaving and what time they were expected to be in Mayaro. We would be there around four o'clock in the afternoon and the others should be there by seven o'clock. That would give us lots of time to unload the vehicles, clean the house and set up for dinner by the time the bandwagon rolled in.

    A honk of the scooter's horn told me that the pizza had arrived. I paid the guy and called everyone to the table. Mario's pizza was always good and I had ordered garden veggie and Hawaiian. Over lunch we chatted about the plans to get Ms. Dorothy in to help us with the chores. Ahamad and his boys, Bari and Javed, arrived as we were eating and they joined us. With lunch finished, we helped ma and pa into the car and locked the gate. We set off down Ramgoolie Street, turned right onto the Southern Main Road and merged onto the Churchill Roosevelt Highway going east. Once more we were on our way to Mayaro. This time, I was an adult and I was the one doing the driving. Yet still that childish excitement that I felt years ago bubbled back to the surface and I could not wait to get there.

By the time we left Curepe and hit the highway, there was no traffic and we sped along at a decent clip. As I kept my eyes on the road, I saw some of the old landmarks that I remembered looking for as a child on this drive. Some of them had changed over the many years that had passed. The old roundabout at the Piarco junction had long since gone and the road ran straight towards Arima. The stench of the chicken processing plant near to Mausica was still there but not as strong as I had remembered. The Santa Rosa Racetrack was now walled all the way around and you could not see the track and rails. The stone pillars into Wallerfield however were still there. The Ponderosa was still there and very busy. I pointed these observations out to Vashti who seemed lost in taking in the scenery. Maybe she was recording these images into her memory as she was also preparing herself to leave Trinidad.

As I drove into Sangre Grande for the second time in a week, we stopped this time at the Seaway Bakery to purchase bread for the weekend. We chose loaves of plait bread and hops for the meals, and biscuit cakes, coconut drops and turnovers for treats. After a quick chat to verify that we did not need anything else, we agreed to continue the drive straight to Mayaro with no more stops and we set off once more. Just a few days earlier I had been this way with Ahamad but I still marveled at the excitement I felt as I saw First and Last come into view again. Once more the sight of the Atlantic took my breath away and I could sense that Vashti was equally enthralled. I was eager to get to our destination and with the road ahead clear of traffic we soon arrived at the Plaisance Junction. I could not bring myself to glance down Plaisance Road as I normally would have done. I was still disappointed at the changes that I had seen a few days earlier. I would have to find a way to reconcile myself with the memories of Gill Street.

About six minutes later, I turned left into Church Road and pulled into the driveway of the beach house that we had rented. It was three forty-five in the afternoon and we were fifteen minutes early. The agent was there with a lady who we assumed was Ms. Dorothy. Kamini, Ahamad, Vashti and I alighted from the three vehicles and greeted them. Ms. Dorothy introduced herself and insisted that we drop the Ms. and just call her Dorothy as she said the Ms. made her feel old. We laughed and agreed and the ice with her was broken. Lots of willing hands made quick work of unloading the vehicles.

The first matter was to assign the bedrooms. Kamini and Vashti took on that task and with the help of a few sticky notes and a marker they put names on the various doors. Ma would have one room and would share with Nishi, Vidya and Kavita. Pa would have a room and would share with Avin, Rajiv and Bari. Kamini and Ahamad with Javed, Nikki and Fari would have another. Raj and Aruna with Shivana and Anuka would have another. Vashti and I would share one with Kumarie and Rennie. Franklin would have the day bed on the lower level. With the sleeping arrangements finalized, Javed and Bari were tasked with sweeping the two levels of the house and we unpacked the rest of boxes.

The pots and pans, foodstuff and pantry items were taken to the main kitchen on the ground floor and unpacked. Dorothy took charge of the food items and she packed the fridge. There was a large box with an enormous iron pot which Franklin brought out from Kamini`s car. There was another smaller box next to it. Curiosity won and I asked about these as they were not in my vehicle. Kamini happily announced that she had already cooked dinner for everyone. Knowing that by the time we got to Mayaro, cleaned and settled down, it would take too long to get dinner going for more than twenty people. So, as a surprise, she made a huge pot of curried mutton with potatoes, and paratha roti for dinner. She also made baigan and tomato choka for Pa and Ahamad. This was certainly a treat and a surprise. She beamed with a huge smile as she saw our appreciation. As dinner was already prepared, she told Dorothy there was nothing to do this evening but wanted her to stay with us to meet the rest of the family as they arrived and to have dinner with us. They were getting along just fine. By five o'clock we had settled in, the chores were done, the house was ready to welcome the others and there was nothing else to do but sit back and relax a bit. Dorothy and Franklin busied themselves around the kitchen while the rest of us retired to the upper porch.

    I took a chair, sat down and put my feet up on the banister. Ahamad joined me and clapped me on my back saying that we did it. We certainly had done it. In the past Vashti's family would go only to Manzanilla on day trips. They would not go to Mayaro and never overnighted. This extended weekend was going to be special on so many fronts and Ahamad was pivotal in making it happen. I shook his hand and thanked him for arranging it and told him what it meant to me to do this before Vashti and I left for Canada. Normally Ahamad is not visibly emotional but he grasped my hand, squeezed it and there was no need for words as his touch said what he felt. I knew he was a bit overcome so to transition I rebuked him that my hand was empty and there was no glass in it. That spurred him back to the moment and we got a bottle of scotch and mixed two drinks, clinked glasses and toasted to a memorable vacation. As we were sipping our scotch and Peardrax, Kamini and Vashti came out to the porch and chided us for excluding them with the drinks. I mixed two for them and they joined us. Ma and Pa came out as well and sat on the sofa on the porch. The kids took to the table on the porch and started a game of cards. It was certainly very relaxing and the holiday was off to a wonderful start.

Chapter 16

Making New Memories

Javed brought out a bag of potato chips and we nibbled while we enjoyed the beautiful vista before us. From where we sat, I could see a panorama all around. The yard below was huge and there were ten coconut trees planted in two rows alongside a concrete walkway that led down to the beach. The wide yard was sandy and covered in shade from the trees. There was a low picket fence all around the property with a gate that opened out to the beach. I observed the coconut trees and remarked that two in particular on the right side would be perfect for a hammock. As I said that, Ahamad exclaimed loudly and called for Franklin. He asked him if he had packed the two hammocks. Franklin confirmed that he did and that he would soon have them up. I called dibs on the hammock for the next day. I turned my gaze back to the horizon as the sun began to set. With the light fading, I looked to see if the glow of the oil platforms were still there. Slowly as it got darker, I saw the orange glow and counted seven as I kept my gaze on the horizon. Night came quickly and we put the house lights on.

Despite there being a breeze blowing in from the ocean, there were mosquitoes so we set about lighting the coils and citronella candle buckets and plugged in the bug mats in the bedrooms to try and keep them away. Kamini and the others were downstairs tending after dinner. We heard the honking of horns and we knew the others had arrived. We went out to the carport to greet the arrivals. Raj was his usual boisterous self and immediately found the bar and poured him and Rennie a drink. The cousins greeted each other and many hands brought their stuff indoors in a flash. Vashti directed everyone upstairs to find their rooms and install their belongings. That was accomplished in quick time and as everyone was there, Kamini called us all to dinner. We were famished and looked forward to tucking into a delicious meal. Dorothy and Vashti took charge of dishing out as everyone lined up with their plates in cafeteria style. Dinner was informal and everyone sat where they could find a seat and we delved into the curried mutton and paratha. Dorothy had made a simple salad of watercress, cucumbers, onions and tomatoes seasoned with lime, garlic and salt and it went well with the meal.

As we sat eating, my mind floated back to my first dinner and first night in Mayaro back when I was a child and compared that to the one I was having now. I remembered the fried fish and platter of bread and butter and could see in my mind's eye the two mugs of tea and cocoa. Now more than twenty years later here I was, having a luxurious dinner of curried mutton and roti. Back then we had to get a ride from Chestnut and Selwyn. This time there were six vehicles parked in the driveway. Times had certainly changed and I felt a mixture of sadness and pride inside. I was sad because there was something inside of me that longed to be here again with my mother, my father, my brother and sister and feel that wonderful warmth I experienced as a child. I knew I could not turn back the sands of time and somehow it choked me up inside. At the same time, I remembered the sacrifices that my parents made to provide for us, to take those vacations and to support our education and I was grateful for and proud of all they did to help make me into the man that I had become.

Now that I was married and part of another family, I battled with the emotion of somehow feeling that I abandoned my family as I embraced

Vashti's family. But as I glanced around the room and listened to the snippets of banter and watched their faces, I knew that I was fortunate to be part of another close-knit family and while I could not have my own family with me, my family time in Mayaro years ago with them held a special place in my heart. I was grateful to and proud of my parents for giving me that. I snapped out of my reverie as I heard Raj calling to me to pass the pepper sauce and I refocused on the delicious meal in front of me.

Dinner was a leisurely event that first night. Almost everyone helped themselves to seconds and we thanked Kamini for preparing such a feast. The kids cleared their dishes away and retired to the upper floor for some board games and cards, much like I did when I was a child. Dorothy and Franklin cleared away ours and we also went upstairs. We went out to the porch and brought the sofas and chairs and set them up in a semi-circle. Rennie placed a few mosquito coils and citronella candles around us and we settled in for a relaxing evening. The moon was out and sent long silvery beams of light through the coconut branches. The tide was out and I saw the wide beach and heard the waves as they broke and gently lumbered to the shore. There were a few houses adjacent to ours with their lights on but no one seemed to be about. I was drinking in all the sights, all the sounds, all the vistas when I caught a bit of Ahamad talking about going to find a seine the next day. I enthusiastically chimed in and echoed my own excitement and the conversation gravitated to this. I called the kids out and asked them if they had ever been to a seine and as they all said no, I told them to sit and I explained in great detail the whole mechanics of it. As I was recounting this to them, I felt warm inside as I remembered explaining this to my cousin Derek over twenty years ago.

As the night wore on, one by one the kids, Ma and Pa and the ladies all turned in for the night. Ahamad, Raj, Rennie and myself though stayed up and huddled our chairs closer as we sat talking. It's funny the way some things never change. The cool salty night air, the breeze coming from the ocean, the gentle rustle of the palm branches, it was just as I remembered from so many years ago. But this time I had a glass of scotch in my hand and I was relaxed with my brothers-in-law. Rennie was the entertainer in the family and he could always be counted upon or inveigled to start dancing or singing at all our family functions. He used to call me Mr. B, why, I don't know. It was Rennie's turn to refresh our drinks when he turned to me, pointed his finger in my direction and started to sing "Fly Robin fly." We burst out laughing at that. He stopped, said to me "isn't your name Robin and are you not going to fly to Canada soon? So Fly Robin fly." It was infectious and we chimed in as it was a popular old song. We sang the words we remembered and hummed where we forgot.

As we finished that song, we burst out laughing as Ahamad told Rennie he was a clown. That brought me to life and as I also loved to sing, I looked at Rennie and started with "Sad Movies" in the same up tempo soca beat that Ronald Procope used to sing it when we were working in French Guiana. Rennie quickly caught the beat and we had a blast with this oldie. One by one Ahamad and Raj started their favourite oldies and we all chimed in the nostalgic sing along. As the old songs came up, we reminisced about what we were doing when that particular song was on the charts. While everyone else slept, we sipped on scotch and peardrax, sang old songs and had a wonderful time with each other's company.

It was around two o'clock in the morning when we heard a noise inside the house, turned around and saw Avin, Raj's son, coming out onto the porch. He said he was sleeping lightly, heard us laughing and came out to see what we were doing. By this time Raj was very merry so he told Avin he could stay up with us but he had to warm up some mutton and roti for us as we were hungry. Avin laughed, agreed, did as he was asked, and soon came back out with a huge plateful of curried mutton drizzled with some pepper sauce and some paratha. We shared this community plate as Avin got a blanket and cuddled up on the Morris chair next to us. That meal hit the spot and we licked our fingers clean.

As we were finishing up, Vashti came out and scolded us that we were making noise, that it was late and that we should go to bed. All four of us looked at her, laughed loudly and Rennie started up a version of "mama look a boo boo dey." As he belted out the words "shut yuh mouth, go away, mama look a boo boo dey" Vashti shook her head in defeat, gave a smile and went back to bed. That set the tone for the old calypso session. I was waiting for this and launched into the popular old medley starting with "Jane it is four o'clock in the morning" and we ended with "the last train to San Fernando." I felt as if it was twenty years earlier and we were there with Gatch and Selwyn in the driveway at the old Thackories house, and with Leon and Errol at Charles' house belting out the old familiar calypso medley.

We continued for a while longer but inevitably, sleep started to catch up with us. I looked at my watch and realized it was almost four o'clock in the morning. We had planned to be up early to watch the sunrise and to go to a seine. I needed to get a bit of sleep as did Rennie and Ahamad. Raj wanted to stay up and teased us about being too soft, but we convinced him to do so as well. We agreed that we would all be up at five thirty to head down to the beach to watch the sunrise and Rennie said that he would wake us all up. I helped to close the windows and doors, double checked that the lights were off downstairs, and bid the others a good sleep. I made my way to my room and quietly climbed into bed. The sheets were cool and comfortable and felt exquisite to my skin. As soon as my head touched the pillow, I fell asleep. I was tired but happy.

I must have been in a very deep sleep and must have thought I was dreaming about eating peppermints when I felt something wet on my face. I jumped up startled only to find that it was Raj pasting toothpaste on my lips and laughing loudly. Instantly my uncle Kelvin crossed my mind when he did the same to me. That woke me up and I conceded that round to him. Raj had not gone to sleep. He stayed up by himself and was anxious to wake us. He had already put a pot of coffee on the stove to boil. I brushed my teeth, washed my face and made my way out to the living room. Ahamad was just coming out of his room and we joined Rennie at the table. It was still dark out but we knew it would soon be light. Raj brought out four cheese sandwiches wrapped in paper napkins and called to me to help him with the coffee. I got four large enamel cups and poured the coffee from the pot into them. Raj had made it strong and had added the milk and sugar to the pot. It was the local Hong Wing brand and it smelt good. We were ready to head down to the beach. Ahamad and I grabbed our smokes and we made our way down the stairs with the others.

  The sand was cool to our bare feet and I tasted the salty air on my lips. There was a fishing boat parked on the sand just to the side of our house and we settled down in the sand against it. As we settled into our sandy spot on the beach, I opened my sandwich and munched hungrily. The coffee was strong and piping hot and the cup warmed our hands. As we were sitting there talking with our eyes fixed on the horizon, we gradually saw the sky lighten as it took on a dull crimson tinge. I remembered when I was a child looking at this same vista unfold before me and I could see my uncle Roy sitting with me and my cousins, the clandestine enamel cups of coffee that he gave us and the scent of the tobacco from his cigarette. Now here I was, probably just like my uncle back then, enjoying my coffee and my cigarette and drinking in the spectacle of the rising sun that was unfolding before my eyes. I was silent as I took in every last detail about this snapshot in time and place and recorded it into memory especially for when I would no longer be in the land of my birth.

I was grateful that the others were also quiet and did not spoil this moment with needless talk. Even though we lived on an island, getting to the coast to watch the sun climb into the heavens from beyond the watery horizon is not something we did every day, so this opportunity to drink it in was special for the others as well. Rennie eventually broke the silence with a comment about the greatness of God and His creation and we all nodded in agreement. We had been sitting for about forty-five minutes and I needed to stretch my legs. I stood up, looked down the beach and glanced back at the house. It must have been timing but there was Aruna waving and calling to us. Something must have happened so we ran back to the house to see what was wrong. It was my mother-in-law. She had woken up and was in the kitchen when she experienced cramps in her leg. We were relieved as it was not serious. Ma got these cramps from time to time and Raj tended to her. In a few minutes she was fine and apologized for dragging us from the beach.

The mild commotion awoke everyone else and soon the living room was full. Dorothy arrived just at that same time and she set about in the kitchen to organize breakfast. I poured another cup of coffee and pulled up a chair on the porch. Pretty soon everyone else came out and just like me, I assumed they were drinking in the beauty of the morning. Kamini brought out the playpen, opened it up and brought the twins Nikki and Fari out. I pulled my chair closer to the playpen and smiled at the girls as they stood up and each grabbed my arm nestled on the playpen. Franklin was up and about in the yard and he called to us to help him. He had two hammocks and was hanging them between the coconut trees. Ahamad and Rennie helped him secure them and I was given the choice of the two. I selected one closer to the fence that had a good canopy of leaves overhead to provide shade. I was tired from lack of sleep the night before and I climbed in to test it out. It was perfect. Ahamad gave my hammock a push and went back into the house leaving me gently swinging. The motion was therapeutic and I must have closed my eyes and drifted off to sleep. I don't know how long I was out for but I felt someone shaking me. It was Vashti waking me up that breakfast was ready. I pulled myself out of the hammock and made my way to the breakfast table. A truly familiar and nostalgic scent hit my nostrils and I felt transported.

There was a huge platter of fried fish and a platter of sliced bread and butter. The kids were seated around the dining table and were helping themselves. I saw the ketchup and mustard bottles and the pepper sauce and instantly I relived my breakfast in Mayaro twenty years ago. I looked at the delight on their faces as they delved into their meal and I remembered my brother Gerry, my sister Sherry, and my cousins Hayden and Ronald. I helped Shivana and Anuka with their plates, then dished out my own and moved to the porch to have breakfast. Nikki and Fari were still in the playpen and Kamini was seated on a chair next to them. It was a sight to behold. The twins were standing and holding onto the playpen while Kamini flaked the fried fish, double checked that there were no bones, and fed each of them. They seemed to enjoy it as they stood with their mouths open waiting on the next handful from their mother. It was so like a mother bird feeding her little ones with their mouths wide open. The fish was delicious and it instantly transported me over the years to when I was a child here in Mayaro with my parents and my family.

Breakfast was leisurely and no one was in a hurry, except of course for the kids. They clamoured to go to a seine. I was anxious to go as well but the drinks and the lack of sleep the previous night had caught up with me and I just did not have the energy to do so. I know Raj, Rennie and Ahamad were also tired so we called the kids and made a deal with them that for sure the next day we would go to a seine. Instead, they could do whatever they liked on the beach today. As we said that to them, it struck me at how times had changed. Twenty years ago, as children we were allowed to go a few kilometers down the beach to a seine all by ourselves. We had rules to follow of course, but we were safe. Now with crime on the rise in Trinidad and the upsurge in kidnappings and other crimes, the kids were not allowed out without adult supervision and someone to accompany them. It was a sign of the changed times. With that settled, I found my hammock and climbed in. The gentle breeze rocked the hammock and the branches provided delicious shade and soon I fell fast asleep. By the time I awoke, the sun was high overhead and I judged it to be around noon. I looked around at the house and there seemed to be no one about. I got up and walked over the cool dry sand to the fence and there I saw all the ladies with the children and grandparents on the beach.

  I made my way over to where Vashti and Kamini were sitting on a log as they teased me about falling asleep. I took their teasing with a smile and asked about Ahamad and the others. I found out they had gone upstairs to the bedrooms and were still asleep. Just then Rajiv and Avin ran up to me and begged me to accompany them into the water. The tide was out and the water looked inviting. I took off my shirt and raced them to the water. I plunged my head into a wave and let it cascade over me. It was warm and felt luxurious. The boys came up to me and started splashing me and that invited the others to surround and gang up on me. There were squeals of laughter as they used their little hands to scoop and throw water on me and screams from the girls as I splashed them back.

  I called out my surrender and told them they had won which make them cheer in delight. I called them nearer and asked them to show me how they splashed me. Avin demonstrated with cupped hands. I laughed and told them to watch how it was done properly. I showed them how to use the flat of their palm, with fingers pointed up, to strike the top of the water and direct a jet into the faces of their victims. I had them show me if they understood and very soon they had the action learned. I told them that when Ahamad, Raj and Rennie woke up and came into the water, they should try this new action. They again cheered and said yes. I let them go on with their play as I floated in the water. I could not help but remember my uncle Kelvin who taught me all these things and who romped with me in the water when I was a child. I think now with Vashti's nieces and nephews, I had become my own uncles Kelvin and Roy. That made me smile and feel happy as I could not hope for a bigger compliment than to be regarded by these kids the same way I regarded Kelvin and Roy.

  I heard someone call me and saw Aruna and Kumarie on the beach calling everyone out of the water. They had something in their hand. I rounded up the youngsters and we waded out onto the beach and ran up to see what they had. There was some kachourie and sponge cake and three bottles of icy cold juice. It was exactly like my aunt Radica and my mother calling us out for a snack over twenty years ago. It was uncanny that so many things now were reminding me of when I was a child vacationing in Mayaro. I took a kachourie and as I was biting into it, I heard Raj's voice, looked up and saw him, Rennie and Ahamad coming down to join us on the beach. They told us they had woken up and were coming to join us when a vendor who knew we were at the house came knocking. He was selling crab and they were big and looked juicy. Dorothy was in the kitchen and she inspected the crab and gave her approval. So the guys purchased five strings of crab and Dorothy said she would do curried crab and dumplings Mayaro style for us for dinner. It was again a very strange coincidence as over twenty years ago, Roy took us to catch sireek crabs and we made crab and dumplings for dinner with Peter one night. We would be having the same dinner tonight except that the difference this time was that we purchased the crab instead of catching them. It was something to look forward to later.

  The rest of the afternoon went by quickly and by the time we had all showered and changed, the sun had set and night had fallen. There was a delicious aroma permeating the house and we could not wait for dinner to be ready. A bottle of split channa served to take the edge off our hunger for a short while and it was a welcome sound to hear Dorothy call us for dinner. There was an enormous pot set up on the concrete counter and she and Kamini dished out for us in turn. We put a few bowls on the tables to put the crab shells. I took my plate and sniffed at the wonderful aroma. The sauce seemed thicker and Dorothy told us her secret of using cooked dhal to thicken the sauce which also helped to mellow out the curry. I found a seat in the living room and used my spoon to delve into the delicious food. While my mother's cooking was the benchmark by which I measured all cooking, Dorothy's crab and dumpling was exceptional. Vashti got her recipe and it is one that we use up to the present day.

The old saying about the more things change the more they remain the same sometimes would manifest itself when least expected. We were twenty-two persons staying in the house. After dinner, we all stayed downstairs as the kids put the television on and were watching a movie. Vidya and the other girls started a game of all fours. That left the men on our own on the porch. I think we may have had a bit too much to drink the previous night as no one seemed interested in mixing a scotch. I listened in to the snippets of conversations around the house and I felt happy. I was in a new family and I felt accepted. I got up and looked out at the beach which was lit up by the shiny moonlight. The tide was out and the beach was wide and I had a great idea. I called out to everyone that we should stop what we were doing and we should all go down to the beach for a walk in the moonlight. Some wanted to stay and finish the movie, so Franklin stayed with them and with Ma and Pa. The rest of us quickly organized and we trooped out down the pathway, opened the gate and set out for a walk to our left towards Plaisance.

The moon was almost full and it shone brightly in the night sky. It lit up the wide beach and showed us the way forward. The kids trooped ahead of us and we all walked abreast of each other. I listened to the conversations around me and marveled that for some of the others, this was their first time overnighting in Mayaro. I recounted aloud to them what I remembered of this same walk in the evening years ago after dinner with Alloy and Mrs. LeeHa. As we walked, I heard a bubbling noise and my heart leapt for I knew it was the old river where I used to catch crabs. Like an excited child, I raced ahead, caught up with the children and led them to the narrow shallow channel that flowed out from the river to the beach. I looked to the left and made out the outline of the bent old coconut tree. It was still there. That made me smile. I pulled the children around me as we waded in the shallow channel feeling the warm river water flow around our ankles. I took them to the old tree and showed them where I used to catch crabs when I was their age. The moonlight lit up the river bank and I could see that not much had changed here over the years and I was silently grateful.

    We left the river bank and continued our walk down the beach and I wondered if the old tree was still on the beach? I squinted in the darkness to see if I could make out anything up ahead, but alas, the tree was no longer there. Somehow I remembered the tree being so huge and so heavy back then, that I thought it could never be moved. I think I must have been more disappointed in not being able to show the others my tree. As we walked, I knew we were getting closer to Plaisance and where the Thackories beach house used to be. My heart raced. I could not drive into Gill Street the week before with Ahamad as I saw too many changes. This time, I would be walking past the old spot where the house used to be and I felt a bit of dread and sadness in the pit of my stomach.

    A short distance away, I spied a few boats parked high up on the beach and knew we were just feet away from where the old beach house used to be. I steeled myself and walked alone ahead of the others. I stopped and looked and saw the remnants of the old steps, the old retaining wall and some of the asphalt from the driveway where I used to play cricket. I closed my eyes and saw the beach house like it used to be and heard the laughter and voices of my family. As I opened my eyes to the reality that the house was gone and no longer there, I knew that the memories that I had of that happy place were part of me to be summoned as I had just done. I was sad and with a final look at the old place, I made my way back to the group and continued our walk.

Another couple hundred yards brought us to the boats and the point where the Plaisance Road met the beach. I looked at the names of the boats somehow hoping that *Spartacus* would still be there. It was not. As I noted all the changes around me, I felt the feeling of anxiety and dread flow out of my body and an inner peace settled into my mind. The memories that I had were mine and I could call upon them whenever I needed them. I thought I would be more anxious about the changes, but instead I found myself telling and describing to the others what used to be here over twenty years ago. I think that was my way of accepting the changes and in that moment I knew I had reconciled the present with the past. We walked around a bit looking at the comings and goings of the local folk and walked as far as Mr. James' shop. It was closed, but the lights were on outside and I could see the same building that I remembered. I felt comforted by that. With not much more to do, we decided to retrace our steps along the beach, walked past Gill Street and made our way back home to Church Road.

We got back to the house to find those who stayed back, fast asleep on the couch. Ahamad and I retired to the upper porch sat down and relaxed with a drink. It was a quiet night with hardly any man made noise to spoil the serenity. As we sat there, I heard crickets chirping and the gentle rustle of the coconut branches in the breeze. The ladies came out to join us and brought out a few cardigans to cuddle up with. Kumarie had made coffee and brought out a few cups for them to sip. It had been a long day with little sleep for some of us, but that was to be expected amidst the excitement of the first night and first day. I told the others that we should get a good night's sleep as I wanted to wake the kids early in the morning to go find a seine. I was surprised when everyone said they also wanted to go. So with that settled, we locked up the house and retired to our beds and were soon fast asleep with a light salty breeze cooling us and sending us into dreamland.

Chapter 17

From Trinidad to Canada

I was up early the next morning and was making coffee downstairs when I heard my mother-in-law coming into the kitchen. I made a cup of tea for her and sat with her to enjoy the stillness of the morning. It was just past six o'clock and I went upstairs and knocked on each door to wake everyone up. It was time to go down the beach to find a seine. I called out loudly to everyone that they had twenty minutes to meet me on the porch downstairs. Franklin was up and he met me on the porch. I had an idea which I told him about. We found a fallen coconut branch and he and I stripped it of all its leaves. We took a small knife and one by one, stripped each leaf and kept the rib. To the end of the rib, we tied a small piece of twig. Franklin knew exactly what I was doing and in ten minutes we had made about twenty of these. As the children came out followed by the adults, I took the stripped coconut branch strings that we had made and handed them to the kids. They had no idea what it was for so I explained that when we got to the seine and if they foraged for any fish, they could string one end of their branch through the gills of the fish and it would slide down and rest on the twig and not fall off. That way they could get many fish and each have a string to carry their catch. That made them excited and they were eager to set off.

As we walked onto the beach, I looked left and right to see if there were any seines. There was nothing to our right, but to our left, about half way between Church Road and Plaisance, there was a seine. It was very close and we would not have far to walk. We set off briskly and as we walked, Avin and Rajiv asked again about how the seine worked. I was delighted to explain it once more, just as I had done with Derek over twenty years ago, but this time to my nieces and nephews. The seine had just started and the boats were on the shore. I pointed and illustrated as I explained and I could sense they were excited. In a few minutes we were at the seine and I waded into the water and took hold of the rope. Bari and Javed took up places next to me. Everyone spread out along the two sides of the ropes and we joined in the cadence of pulling the seine. As I grasped the wet rope and clasped my hands around it, I saw the waif of a little boy doing the same thing over twenty years ago. I had not pulled seine since the last time I was in Mayaro with my mother and father. As I thought about that, a wave broke against me and splashed my face and no one saw the tear that had rolled down my cheek.

The kids were enjoying their first experience at the seine and I relived my memories through their youthful exuberance at the task. Shivana let out a loud squeal as she felt something brush against her feet. It was just a piece of seaweed and the others teased her about being a baby. Rennie was in front of me and he shouted that he saw the corks. Soon the nets came into view and the seine workers took control of the lead. Anuka was standing next to her father Raj and she called out loudly that there was a fish in the net as she pointed to a carite caught on the side of the net. As the nets came in and the arc narrowed, we let go of the ropes and allowed the workers to get in. The water was splashing with writhing fish and I could see the children drinking in the spectacle. Ahamad was on the beach and was talking to someone and beckoned to me. I ran to him to see what was up. He had been talking to the owner of the seine and had arranged for our kids to go into the nets and pick a few small fish for their strings. Times had certainly changed but I was glad that he did as it would give the children an experience they would never forget. We called to Franklin, Rennie and Raj and told them.

As the nets came in and the bigger prized fish were extricated and tossed into waiting baskets, Franklin called to the children to follow him and showed them how to pry the small fish from the net and how to put them onto their coconut branch strings. I spied a small butterfish, freed it from the net and handed it to Anuka. She squealed at the slippery feel of the fish and let it slip from her hands. It fell into the water and deftly swam away. She was amazed that it was still alive. We let the kids forage for a while longer and they got a decent haul. Meanwhile, Ahamad and I purchased some kingfish, baichine and red snapper for us to take back home. The kingfish was still wriggling and we let the boys hold it by the tail to feel the weight and strength of the fish. As we walked home all they could talk about was how they got their fish from the nets and how they put them on the strings. I knew this was an experience they would never forget and I was glad that I was able to be part of it with them so that maybe one day they would include me in that memory as well.

When we got home, unlike when I was a child, the kids were not interested in cleaning the fish. So Franklin took all the strings, set up shop at the outdoor sink in the carport, and started to clean all the small fry that they had foraged. While he was doing that, the kids had cleaned up and were sitting down to breakfast. We joined them and partook of a delicious offering of eggs, vienna sausages and avocado with toasted hops bread. Instead of cocoa like I had when I was a child, they were served instant hot chocolate. Some old, some new, but the same ambiance around the table with lots of chatter, joking and teasing. Every fleeting moment was a memory that someone was registering either consciously or unconsciously. I took my breakfast on the porch as I wanted to drink in as much of the vista as I could. I felt that I had to store up as much as I could for the times when I would no longer be here in this land. As I ate, I heard a sound and looked in the direction of it. It was an old dry coconut that had somehow fallen from one of the trees and it landed with a slight thud on the soft sand. Franklin came out from the carport and walked over to where the coconut fell to retrieve it. As he walked over the sand, I heard his feet crunch the old chip chip shells strewn about the yard. As I sipped my coffee, a slight breeze blew from the ocean and whipped up some of the dry loose sand in the yard. I became aware of everything around me and even the seemingly mundane was an opportunity to register and record into memory.

With the day stretching before us, after breakfast, it was time to hit the beach. Unlike at the old Thackories beach house, there was no long asphalt driveway at this one. But the tide was out and there was a wide beach and we decided on a game of cricket. Everyone came out including Ma and Pa. They set up chairs in the shade where they could see everyone. We decided on playing a match and we let Avin and Bari be captains and they chose their teams. We established the rules including the boundaries and proceeded to start a noisy, rambunctious, contentious game with lots of laughter, teasing, challenges and good old Trinidadian picong. I was fielding at the edge of the water and felt the ebb and flow of the water around my ankles. The sun was shining brilliantly, there were hardly any clouds, and the blue vault of the heavens seemed to go on forever. The cacophony of noise from the gulls and corbeaux overhead were drowned out by the squeals and shouts of the players on the beach as they also competed with the sound of the rolling surf. My auditory and visual senses were inundated with stimuli that I gladly received and stored.

When the game was over and the winner declared, it was time to bathe in the ocean and everyone dived into the surf and luxuriated in the warm water of the Atlantic. I had brought a bottle of Bundenberg rum from Australia which was a gift from one of my friends, Kemp. Rennie had gone back into the house to fetch something, found the bottle of rum and brought it out to the beach. He wanted us to take a swig, but we declined. Even though it was a sunny day earlier, the skies had quickly darkened with clouds rolling in and suddenly they burst open. It was a typical tropical rain shower, fairly heavy, but no thunder and lightning. At first some of the ladies wanted to retreat to the house. I teased them that they were already wet and the rain wasn't going to melt them. So they stayed in the water and on the beach with us. That egged Rennie on to take a swig out of the bottle to warm up. Surprisingly Vashti and Kumarie joined in and they each took a sip. That caused a lot of laughter to see their faces contorted after the strong liquid hit their throats. Inhibitions were cast aside as everyone was totally relaxed with so much family around. Then as suddenly as it had started, the rain stopped, the clouds dissipated and the skies cleared. The sun came back out and the warmth of its rays caressed our faces and bodies with a gentle touch.

As the afternoon rolled on and it was time to come out of the water, we sent the children to shower and change. With a last duck under a wave, I slowly made my way out. The dry sand in the yard clung to my wet ankles and crusted and covered my feet. I used the pipe in the carport to rinse my feet and joined the others on the porch. As I wrapped a towel around my shoulders and felt the delightful sting of a bit of sunburn, I saw five children doing the same and feeling the same sunburn at Thackories years ago. I took my turn to shower and change and then joined the others in the living room. The skies had clouded over again and there was a slight drizzle. I could hear the sound of the rain on the zinc awning of the porch and I walked out to look at the rain. A slight breeze from the ocean blew the rain onto the porch and it was wet. As I retreated back into the house, I felt the change from the coolness of the porch to the warmth of the living room.

My senses came alive as a delicious aroma wafted from the kitchen, one with which I was very familiar. Franklin and Dorothy had cleaned all the small fish the kids had foraged for in the seine earlier in the day and she prepared a huge platter of fried fish. For the kids, she filleted a kingfish, made sure all the bones were removed and prepared that for them. The adults were capable of managing the small fry and the bones. Fresh fish just caught by our own hands this morning, it was just like over twenty years ago.

After dinner, we all gathered in the living room, switched off the television and talked. Conversation was easy and the highlight was Pa telling everyone stories of when he was a child, when he was growing up and some of his adventures and misadventures. That drew laughter from everyone. Kamini, always the one to be emotional and expressive, spoke about how special and this time was for all of us to be able to spend it with each other. Her words touched me deep inside and a quiet pervaded the room as she spoke. I knew everyone was processing what she was saying and were appreciative of her ability to express what I am sure everyone felt. As she concluded and the silence continued, Raj, in his usual manner, made a loud comment about this not being a wake. That caused ripples of laughter and he changed the mood immediately. Rennie and Shivana, father and daughter, broke into song singing some of the old hits from the Bee Gees, with Shivana doing a few dance moves. It was brilliant and of course I jumped right in with an air mike and lent my lusty voice to the chorus.

We spent the next two days doing pretty much the same, getting up early to watch the sunrise, taking walks on the beach, pulling seine one more time, playing cricket on the beach, swimming in the warm ocean, enjoying each other's company, being a family. This trip to Mayaro was organized on my request. Mayaro had held a special place in my heart and my memories, created from my holidays here with my parents and my family over twenty years ago. Those memories were deeply etched and I wanted to remember them as I did when I was a child. Coming to Mayaro this time as an adult, married, and with a new extended family, I hoped to recapture some of those distant memories. Instead, I was confronted with physical changes to some of those memories and I found it hard to accept. But as I looked at the new family around me when we walked on the beach to Plaisance that second night, I was able to reconcile my past memories with the present, and I embraced the new memories I was adding to my collection of Mayaro. Back then, when it would have been time to leave, I would have gone to all the old places one last time to say goodbye in my own childish innocent way. This time, I simply walked out to the beach, looked around, looked in the direction of Plaisance, and said goodbye to this wonderful place. I was content and I was happy.

When we got back to Tunapuna and Curepe, we had about two weeks to prepare for our departure for Canada. After my jobs in French Guiana, Dominica, Nevis and Montego Bay, returning to Trinidad to continue work did not promise much in terms of a future. Vashti and I had discussed it and she thought about Canada. She said that if we had to make a new start at a life together, why not make a new start in a new country with more opportunities for the future and better opportunities for starting our own family. I went along with her plans and we took the screening tests offered by the High Commission. We scored very high marks and we were invited to apply for Canadian emigration. Upon return to Trinidad from Montego Bay, we submitted our applications and within six weeks we were interviewed, processed and approved. That was in August of the previous year nineteen ninety-seven.

After speaking with Rolph and Deanne Hosein, friends of my mother and my godmother's brother, we decided to move in April nineteen ninety-eight. The departure date was fast approaching and everyone in both families were anxious and torn. It was particularly hard on Vashti's family. When we were married in nineteen ninety-five, the day after our wedding, we left Trinidad for Dominica where I was working. We then spent the next three years away from Trinidad on my job postings. So she lost three years with her family. After Montego Bay when we had returned to Trinidad, she had only six months with them before we permanently left Trinidad.

My family and especially my mother, was torn about our decision and she was very emotional about it. Since I was nineteen years old, I was away from Trinidad for about ten years. I spent three years away at university. I came back and spent four years at home. I then left and spent four years in French Guiana followed by three years around the Caribbean. So she also lost ten years of my life and I understood what she felt and what she was going through. But she held me one day and told me that she would always be there for me, to be the best that I could be, and to never forget God in my life. Those words stayed with me to the present. I knew it was her way of giving me her blessing as I was preparing to set forth on my new life away from her and from my family.

The day of our departure came all too quickly and we were not prepared for the emotional roller coaster we would experience that night. Vashti's entire family came over to my house as we would be leaving from there for the airport. We were going to leave the house at eleven o'clock. They came around seven p.m. My mother prepared to receive everyone and made chicken pelau for dinner. Rennie and Raj made themselves at home, poured drinks for everyone and toasted us. Ma and Pa chatted with my parents and everyone was engaged in conversation. But the atmosphere was heavy and the laughter was subdued. I knew everyone was dreading that moment when we would leave.

Vashti and I went around to each family and chatted with them. At about nine thirty p.m. Vashti and I called everyone together and I said a few words to thank everyone for all they had done for us. We thanked our parents for all their guidance, support and love that helped mould us into the adults we had become. When I was done speaking, Kamini came up and said a few words on behalf of both families and reiterated to us that we could always count on them and that they would always be there for us. It took all control on our part not to crack at that moment, and we held it together. But not for long though. My two nieces Anuka and Shivana had practiced a song to serenade us with and they wanted to sing for us. Their choice of song was poignant and it caused the tears to flow from everyone. They song was Celine Dion's "*My Heart Will Go On*" from the movie *Titanic*. Their young voices and their hearts that they put into it along with the powerful lyrics was too much and Vashti broke into tears. It was an appropriate song and I remember them singing it up to today.

      Our luggage was taken to the car, documents were double checked and we were dressed. It was time to leave for the airport. My father was never one to be very expressive with his feelings and emotions. But on that last night before we left for the airport, when he spoke to me his voice broke and tears rolled down his cheeks. I hugged him and my mother tightly as we embraced each other. My sister Sherry and her husband Rudy embraced Vashti and I. My brother Gerry and his wife Alicia hugged us tightly. I kissed my six moth old niece Sarah who was asleep in her cot. I picked up my five-year-old niece Gerarda in my arms and hugged her tightly, kissed her cheek and could not hold back my own tears.

      I went back to my mother, held her hands, looked her in the eye, told her that I loved her and hugged her one more time. I held Vashti's hand, turned away, walked down the stairs and got into the car. As we drove out of my driveway, I wanted to look back, but I couldn't, it was too hard. I was leaving the home I grew up in; leaving the parents who nurtured, raised and loved me; leaving the family who cared for me. All I would have from here on would be the memories. I wiped the tears from my eyes as the car turned on to the highway and we sped towards the airport and the flight that would take us to a new land, a new home and a new life together.

Chapter 18

The Last Days with My Mother

Moving to Canada was a big decision for us which we had thought about long and hard. While we were away from all our loved ones back in Trinidad, Canada gave us the opportunity to build a new life and start our own family. Three years after coming to Canada, our first child Joshua was born in June two thousand and one. Vashti took the full maternity leave and we shared the parental leave with me taking four weeks. She wanted to go visit the family back in Trinidad and of course take Joshua to be introduced to them. She had planned on going just before Diwali in November that year. It was going to be special as she wanted her grandmother to hold Joshua. But as life would have it, one week before her departure, her grandmother passed away. Vashti was distraught and inconsolable as she was very close to Nan, and her grandmother would not meet her first born son. Vashti was devastated by that loss.

    When Vashti took Joshua with her to Trinidad, he was five months old. She would go on ahead and I would join her a few weeks later just before Christmas. I heard the stories and saw the photos of Joshua being cuddled and spoilt by all the family in Trinidad. I missed my son and was anxious to join them. I had not been back to Trinidad since we left three years ago. I was also anxious to see my parents as well. Early in December, my father and mother called me to tell me that my mother was going to have surgery to remove a hernia and that it was a routine procedure. The surgery was scheduled for one week before Christmas, a few days before I arrived, and after the surgery, she would have to rest up for a while. We had not baptized Joshua as yet as we wanted to do his Christening Ceremony in Trinidad. I wanted it done at my old parish church where I was an acolyte and where I went to church. So with the date for my mother's surgery set and the date for the Christening set, I counted down the days to my departure back to Trinidad.

When I arrived at Piarco airport, Vashti brought Joshua to the airport to meet me. I had missed my son and took him in my arms and hugged him for a long time. We drove to my parents' house in Hackett Lane and I rushed up the stairs to greet my parents. My mother had had the surgery and was recovering well. She was sitting on the couch and could not stand because of the healing surgical incision. I hugged her as she held onto me in a tight embrace, seemingly drawing strength from my physical presence. I hugged my father and kissed him on the cheek. Vashti came up the stairs with Joshua and even though she had seen and met him before, I wanted to present my son to her. Because of the stitches, she could not hold him as yet so I held him close to her as she held his hands, touched and kissed his cheeks. The circle was completed as I presented my son to his grandmother and his grandfather.

Christmas morning came all too quickly. We were staying at my parents' house and I was up early. My sister Sherry and her husband Rudy were also there as they had spent Christmas Eve with us. Mummy was up and wanted to come out to the living room so we helped her. Joshua was up and Vashti was seeing after his bottle. Mummy said that she wanted to hold Joshua and assured us that she was strong enough to do so if we put him across her lap. I knew this was extremely important for her so I picked him up from the playpen and with Vashti's help, laid him across her lap with his head cradled in her arms. It was a beautiful moment as this was the first time she held him. She smiled at him, spoke to him, and sang a song to him. He looked up at her and cooed and held on to her finger that she was using to caress his face. I grabbed my camcorder to record the moment. She said this was her Christmas gift, to have the strength to hold her grandson. It was indeed a wonderful Christmas.

As usual the festive season goes by in the blink of an eye and before you knew it, the New Year was rung in at Vashti's parents' house in Curepe and it was only days away to Joshua's Christening and our departure back to Canada. He was being baptized on the sixth of January and we were leaving on the eighth. Father Reggie Hezekiah was doing the Baptism and the reception was being held at Kamini's house. Kamini was his godmother and Rudy his godfather. My mother made the best Spanish Rice and I wanted her to do it for Joshua's reception. But alas, she could not because of the surgery. She made a huge effort to make it to the Church to attend his Baptism and we took photos at the Grotto in the churchyard. When we got to Kamini's house and everyone had changed into more relaxing clothes, I brought Joshua to my mother who was seated in the living room with my mother-in-law, my sister and a few others. She asked to hold him again and I obliged. She made the sign of the cross on his forehead and prayed that God would watch over him as he grew and she told him that she loved him with all her heart. Little did we know that would be the last time she would hold him.

The next day, we were sitting on the porch with my parents having breakfast. Rudy was holding and playing with Joshua. I had my camcorder going and was taping everyone chatting. I asked my mother if she had anything to say before we left. She looked at the camera and said that her only regret was not being able to hold Joshua more and not being able to do more for us while we were there. She was choked up and I sensed it was very emotional for her. I told her she did so much for everyone when she was stronger, now it was our turn to do for her as she recovered from surgery. I told her to hurry up and get better fast so that she can come up to visit in

Canada. We had planned on her coming up in July to babysit Joshua for us for a few weeks. She said she was looking forward to it and a tear rolled down her cheek. In retrospect, I did not foresee what was to come and that tear, when I think back on it, represented what she knew was coming.

It was a very emotional farewell as we prepared to leave for the airport. Mummy was not feeling well that morning so we said goodbye to her in her room. When I went to hug her, she held me very close for a long time and cried. Her emotions and ability to express her feelings was an intrinsic part of who I was and I reacted to her in much the same way. Before I left, she held my face in her two hands, looked at me and told me that she loved me, that she was proud of me, to protect my family and never forget God in my life. I held her hands, kissed her cheek, told her goodbye and with tears in my eyes, I turned around and left my old home in Tunapuna. Little did I know that would be the last time I would have seen, touched and held my mother. I left Trinidad on the eighth January two thousand and two. I returned one month later, on eighth February to bury my mother who had passed away.

My mother died on sixth February, one day before her birthday. She succumbed to post-surgical complications. My mother's death had a profound impact on me. It was too sudden and because I was not there at her side when she passed, it was so much harder. I remember speaking to her on the phone the night before she succumbed and her voice still echoes in my mind. When I received that phone call the following morning and I heard my father's voice shake with the news, I collapsed in grief and despair. The woman who gave me life had now been taken away from this life and I would never be the same again. She had shaped me into the adult that I had become and her empathy, expressiveness and emotional intelligence is something that she had passed on to me. I would be eternally grateful to her for that. When she died, a huge part of me died as well. It was hard to reconcile that just one month before I was with her and now she was gone and I would never see her again.

The loss of my mother was the most devastating event in my life. When we arrived in Trinidad, I went with my father to the funeral home to see my mother. I was an emotional wreck and he held my arm as I viewed her body. I touched her forehead and silently wept. He wanted me to help him choose the casket for her burial and we selected one which we knew she would have liked. When my father asked me to do the eulogy for her, I gladly accepted to do it. I stayed up that night and wrote six pages. At the church, as everyone filed past to pay their last respects, I kissed her forehead one last time. As I read the eulogy, I tried hard to keep my composure and did so very well, until the final paragraph when my voice broke on the altar as I said a final goodbye to her. At the cemetery, looking at her casket being lowered into the grave, I cried as I held the clump of earth in my hand and threw a handful in. The matriarch of the family, the woman who gave me life, my mother, was gone from this life. After mummy's funeral, I stayed in Trinidad for ten days more. My sister Sherry was pregnant with her first child and near term. She was looking forward to and planning with mummy for when her son would be born. Sherry was devastated that mummy would never see her first born child. Ten days after mummy passed away, my nephew Adam was born.

I returned to Canada with Vashti and Joshua and tried to get back into my routine. Joshua kept us busy as he was growing and in a way that helped the time to go by quickly. I was looking forward to July as my father, Sherry, Rudy and Adam were coming to visit for a month. Before mummy had passed away, we had made plans for them to come up to Canada to help us babysit Joshua during the summer. I was glad that they stuck with the plan to visit as it brought our family closer together during those four weeks they were with us. I knew it helped my father immensely to cope with the loss of his life partner. It was a happy yet sad time for us. We were happy to be with each other, but sad because of the void left by my mother not being there.

Everyone carried their own emotions and it manifested itself on our faces when we sat and talked, looked at pictures and watched the videos that I had made at Christmas. We played back over and over her last words to me that morning on the porch. Every time we played it, even though it pained us to the core, we were able to smile a bit and somehow we knew she was preparing herself and telling us goodbye. When it was time for them to leave to go back to Trinidad, it was another tearful goodbye. I had begged my father to stay in Canada with us but he would not. He was used to his ways and his routine in Trinidad. He was not comfortable with the cold weather. But most of all, he did not want to leave his house, his home. So with tears in our eyes once more at Pearson airport, I looked at them retreating beyond the security gates until they disappeared from sight. I would not see them again for two years.

Joshua was growing into a toddler and he was the centre of our lives. Vashti's sister Kamini and her family came to visit us in summer of two thousand and three. It was a joyful reunion with them and because of their visit we did not go to Trinidad that summer. Just before they came to visit, Vashti found out that she was pregnant and we were expecting our second child, news which delighted everyone in both families. We knew the baby was going to be a boy and I chose the name Aaron for him. Aaron was born in March two thousand and four and we had planned on his Baptism in July. As fate would have it, my father and Vashti's father would both be in Canada for the occasion. When Joshua was baptized in Trinidad, all his grandparents were there. Now that Aaron was going to be baptized, this time in Canada, it was very special that both his grandfathers would be there to celebrate with us. It was a joyful reunion once more with Vashti's sisters Kamini and Vidya. This was the second consecutive year that Kamini and her family came to visit us. I was delighted that my father was able to come and that he and my father-in-law were there to witness Aaron's Baptism in the church. The Christening party at our home was indeed very special.

In the year that followed, both boys were growing fast and we wanted to take Aaron on his first visit to Trinidad. Plans were made to travel in summer and flights were booked. Aaron had started walking, Joshua had just turned four, and I was particularly excited about this trip. I would have the opportunity now to take both boys to Mayaro, something that I very much looked forward to. Visiting Trinidad brought on a lot of emotional angst for me. Knowing that when I got there, my mother would not be there was very hard for me to cope with. I looked out of the aircraft window on the port side as the pilot lined up with the runway and we flew parallel to the east-west corridor. I saw Mount Saint Benedict and my eyes followed the terrain to make out Tunapuna, the old Lever Brothers grounds and the Tunapuna cemetery. Silently I said a prayer for my mother and wiped a tear from my eye. I was holding Aaron on my lap for the landing and his head against my chest and heart comforted me. I had my left arm around him holding him while with my right hand, I held Joshua's hand sitting in the seat next to me.

Our arrival in Curepe was a bit muted for me as the day before we left, I had received a phone call from my sister to let me know that my father had a slight accident. He had fallen down the stairs at the house in Tunapuna, was bruised and was in the hospital. Vashti's entire family was at her mother's house and they were eager to see, greet and hold Aaron. I helped Vashti settle the boys down and then borrowed a car and drove to the hospital to see my father. When I got there, Sherry, Rudy and my sister-in-law Alicia were there. I hugged my father and looked at him. Fortunately, there were no broken bones or sprains, but he had some nasty haematoma bruises on his neck, shoulders and arms. We decided that it would be best for him to stay at Alicia's house while he recovered. Her mother was usually there during the day and would be able to tend after him and keep him company as well. With that settled, I returned to my family in Curepe.

I was torn between looking after my father and making a memorable visit for my children. I wanted to spilt my time with all of them but was afraid of them feeling like I was neglecting them. I was agonizing over this and alone in the garage in Curepe when Kamini came and sat with me and asked me if everything was alright. I opened up to her and she had a sobering conversation with me. I was feeling immense pressure with my family after my mother's death and now with my father's accident. Rudy and Sherry had separated and were going through a divorce. Gerry and Alicia were estranged and I felt like my family was crumbling before my eyes.

As I spoke with Kamini, I realized that it was my mother who was the glue that held the family together. Now that she was gone, I was trying to be the glue in her place. But lots of things were outside of my control and I had to let go. The love that we had for each other was still there, no one could doubt that. It's just that the partner decisions my siblings had made did not work out and I had to accept that. Kamini said to me that with my father settled and recovering, I had to make sure I go visit him often and spend some evenings with him. But during the day, make the most out of the vacation for my sons and make my own memories with them. I was grateful for the talk with her as Kamini could connect with me on a spiritual and emotional level.

A couple days later, Kamini and Ahamad took us on a trip to Tyrico Bay with the mandatory stop at Maracas for Bake and Shark. The boys were excited as we piled into the minivan for the drive up and across the hills of the Northern Range. Just as we passed the Saddle Road, the minivan started to overheat and we had to pull aside on a grassy fringe while Ahamad tended to the problem. We could not have picked a better spot for a vehicular breakdown. In front of us there was a magnificent vista of the hills of Paramin. I pointed out the tiny houses way in the distance on the hills and told Joshua and Aaron that this was where Aunty Deta was born and grew up. Deta was Vashti's best friend and Aaron's godmother. Pretty soon Ahamad had the problem fixed and we were off once more. We had to stop at the Lookout and I took my first photos with Joshua and Aaron there. Over the years we would always stop at the lookout with Kamini and her family every time we went to Tyrico, and we would always take a photo. After the lookout, as we descended, I saw Maracas Bay and pointed it out to Aaron. Joshua was sitting with his cousins Anika and Farhanna in the back and he was as excited as can be. We stopped at Richards, purchased some Bake and Shark and drove on another five minutes onto the beach at Tyrico.

 I was excited to smell the salty air and feel the sand between my toes. Joshua jumped out of the van and ran onto the beach with Nikki and Fari. This was Joshua's first time at the beach and he was excited and delighted. I wanted to take Joshua into the water, but he was so happy playing with his cousins on the sand that I left him alone with them. I took Aaron by the hand and we walked towards the surf. This was his first time in the ocean and he seemed a bit scared. I lifted him up and took him to the water's edge and let a wave splash me. As the water hit me and splashed on him, he looked scared but I was talking to him all the while and that seemed to calm him. Of course the water had splashed onto his face and he put out his tongue and tasted the salty water and made a face. Inch by inch I sat in the water and eased him with me. The waves were gentle and he stood up in the water while I held his hands. Then he smiled at me and my heart melted. Just then Vashti came up and squealed his name and he laughed out loud, let go of my hand and waddled towards her. She scooped him up and then bounced him up and down in the water. Meanwhile, Joshua and the girls had started building a sandcastle and he would not come into the water despite all my pleading with him. So when I look back at that first trip to the beach with my boys, Aaron was the first one in the surf.

A week later, Vashti's family organized a day trip to Manzanilla. I tried to get them to go to Mayaro, but they all preferred Manzanilla. On the morning of the outing, it was very overcast and rainy. One by one the other family members opted out of the trip and while I understood it was because of the rain, I was disappointed. But Ahamad and Kamini would not let it spoil our plans and they were adamant we would still go on the trip. As it was only us, we decided on going to Mayaro and I could not be happier. I would finally get the chance to take my sons there. We stopped off at KFC, ordered some food and we set off towards the east coast in pouring rain. Ahamad and I were optimists and we felt strongly that it would be clear when we got to the east coast.

With the windshield wipers working at a pace, we swallowed up the miles as we drove past old markers. Because of the rain, it was not much of a sightseeing trip for Joshua who was content to be with his cousins in the back seat. Aaron was asleep in Vashti's arms while she and Kamini chatted. I sat in front with Ahamad. As we got past Sangre Grande, the rain had stopped but it was still overcast. We agreed the ocean may not be the best for bathing as the water may be rough. So then and there we decided to make it only to Manzanilla for a short stop. Mayaro would have to wait a bit longer.

Chapter 19

A Final Journey to Mayaro with My Father's Ashes

The year two thousand and six brought with it two trips to Trinidad. One was a planned vacation in July of that year; the other was the second devastating loss in my life. The first loss was that of my mother. Her death affected me so profoundly that I felt as if a part of me also died with her. I never could bring myself to visit her grave in Tunapuna because the pain was just too deep. I could not bear to remember her casket being lowered into the grave and then being covered with earth knowing that I would never again see her. I have lived with that pain and that loss ever since. The trip in July of that year was planned because we wanted Joshua and Aaron to spend time with the family and I wanted to see my father again.

In two thousand and five, just after we returned from our trip to Trinidad, my father visited us twice in Canada. He came up towards the end of summer when we were doing a project to have our basement finished. He looked after the house while the contractor did the work. He spent ten days with us and it was a wonderful visit with him for us. Then later that year, in December, he came to visit us for four days just after Christmas and he left before New Year's Day. Even though it was a short visit, he spent some quality time with his grandsons and we were blessed to have him spend it with them. When it was time for him to leave, it was a sad departure again, but he kissed us all and said that we'll see each other again in a few months. Little did I know that the hugs we exchanged at the airport that night would be the last time I would hold and touch my father. June of the next year brought the second shuddering blow to my life.

It was Saturday fourth of June and I was getting ready to take Joshua to his swimming lesson. Before we left though, I called my father for our weekly chat. He was sitting on the porch at home in Trinidad when he took my call. He was having his morning coffee and reading the newspaper. I let Joshua chat with him and tell him about his swimming lessons. When I took the phone from Joshua and spoke to him, his voice sounded a bit odd and I asked him if all was well with him. He said yes, that he was just a bit tired as the day before he was out liming with Selwyn and some of his friends and may have had a bit too much to drink. He said he was fine and was going to make some soup and have a quiet day at home watching sports on television. I chatted with him a bit longer, told him I would call him the next day, and then hung up. The next day as I was helping with the preparation for Sunday lunch, I decided to call again and see how he was doing. But the phone kept ringing with no answer. As he lived alone at home, after several tries, I called my sister to ask her to check on him, but I could not get through to her as well. I tried a few more times during the day but no luck as the phone kept ringing. I thought that he may have gone out with his friends again and I left it at that.

I was at work on Monday around one o'clock in the afternoon when I got a call from my brother-in-law Rudy who called me to tell me that my father had died. Time slowed as those words came into my ear over the telephone line. I cried in disbelief as I collapsed into my chair. My father was gone, and I was not there with him. Two parents had now been taken from me and I was not there with them. The pain seared through my eyes and my heart as the tears flowed. I spoke to my boss and then called Vashti with the news. I called my travel agent and fortunately there was a flight to Trinidad that very night which she booked us on. I had a friend, Terry, pick up the tickets for me as his office was close to the travel agent. The ride on the GO train back to Oakville seemed interminable as I played back every memory I had of him in my mind as the tears flowed down my cheeks. I picked up Joshua and Aaron from daycare and got them home. I sat them both down and told them that their grandfather had died. Joshua burst into tears, looked up at me and asked innocently "so now he will be with mama in heaven?" Aaron, seeing both Joshua and I crying also started to cry as well. Joshua's words resonated in my heart and I said to him, "yes, he will be with mama in heaven." I hugged both boys as they laid their heads on my chest as we waited for Vashti to get home. When we arrived in Trinidad the next morning, Vashti's family met us at the airport. My sister and brother were not there. I had been in contact with Rudy and we agreed to meet at the house in Hackett Lane so we went there straight from the airport. Kamini drove us to Tunapuna and Rudy was already there. He hugged Vashti and the boys, I kissed them goodbye and told Kamini to take them to Curepe. I was going to stay in Tunapuna with Rudy as we had a lot of work to do. I would see my family later in Curepe. I was anxious to find out from Rudy what had happened.

Rudy was at work when he received a call from my father's neighbour to come quickly to Tunapuna. My father had given Rudy a key to the house. Apparently on Sunday, some of my father's friends came to the house calling for him but got no answer. They assumed he was away and they left. On Monday, they came back calling for him. Still there was no answer. One of them opened the gate, went up the stairs and knocked on his bedroom window. Still there was no answer. As the louvres were slightly opened, he put his hand in and pulled back the curtains. He saw my father laying on the bed. He called to him, and still no answer. So he went to the neighbour's house and called Rudy. When Rudy got there, he opened the door and they went in. My father was dead. They called the police who came to the house and eventually my father's body was removed after the district medical officer came, officially pronounced him dead and gave the consent to remove his body. He had died in his sleep. Rudy's recount of what happened made sense to me as I recalled trying to call him several times on Sunday after he said he wasn't feeling so well on Saturday.

I looked at the sheets and touched the bed where he would have laid and the tears welled up again. But for the time being I had to put away my emotions as there was a lot of work to be done. His body was at the morgue undergoing an autopsy and we had to be there to get the results and have his body released to us. There were people to be informed, the undertakers to be contacted, the church to be arranged and a wake to be organized. Rudy told me to stay in Tunapuna and take care of all the administrative work and that he would go to the morgue and get the release papers. I was grateful for his help and his support more than he would ever know. Without Rudy's steadfast and solid support during that time, I would have been overwhelmed. I set about the task of going through my father's phone book and making calls to let everyone know. By mid-afternoon I had taken care of most of the arrangements including the church and the undertakers. Around four o'clock, Rudy returned with the documents. We went to Dr. Hosein to sign some forms and then to the Police Station to apply for a cremation permit. Rudy then gave me a lift to Curepe. I had not slept on the flight and I was exhausted. But I had to keep going as that evening was the first night of the wake. I showered, changed, got a bite to eat, hugged Joshua and Aaron, and returned to Tunapuna. Vashti would join me later with Kamini.

Just as at my mother's wake, the parish prayer group with Sister Deborah, led the prayer session. As I looked around the house, it was surreal that I was doing this for my father when just a few years ago, I was here for my mother. Now I was trying to help my father's passage from this life to the next through the prayers we offered for them. As I looked around the house, it would never be the same again, and neither would I. When the prayers were done and refreshments were being served, I saw my sister who called me over as she wanted to have a talk with me. She wanted to know if daddy would be buried next to mummy as had been mummy's wish. I did not want a confrontation with Sherry, but I had to be firm. I told her that while I loved mummy and respected her wish, daddy had made no secret about what he wanted done upon his death. He wanted to be cremated and his ashes sprinkled in Mayaro. She did not agree with me and it caused an argument. That made me even more upset as I did not want to bicker with her during this time of transition of my father's soul. So, I walked away.

    I saw my uncle Latiff, daddy's eldest brother, who beckoned me to come and sit with him. He sensed something was wrong and I told him about my conversation with Sherry. He looked at me and told me that I had to trust my heart and make sure and do what my father wanted, not what anyone else wanted. He reminded me that I was the eldest, that the decision was mine, that everyone else knew my father's wishes and that he would support me. I was glad for his words and his support. And so, the next couple of days, with Rudy's help, I finalized the arrangements.

    The church was filled to capacity with lots of people standing outside. There were lots of friends and colleagues from the airline who he and I both worked with, and whose presence and kind words served to reassure me that my father did have an impact on so many peoples' lives. Once more I did the eulogy and with so many familiar faces in the pews, my story about his life touched many on a very personal note. Even though I fought every emotion to keep my composure, just like I did during my mother's eulogy, towards the end, my voice broke and the tears flowed. I was glad that Sherry and Gerry were there at the crematorium even if she did not agree with the final rites. I stood with my family as we watched his casket being conveyed into the fire and I said goodbye to him as the doors closed.

We then went back to the house as was customary, and had a meal with those well-wishers who returned with us to keep us company. The somber mood changed as some of them spoke of their fond memories of him, of his quirks, of his professionalism and pride in his work, of funny stories. I sat and listened to everyone talking and somehow knew that even though he was gone, his memory would live on. Unlike when my mother passed away, I did not stay in Trinidad for a long period after the funeral. I returned to Canada with Vashti and the boys as we had other commitments there to take care of. As fate would have it, our annual vacation that year was already planned and booked for July, and it would coincide with my father's forty-day period. Because I had to leave, I arranged with the funeral director, Ronald Lee, who was also a friend of the family, to collect and keep his ashes for me until I returned in July. I had already decided on what I was going to do. There would be one final trip, with my father, to Mayaro.

The couple of weeks back in Canada flew by quickly and very soon we found ourselves once more on a flight to Trinidad. This time it was a planned vacation. Joshua was excited and could not wait to be reunited with the family back at home. Aaron was two years old and was developing his own personality. We were going to split our stay between Ma's house in Curepe and Kamini's house in El Socorro. But I had a few responsibilities to take care of to complete the rituals for my father. Traditionally, to mark the forty days after passing away, the family would hold a prayer at home and then a feast. However, instead of a prayer at home, I decided that I would do a simple mass at the church. Instead of a feast at home, I opted to feed the children at the Cyril Ross Home for Children. Rudy told me this was what my father told him he wanted done and with his help, we planned this.

On the day of the mass at the St. Charles Parish Church, my aunt Radica, my uncle Kelvin and my uncle Latiff were there to celebrate his life and offer prayers for him. After mass, we all went to a nearby Chinese restaurant on Jubilee Street where he frequented, and we had dinner. It was just my family Vashti, Joshua and Aaron with Alicia, Gerry, Gerarda, Rudy, Kelvin, Radica and Latiff. We spent several hours with Latiff talking about the old days when he and my father were growing up. He told us stories of their misadventures that caused us to laugh. In a way, it was cathartic that we should spend that time together with Latiff as he was also hurting at the loss of his brother, and those few hours with us brought me closer to him. When it was time to leave the restaurant, as we hugged each other, Latiff made me promise to keep in closer contact with him. He kissed Vashti and held my sons and gave a blessing to them. I had never been closer to Latiff as at that moment.

  Two days later, Rudy picked me up in Curepe. Vashti and I took Joshua and Aaron with us. We had ordered one hundred boxed lunches from a restaurant in St. Augustine and we were going to the Cyril Ross Home for Children in Tunapuna to feed the children there. The home was name after Fr. Cyril Ross who was one of the longest serving priests at St. Charles Parish in Tunapuna and I served as an acolyte while he was there. Fr. Ross was the one who did the instruction for my father when he converted and became a Catholic. We took Joshua and Aaron with us as we wanted them to be able to see children less fortunate than themselves. As we brought the baskets of food and the cooler of drinks out from the car, the teachers at the home organized the children at their tables. We sat with them and ate lunch together. My heart felt happy at doing this and I was grateful to Rudy for telling me about this wish that my father had. There was just one more obligation that I had to perform and I dreaded that one with all my soul.

  It was no secret that my father wanted his ashes scattered in Mayaro. At the wake in June, everyone without exception, told me it was not me that he wanted to throw his ashes. He had a friend named Chano who was a lifeguard in Mayaro. He wanted Chano to take a boat and go out past the breakers into the very deep water, and there to throw his ashes. But I was to take the ashes to Mayaro. I called Selwyn Tinto to contact Chano and set the date and time. I also called my uncle Kelvin, and my cousin Sunil to let them know. When Selwyn called me back to finalize, I contacted Sherry and Gerry and let them know. Everything was set for the final journey to Mayaro.

I wanted this to be the three children doing this together. But with the estrangement and tension with Sherry since the funeral, I was not sure about unity. Nevertheless, I arranged to meet Gerry and Sunil in Tunapuna at eight o'clock that morning. They would first stop at Lee's to collect the Urn with his ashes. I arrived a few minutes early in Tunapuna and proceeded to wait at the Bulldog Bar for Kelvin and Selwyn. To my surprise, the bar was already open and they were there and they called to me to come in. One of Gerry's friends, Johnson, was also there. Johnson lived with us for a few years in Hackett Lane and was part of the family. Johnson said he was going with us to Mayaro to say goodbye to uncle H, as he fondly called my father.

Even at that early hour of the morning, they were already having a drink. I took a beer with them. A few minutes later, Gerry and Sunil arrived, came in and we all drank a toast to my father Hafiz. Then it was time to leave. As I was getting into the back seat of Sunil's SUV, I stopped suddenly, for there on the seat was the urn that held my father's ashes. It then hit me that this was all that was left of his physical being. I slowly entered the vehicle, placed the urn carefully on the seat next to me, buckled up and we drove off. As we pulled out onto the Eastern Main Road, Sunil drove a few hundred yards and then turned left into Hackett Lane, drove up to the old house and paused a while. It was a symbolic farewell for my father to depart one last time from his house. I could barely see through the tears that welled up in my eyes and I urged Sunil to drive on.

The weather seemed ominous as black clouds gathered densely in the east. It was raining heavily as we made our way onto the highway. We had arranged to meet Chano at ten o'clock. I was very familiar with the drive from Tunapuna to Mayaro. This time, sitting in the back seat of the vehicle, I rested my hand on the urn and gazed out of the window. Things that I had remembered from long ago had changed, just as I had changed from a boy into a man. I stared silently as we passed the familiar markers along the trek to the east coast. The wind was blowing furiously outside and the rain was very heavy as we drove past Valencia and down the Stretch towards Sangre Grande. I was a bit worried about the weather and being able to go out onto the ocean. The radio was on and I picked up the bulletin that said it was a tropical depression affecting the island, but it was expected to pass soon. As we approached First and Last Bar, we slowed down. Kelvin, Selwyn and Johnson in the car in front of us had stopped at the bar and we pulled over to join them. It was a symbolic stop as Selwyn said this was always a mandatory stop with my father when they came to Mayaro and he wanted to do so with my father for the last time. They grabbed a beer and drank another toast to H, as everyone fondly called him.

We continued the drive down the hill and as the Atlantic came into view, I felt a dread come into the pit of my stomach as I knew there were only minutes left with the physical remains of my father. As we descended the hill, the rain eased and stopped altogether. As we drove into Manzanilla, the clouds cleared and the sun poked out. What a glorious blessing as I looked at the silver rays of sunlight radiating from the edge of the clouds as if to beckon us, and my father, to the heavens. Then up ahead at a popular spot, we saw Sherry stopped on the sandy shoulder. We pulled aside and got out to speak with her. Because of the heavy seas and choppy waters, all the boats were grounded. She had seen and spoken to Chano who said that we would not get a boat to take us out. That caused me to panic as I was already hanging on by an emotional thread, and the thought of not being able to do this today filled me with angst. She also said that Chano asked for us to wait for him in this spot. Chano was coming with his jet ski.

We walked out to the beach and soon saw Chano approaching on his jet ski from the south. He slowed as he approached us. I had never met him before and Selwyn introduced me. I clasped his hand and shook it gratefully. He reminded me of our friend Peter the fisherman back when I was a boy. Chano explained that no one would agree to take their boats out on the water. But he knew how important this day was and what it meant to my father to have his ashes thrown into the deep water. He explained that he could take the urn out on his jet ski, out past the breakers. He estimated it would take about ten minutes to get out there and back. I asked him if I could go out with him sitting behind him on the jet ski. But he said no, it was too dangerous. I was aghast and pleaded that I had to do this myself. After deliberating with the others, he agreed to take me with him. I was ready for the final trip with my father.

Gerry retrieved the urn from the vehicle and brought it down to the beach. Sherry gathered us all around and we recited one decade of the Rosary as we prepared to bid him goodbye. I took the urn from Gerry and followed Chano. As he got on the jet ski, I handed the urn to Gerry as I settled in behind Chano. He made me wrap my left arm around him to hold on tight and use my right arm to hold the urn between my body and his. He told me it would be bumpy and that the jet ski would jump into the air as we hit the waves and the breakers, but I promised to hold tight. With a nod to the others, he revved the engine and we drove into the surf. The waves were big and it was indeed a bumpy ride. Once I thought I would fall and lose the urn, but somehow I kept hold of Chano's shirt and stayed on. As we jumped past the breakers, the water seemed darker blue and was noticeably calmer. Chano drove on a bit further and then slowed and brought the craft to a stop. He told me here was deep enough. It was time to let go. I closed my eyes, said a short prayer, opened the urn and emptied it into the deep blue water. I saw the ashes float upon the waves and the current carried it out southwards. My father was home, just as he always wanted. He would take his final resting place in Mayaro. I threw the urn into the deep water, watched it sink out of view and said my final goodbye to him. Chano then told me to hold on and we turned back for the shore. I had done my duty for my father.

As we got back to the shore, the small group drank a final toast to my father and we left the beach. On our way back, we stopped off at a restaurant that my father always stopped at on his way home with Selwyn. The owners apparently knew we were coming and they prepared a simple meal that my father had enjoyed: fried bake with smoked herring. I listened to them talk about my father and I smiled inwardly. These were people who I did not know, but who seemed to know him very well. I was moved and knew that he touched many people's lives and that in their memories, just like mine, he would live on.

The rest of the vacation in Trinidad went by quickly. My sons enjoyed their visit with their families. It was a sad time for everyone when it came time for us to leave. For me, I felt a void deep inside. It was as if I was leaving a part of me here. Part of me wanted to stay in Trinidad, part of me wanted to flee back to Canada. I was torn. I did not see my brother nor my sister before I left. They did not come to see me in Curepe. There was a family dispute that was born when my father died and it would fracture the relationships with Sherry and Gerry for years to come. As I sat on the aircraft as we taxied along the apron, as we turned to line up for takeoff, sitting on the port side, I glanced west and saw the hills in the direction of Tunapuna. I closed my eyes, said goodbye to my mother and father in my heart, and held my children's hands as the aircraft soared eastward and turned north. I silently said goodbye to Trinidad once more.

Chapter 20

The Tide Still Beckons to Me...One Last Time

After my father's death, the magnet that drew me to Trinidad seemingly vanished. There was no desire to visit and instead I refocused on my own family. The boys were getting older and I wanted us to build our own memories with them. Vashti and I started our family vacations to other islands in the Caribbean. The boys enjoyed these vacations immensely, but they always asked when were we going to visit Trinidad again. They missed their families and were eager to go visit. I knew Vashti was eager to do so as well. Even though I was reluctant, it was only because of Vashti's family and my sons that we planned the next trip four years later.

    As the time drew near for our departure, I delved into planning things to do with Joshua and Aaron. I could sense their excitement and I buried my angst. The time lapse since our last visit served to heighten the anticipation and as the aircraft lined up parallel to the hills of the Northern Range on our final approach into Piarco, I glanced out the window with the boys. Joshua pointed and asked if that was Tunapuna, just as we flew past it. This trip was about them and I resolved inwardly to set aside my own feelings and devote myself to them on this vacation.

    It was a wonderful reunion with Vashti's family. The banter, the joking, the picong, the genuine love that they felt for each other was contagious, and it was very easy for me to slip into the cocoon of their familial warmth. The closeness of their bonds evaporated the years and time that separated us. I sat in in the garage in my usual spot near the gate with Ahamad, Raj and Rennie. There was a new addition to the family of in-laws with Raj Biptar who married Vidya. It was such a small world because Biptar and I went to the same Tunapuna Hindu School and were in the same class for seven years. Now we were brothers-in-law. I looked at Joshua and Aaron as they reveled in the attention, the hugs and kisses that they got from everyone. I looked at Vashti sitting next to her parents, a smile of contentment on her face. Their happiness was the reward for me swallowing my own feelings about this trip.

But I still had to confront my own hurdles and face my own family. I had not spoken often with Gerry and Sherry since the funeral and it seemed like there was a chasm in between us. I had accepted that our relationships had changed from when we were children and that as each of them continued with their own lives, I could no longer try to be the glue to hold everyone together. But I did resolve that I will be civil and that I would reach out to them. I was the eldest and I needed to try. I called Sherry first and I could hear the joy in her voice as she spoke with me on the phone. Her voice tugged at my heart and I looked forward to seeing her, despite our past differences. We arranged for me to come and spend two nights at her house and I would bring Joshua and Aaron. Vashti did not go to Sherry's house. The boys would spend some time with their cousin Adam. I next called Gerry and he agreed to meet me at the house in Trincity with Alicia, Gerarda and Sarah. With the arrangements made, I anxiously awaited the reunion with my brother and sister.

The reunion with Sherry surpassed my expectations. As I hugged her, I felt her tremble and shake as she started to cry. There was no need for words. Her tears said a thousand words to me and as she wiped them away, she told me she was happy that I came to her house. I too was glad that I reached out to her and made the effort to come and spend some time with her and her family. Joshua and Aaron were excited to be with Adam as they romped in the yard. I could see them enjoying each other's company. Then there was a surprise as my brother Gerry arrived. Sherry had invited him to come and spend the time at her house so that the three of us could be together. I was at first taken aback by his appearance as he seemed to have aged rapidly. But his voice was the same as he came up and hugged me. As he exchanged greetings with Sherry, I looked at them and tried to picture the waif of a boy doing cartwheels on the sand for Peter, and the little girl walking along Gill Street threatening to tell my father about our dawdling. And just for a fleeting instance, I saw them and they were smiling back at me.

We talked a lot and looked at all the old photos that I had scanned and saved on my iPad. As we slowly looked at each photo, there was a memory and a story behind each one as we nostalgically recalled them. There was one photo of my mother and father kissing under a coconut tree while Sherry poked her head up looking at them, Gerry was perched on a notch on the coconut tree smiling at them, and I had a towel draped over me like a cape to provide a backdrop to the kiss. It was a beautiful picture of the five of us. Without it being said, I knew we all missed our parents dearly. I do believe that it was cathartic for the three of us to spend that time together at Sherry's house. Life went on and I consigned the past to where it was. We wanted to salvage some of the sibling relationships that we had when we were younger, but we were older and wiser, and we recognized that it had changed. But we were still family and we had to be there for each other. We had buried the proverbial hatchet.

Joshua, Aaron and Adam enjoyed each other's company playing cricket and football. Adam had a pair of budgies and he took them out of their cage while my boys marveled at how tame they were. They squealed in delight as Carlisle put the birds on their fingers to sit and perch. Sherry cooked a lot of our favourites and Joshua said that her Trini stewed pork was the best he ever had. She and Gerry sat with my boys one night and they told stories about me when I was a boy growing up, about some of my misadventures and deeds. That caused everyone to laugh and I was surprised at how much they remembered of those olden days. The three days and two nights were very important as they allowed Gerry, Sherry and I to reconnect as a family. As the time drew near for us to go back to Curepe, Sherry was very emotional. I spoke with Gerry from my heart and bade him try and get his life back on track and remember that despite everything that had happened, we were family and that I would be there for him. Sherry's tears rolled freely as she tried in vain to put on a brave face. I was also an emotional wreck as I struggled to keep my own composure. Unable to speak, I simply hugged them both, squeezed their hands, told them that I loved them and got into my car. With a final glance and a wave to them, I left my brother and sister as two tears rolled down my cheeks.

I was aware of Joshua and Aaron witnessing the emotional departure from Sherry's house and that they were silent in the back seat of the car as we drove back to Curepe. I wanted them to be aware of their own feelings and wanted them to be able to express emotion so I asked them how they felt about leaving. Joshua said he was sad because he would miss them and he did not know when next he would be able to come and see them and spend time with them. Out of the mouth of babes, as the adage went, his innocent summary was a perfect synopsis of how I felt and I was glad he could express it to me. Aaron asked me if it was OK to cry when you are sad and I told him absolutely. He said to me that he wanted to cry because he was sad at leaving them also. As I drove along the highway and listened to my sons talking to me about their feelings, I felt good inside that I was raising them properly.

Since Curepe was our base in Trinidad, it meant we spent most of our time with Vashti's huge family. My family was much smaller. I did not attempt to go visit any of my cousins, or other family as they were distant and we had not kept in contact over the decades. I did meet my uncle Kelvin once and we spent some time together. I was very happy to have seen him again. Vashti and I did go to Trincity to visit my sister-in-law, Alicia, Gerry's ex-wife, and my nieces Gerarda and Sarah. We spent a day with them and had a wonderful visit. Gerarda and I always had a special bond and I always remembered her as a five-year-old on that night when I left Trinidad for Canada, holding her in my arms as she clung to and hugged my neck. Now she was a teenager and doing very well in school having won a scholarship and was about to start university. A couple days later, Gerry, Alicia and the girls all went to dinner at Valpark Chinese Restaurant with me and my family. We had a wonderful meal and a great evening with them. I was glad that Gerry could join us even though he and Alicia were divorced. As we prepared to leave them that night, Vashti and I reaffirmed our support for Alicia and the girls to her. I would see them once more before we left when they came to Curepe to say goodbye.

   As the holiday in Trinidad wore on, we did a lot of things with the families. There were several rounds of family visits. Ahamad and Kamini arranged another memorable outing to Maracas for Bake and Shark and a sea bath at Tyrico Bay. We spent a wonderful family day in Penal at Kavita's house where we played football and cricket. She planned an extremely extravagant lunch and dinner for everyone. Kavita was Vashti's youngest sister. I took the boys on a trip up to Mount Saint Benedict to show them the monastery and the hills of the Northern Range. I showed them Mount Tabor and pointed out the trail I used to hike to get to the top of the mountain with the acolytes and youth group of the St Charles Parish Church in Tunapuna. They enjoyed the view looking across the Caroni plain and seeing most of central Trinidad. But there were two more activities which I wanted to do, both of which filled me with anxiety and dread.

Gerry and I had spoken about this at Sherry's house and it is something that I had never could bring myself to do. But this time I resolved to do it and both he and Sherry were going to go with me. I was going to visit my mother's grave in Tunapuna. This would be the first time since her passing that I would have gone to visit her final resting place. They picked me up in Curepe and there was another surprise in the car. My uncle Kelvin had come along with them. I felt immediately warm as I felt a sense of family and support for the first time in a long while. On the ride to Tunapuna, Kelvin was his jolly old self, poking fun at me about being afraid to go to the cemetery by myself. As we got there, Gerry drove into the cemetery and parked on the road just opposite the grave. I slowly got out of the car and clutched the bouquet of flowers that I had brought with me. We manoeuvred the ditch and made our way to the grave.

A year after she was buried, my father had the grave cast in concrete and a beautiful headstone was erected. I stood there by myself facing the grave while the others stood to the side. They allowed me this moment by myself. I knelt on one knee as I placed the flowers beside the headstone. I closed my eyes and swallowed hard as I fought back the tears. My voice broke as the words escaped my lips as I asked my mother to forgive me for not having come to visit her before. I fell to both knees and sobbed as I poured out all that I kept inside me since she had passed away. As I emptied my heart that day at my mother's grave, it was as though I buried my burden that I had been carrying inside all these years. I rose to my feet, kissed the headstone, and said farewell to my mother one last time.

The one trip I looked forward to but dreaded at the same time was a trip to Mayaro. This time it was only with Kamini, Ahamad and their family with Vashti, the boys and me. We were going to Mayaro for the day and Ahamad had secured a friend's house that we could use. I drank in all the sights on the drive there, making notes about all the changes that I was seeing from what I remembered. As we approached the Junction, Ahamad asked me if I wanted to make a quick stop in Plaisance to see Gill Street. I hesitated for a moment and almost said yes. But I stopped myself and said no. This trip for me was about a new experience for Joshua and Aaron. I urged Ahamad to drive on to our destination which was very near to Church Road. Ahamad's sister-in-law, Linda, was supposed to be at the house and the kids who knew her were anxious to see their aunty Linda. As we pulled into the driveway, Linda came out to greet us as Anika, Farhanna, Bari and Javed rushed to hug her. Joshua and Aaron did not know her, but Linda spotted them and pulled them in to her and hugged them and kissed them. That made them smile as they were now a part of their cousins' extended family.

We took a raincheck on a meal offered by Linda. Instead we unpacked the coolers and chairs from the car and made our way down to the beach. I helped set up our family spot under the coconut trees as Joshua and Aaron busied themselves with their cousins building a sand castle. Vashti, Kamini and Linda got their chairs set up as Ahamad poured them a drink. I accepted one that he handed to me. I did not sit, preferring to stand with my back against the coconut tree. I dug my toes into the sand and felt the abrasion as I rubbed my heel over my foot. It was busy as there were many people out enjoying the sun and the water. I listened in to the snippets of conversation but my mind was elsewhere. I was thinking of my father and the last time I was here. I slowly took a few steps away from the group. I heard Vashti ask where I was going and I heard Kamini tell her to give me a moment.

My eyes were fixed on Point Radix as I looked at the Atlantic Ocean and followed the current flowing south. I walked to the water's edge and stopped. I closed my eyes as I spoke to my father's presence in that water where I had thrown his ashes. With my inner voice, I told him that I was making peace with my brother and sister, that I had finally had the courage to go and visit my mother's grave and say goodbye to her, and that I hoped he could hear my words. I told him that I missed him and my mother so much and wished that they could see my children. I asked him to look down upon us and pray for them as they grew up. A movement on the water, what seemed like seaweed or driftwood in the distance, caught my eye. But it vanished and I could not see it anymore.

I looked out to the vast Ocean and I told my father that I hoped he was happy that I had brought him home to Mayaro. As I stood there, saying goodbye to my father, Joshua and Aaron came up to me and asked me if I was OK because I was just standing there. I picked up Aaron in my arms, pulled Joshua to me and told them that I was saying goodbye to my father and explained to them that it was here that I had scattered his ashes, as he had wanted. Aaron looked across the water and waved and said "goodbye papa." I turned away from the water with my boys and with one a final glance back, I said farewell to my father for the last time.

The others knew what I was doing and Ahamad came up to me and gave me a huge hug as he kissed my cheek and told me to be strong and that my parents would be extremely proud of the man that I had become and how I was raising my family. I was grateful for his support and his words. It was soon time to leave and we hugged Linda before setting off. As we drove down the Guayaguayare Road, I asked Ahamad if he could make one short stop at Gill Street. There was one last thing I wanted to do. Gill Street held some of the best memories of my childhood and I wanted to see it one last time. As we drove down Plaisance Road, Ahamad slowed down as I pointed out everything I remembered to Joshua and Aaron. I told them this was my happy place when I was their age growing up.

The sun, the sand, the sea, the tide, always seemed to beckon to me when I was a child. When I needed to reconnect with my homeland, the tide always beckoned to me to drift my memory back to this place. The tide beckoned to my father to come to his final resting place. Gill Street and

Plaisance Village were central to the beckoning tide. I got out of the vehicle at the corner of Gill Street. As I stood there, I closed my eyes and everything that I did over twenty years ago, when I was a child, in this very place, flashed before me and at the back of those images, I saw my mother and father. I smiled with a new calm. I knew what my parents did for us back then and I knew how much they sacrificed to make that possible for us and I felt pride in being their son. The tide had brought me back to this happy place one more time, and I was content.

www.ingramcontent.com/pod-product-compliance
Lightning Source LLC
Chambersburg PA
CBHW070050080526
44586CB00013B/991